Late Bloomer

A memoir

Erica Scott

Cover photo by Omar:
http://www.modelmayhem.com/Mozer

Cover design by Zelle
(Thank you! ♥)

ISBN 978-1461129783

This book covers many years and mentions several people. In the interest of consideration and discretion, I chose to handle their names as follows:

- For my family members and anyone who could easily be identified by an unusual name or spelling, I used initials. I suppose I could have made up fake names, but I hate doing that.
- For my friends and colleagues in the spanking scene, I used their scene pseudonyms.
- I used a real first name (no last names, ever) only when it was an extremely common one and said usage would not risk exposing the individual's identity.

All quotes from my journals and blogs are taken directly from the sources verbatim.

If you are seeking a trashy tell-all scene book, this isn't it. People have entrusted me with many secrets over the years, for good reason. Because I keep them.

To my father, with love and gratitude. Without the writing gene and sense of humor he passed on to me, this book would not be possible.

And to John, my beloved, who owns my heart.

PROLOGUE

On the evening of September 21, 1957, my parents went to a Hollywood party. My father was a television writer/producer, and he and my mother often attended these types of affairs. Mom was elegantly dressed with her hair perfectly coiffed, and hugely pregnant with me. She started having labor pains at the party and, noticing how quickly they were coming, called her doctor, who said, "For God's sake, meet me at the hospital before you have that baby right there on the floor."

My parents went to the hospital and I arrived at 12:30 A.M. on September 22. I've been told that my birth was so quick and easy, my mother's hairdo was barely out of place. Dad stayed long enough to make sure Mom was all right and to greet his new daughter.

Then he went back to the party. Priorities, right?

It's a funny Hollywood-esque story now. Being just hours old, I was incapable of feeling I wasn't important or interesting enough to merit more than fleeting attention.

However, that feeling came to dog me for a very long time.

* * *

I often say that I've existed for 53 years, but have only been *alive* since I was 36. Before that age, it wasn't much of a life. I was a prisoner of fears and anxieties, undiagnosed depression and eating disorders, and felt like I could disappear and no one would notice or care. There wasn't a place on earth where I belonged.

As if that weren't enough angst, I was baffled by feelings and desires I didn't understand, and which I didn't dare discuss with anyone. Why was I so fixated on... spanking? Something must be terribly wrong with me, along with all the other neuroses.

After many years of various therapies, I was put on antidepressants in my mid-30s and things began to change. I finally had a key that could break me out of my self-imposed prison. Slowly, I embarked upon a real life. The ever-nattering demons in my head started to quiet down a little. And, as I healed, I realized there was a part of me I needed to explore. A part that I'd tried to stifle and deny, but it wouldn't go away. In fact, now that my fog of malaise was clearing, it was clamoring even more energetically to emerge.

This book is my story of personal discovery and freedom, of embracing my differences rather than fighting them, and of finding love, acceptance and fulfillment, at long last, in a most unexpected way. Better late than never.

PART I: EXISTENCE

"I feel like Charlie Brown. Stupid, wants to have friends, but doesn't know how to make them or keep them. Sometimes I wish I was dead. I have this soap-opera dream about killing myself, and in my suicide note, I'll say 'Life without friends isn't worth living,' or some corny shit like that. That would make them sorry they've treated me this way. But there's only one flaw to that plan. I wouldn't be around to see their reactions to my death."

—from my first journal, July 18, 1973. I was 15.

STRANGE LITTLE GIRL

"You were always spoiled with a thousand toys, but still you cried all night."
—"19th Nervous Breakdown," The Rolling Stones. © 1966, Mick Jagger/Keith Richards.

My brother Ken was eight years older than I. He was a force of nature: curious, smart, musically and artistically talented, fearless, and with a very sunny, even-tempered disposition.

I don't think my parents were prepared for a child like I turned out to be. If Ken was a ray of sunshine, I was a storm cloud. I too was bright, could play the piano and loved to draw and paint. But I was fearful. I threw tantrums and cried a lot.

While Ken couldn't be left alone for one minute because he would get into everything, I was happy to be put down with a toy or a coloring book and would stay there for hours, never venturing out of my little space. While Ken thrived on new experiences, I hated change, even on the most superficial level; I would get upset if my mother moved a knick-knack from one end of the table to the other. Along with being high-strung and hypersensitive, I had unusually acute hearing and loud noises made me cry and clap my hands over my ears. Ken embraced life with the joyous abandon of a true extrovert. I was a classic introvert, but with an extrovert's desire for attention. It was not an easy combination.

Perhaps I always sensed that my family was not what it seemed. To the outside world, we looked like the perfect late 50s/early 60s household. A handsome, successful father and a beautiful mother. One boy, one girl. A dog and a cat. Two cars. And, because we were well off, a live-in maid/nanny.

But my father drank and had affairs. My mother was restless and moody, and obsessed with a singing career that never came to fruition. (In order for one to have a singing career, several things have to come into play, but most important are talent and an appealing voice. My mother, unfortunately, had neither.)

My brother and I were cute kids and our parents loved to trot us out to impress their company. All kids learn how to count, but how many do you know whose counting efforts end up as a blurb in *Variety*? True story: At one of my parents' parties, I was showing off my ability to count and I made it up to ninety-nine. "What comes after ninety-nine?" Dad prompted. I hesitated. "Tenty-ten?"

Ken and I would play duets on the piano, and my father would then put me in front of the piano with my back to it so he could play a bunch of notes and have me identify them. I had perfect pitch and was always spot on. The guests would *ooh* and *ahh* and be impressed. And then the adults went to have dinner in the dining room, while we went into the kitchen to eat with Rina, the maid. Because kids were fun to show off, but who really wants them at the dinner table, right?

I was certainly not a physically abused child. I always had plenty of food, lots of toys and games, a nice bedroom, everything material that I needed. As childhoods go, mine could have been much worse. But I was not happy. I did not feel wanted; I felt like I was an inconvenience. I craved attention, but went about getting it in all the wrong ways, like throwing tantrums. I didn't even know why I was screaming half the time; all I knew was that I wanted to be heard and acknowledged.

My mother's attention was conditional, dependent upon her moods. I remember sitting with her at a very young age, as she showed me the newspaper and picked out words to teach me. I learned how to read before I started school. But I also recall times when she was impatient and dismissive, finding me a nuisance, telling me to go away and find Rina.

As for my father, he was affectionate, but for the most part thought parenting was a monetary function. As a small child, I was a chronic bed-wetter. While Mom and Rina fussed and fretted, Dad's proposed solution was to tell me, "Don't do it for a week and you can have any toy you want." Guess what—that didn't work.

When I was around five, my mother had a horrible nosebleed one night. I saw her in the kitchen, lying on the floor. There were small pools of blood all around her head and her clothes were stained. My brother was on the phone trying to reach the doctor and Rina was running around, getting towels and ice and trying to keep my mother from choking on her own blood. I stood in the kitchen doorway and screamed in fear. And screamed, and screamed, and screamed. No one noticed me.

Finally, after several minutes, my mother raised her head—I remember thinking, "Mommy has a red mustache"—and yelled, "Get her *out* of here!" Ken dashed over, grabbed my hand and took me out, bawling my head off, to our neighbor's house.

From that day on, I was scared to death of the sight of blood. Still am. Fortunately, I got out of the habit of screaming in terror every time I cut myself.

My parents divorced when I was six; their marriage had never been a good one, I found out years later. I saw more of my father after the divorce than before, because he would pick me up once a week and take me to amusement parks and for meals. He was kind to me, but he felt like a stranger. My mother dated several men and went on with her life.

My care was mostly in Rina's hands, except when my mother would have one of her fits of wanting to be involved in my life and would try to take a bigger part in it. But I was never quite comfortable with her, and didn't sense that she really enjoyed me all that much. Her affection ran hot and cold, and she was very critical.

Most children hate being sick. I loved it, because I discovered it garnered me attention and love. My mother, being a bit of a hypochondriac herself, fussed over us when we were sick. I got one of the spare TVs wheeled into my room, I got comic books and candy bars, dinner in bed on a tray. My mother or Rina made soup from scratch. I would dread feeling better, because that meant I'd go back to being invisible.

So I learned how to feign illness. I'd force myself to cough until I became hoarse. I poured water up my nose to sound stuffy and make myself sneeze. I'd say I was sick to my stomach, because there was no way of disproving that. Once, I read a book in which the little girl in the story fell down the stairs. She had to stay in bed for a long time and her family doted on her. So one day, I threw myself down the stairs.

Pathetic, I know. I wasn't badly hurt, though, just some bruises. I was desperate to feel like someone gave a damn.

I lost myself in childish fantasies, wishing I were someone else. Perhaps I'd been adopted and my real family was looking for me. Or maybe I could disappear into the television set and join one of those perfect, loving 1960s families, whose problems could always be solved in under a half-hour and where parents understood everything.

When I was in third grade, I found out that my father was getting remarried. I didn't hear it from either of my parents, however. A perfect stranger, a girl who knew my name, approached me on the school playground and, excitedly jumping up and down, told me her mother was marrying my father.

All I could do was stare at her and say, "What?" She got more animated and repeated herself, stamping her foot for emphasis. "I said *your father* (stamp, stamp) is marrying *my mother* (stamp, stamp)!" She insisted that I had to come home with her so she could prove it.

That night, I told my mother that some strange girl told me that her mother was marrying Dad and I needed to come to her house. Her answer? "Well, I'd guess you'd better go, then." No questions about who it was or where she lived. In retrospect, I guess she already knew.

So the next day after school, I walked with this girl to an unfamiliar apartment. The door opened and the most beautiful woman I'd ever seen smiled down at me. I didn't know her, but she knew me. "Hi, Erica. Come in." I walked in and looked around the room.

The first thing I saw was the piano in the corner—with a framed photograph of my father on top of it.

Yes, it was as surreal as it sounds. People are amazed when I tell that story, but such was the nature of communication in my family.

In fourth grade, I developed a phobia of being left anywhere, including school. Whenever I was dropped off, this terrifying feeling would overwhelm me—that no one would come back to get me. As a result, the maid had to pick me up each day at noon and bring me home to eat lunch, because I was too scared to stay in school the full day. Somehow, breaking up the day with a visit home enabled me to stay without having a panic attack.

I hated school, though. I felt like a misfit and an ugly duckling, and I longed to be one of the popular kids in the center of everything. I had few friends, because I didn't fit in with the admired crowd and refused to join my fellow misfits. If kids came to my house, it was because I had a lot of toys, or because we had a trampoline in the back yard. Or perhaps it was our color television—in those days, few households had them. Whenever *The Wizard of Oz* had its annual showing, suddenly everyone wanted to visit me.

By the time I was eight years old, I had already been to my first shrink. I remember little about him except his name and that he specialized in treating kids, and his office was filled with every toy and game imaginable.

There were many reasons why I felt like a square peg. As a little girl, I'd been cute, but then things took a wrong turn. My baby curls became hair that was neither straight nor curly, just sort of wavy and frizzy. My nose grew before the rest of my face did. I had crooked teeth and eventually got a mouthful of braces. And I put on weight. I was not an obese child, but I was definitely chubby. Enough so that kids made fun of me. They called me "Tiny Tim's sister." For those of you who are too young to know that reference, they were not likening me to a Charles Dickens character. Tiny Tim was a novelty act in the late 1960s; he played the ukulele and sang in a falsetto voice. He was also one of the ugliest creatures on the planet—overweight, with a huge nose, prominent teeth and wildly frizzed-out hair. Sometimes, for a change, the kids would call me "Pinocchio." Or they'd ask if I stuck my nose in a pencil sharpener every morning.

Then there was my fearful nature, my desperation to fit in. Kids are smart and intuitive; they recognize the stench of otherness. They are also cruel. I was often the butt of teasing because I'd cry and get upset, which was the reaction they wanted.

My mother, ever trying to get me to socialize, would send me to day camps every summer, when all I wanted to do was stay home and read. I was wimpy and uncoordinated, poor at sports, got sick from the bus rides. I couldn't ride a bike or skate. Just as in school, the camps had their groups of cool kids; I was never one of them. But as in school, I was too proud to befriend my fellow weirdos, so I had no allies. Therefore, I might as well have pasted a "pick on me" sign on my back. One time, we went to the beach and I shrieked when I saw a sand crab. After that, the cool crowd thought it was hugely funny to put sand crabs down the back of my shirt and my shorts.

God, I was such a victim. *I* would have made fun of me, too.

During these formative years, along with all the other discomforts, something strange was happening within me. I had a fascination that I couldn't understand, and that I certainly couldn't verbalize to anyone. I was mysteriously intrigued with spanking.

In my solitary times, which were often, I wrote stories and drew pictures, all of which included spanking. I was riveted to any spanking scenes on TV and I always wanted to hear the details of other children getting spanked. I collected comic books, and every time I bought a new one, the first thing I did was to flip through it, looking for spanking scenes.

Nowadays, spanking is considered "un-PC." But back then, the practice was *de rigueur* and books, cartoons, TV shows and movies were rife with spankings. Whenever I saw one of them, my stomach would clench and I could feel my face grow hot. I felt the same way whenever I heard the word *spank* or *spanking*, and when I looked them up (along with all their synonyms) in the dictionary. When I played with my dolls, inevitably one or more of them ended up getting spanked (Ken spanked Barbie regularly). I made sure I was alone when engaging in this play.

14

Back to the bloody nose story for a moment. Later that evening, I came back home and saw my mother lying on the living room couch. She had been cleaned up and there was cotton stuffed in her nose. The doctor was there (yes, back in those dark ages, doctors made house calls). His name was Dr. Barton, and he was scolding my mother about her bad habit of blowing her nose too vigorously. "The next time you do that, I'm going to have her call me"—he pointed to me—"and I'm going to come over here and spank you." There it went again; that odd jolt in my belly.

Strange how I remember that moment, right down to the doctor's name, even after all these years. Then again, it really isn't. We spankos do tend to file these random events away and keep them permanently.

Of course, now I know that most people with a spanking fetish did and felt all these things. But then? I had no idea. I was embarrassed by my thoughts and was convinced there was something wrong with me. So I kept the obsession to myself. I was different enough as it was.

THE NUT-FILLED FAMILY TREE

"Family is just accident.... They don't mean to get on your nerves. They don't even mean to be your family, they just are."
—Marsha Norman, American playwright

Throughout this book, you may notice that there is little mention of family, aside from the immediate members. There is a good reason for that—my relatives, for the most part, aren't worth mentioning.

I had little family on my father's side. His father had died long before I was born (complications of alcoholism), and his mother passed away when I was eight years old. I was not close to her, as Dad and his mother had had a rocky relationship, which is putting it mildly. His life as a child was pretty much a nightmare and he was out on his own by the time he was 13 years old.

Dad was an only child. There were a few second and third cousins, but most of them were back East.

My mother, however, had several relatives. And aside from her cousin, who will be mentioned often later in this book, not one of them evokes any warm and fuzzy memories. In fact, I could have done without the lot of them.

Mom was the eldest of three; her brother lived with his family in New York and I didn't even meet him until I was 13. Her sister, unfortunately, was local. My maternal grandparents hated each other's guts and yet couldn't live without one another. My grandfather was loud and crude and boorish; my grandmother passive and whiny. She tried to do grandmotherly things, but nothing even came close to the Hallmark Grandma image. Her cooking was dreadful, her cakes dry, and her knitted sweaters were lumpy and misshapen. I once went to their place to spend the night, but they fought so much, I begged to go home.

I have an old black-and-white photo of my grandfather lying asleep on a beach towel in the sand. Hovering over him is my father, pretending he's going to smite him with a baseball bat. I'm sure that desire was shared by many.

There's no kind way to put this—my mother's sister was freaking nuts. She had married twice and had two children with each marriage, and they were all spoiled rotten and out of control. She'd had a lifelong obsessive competition with my mother, always trying to one-up her, making little digs, angry and jealous whenever Mom had something she didn't. She was even upset when my mother had a son before she did.

Holidays were a special treat. We'd either have them at my house or at my aunt's. When they were at home, my mother would drive herself and everyone else crazy, preparing and fretting over details. Everything had to be perfect. But of course, it didn't matter how wonderful the food was, how spotless the house was or how nice the table looked. Her family would do something or another to ruin the evening every time.

My aunt was notorious for being late and holding up dinner. Mom would fume and fuss and the food would either get overdone or grow cold as we waited. I often wondered why she didn't just go ahead and serve dinner to the rest of us, rather than allowing my aunt so much control. I suggested this to her once, and she nearly took my head off—"We don't *do* things like that!"—so I kept quiet after that, although I privately thought my solution made the most sense.

If we went to my aunt's, she still had her way of getting under my mother's skin. If Mom had agreed to bring a side dish, a dessert or whatever, we'd arrive and discover that my aunt had made or purchased a bigger and better version of the same item.

Time after time, year after year, these evenings ended in the same manner, with my mother ranting about her family and then exclaiming, "Never again!" But of course, the next occasion would roll around and she'd be planning another dinner. Fool that I was, I'd remind her of how she'd sworn to eschew these gatherings, and she'd turn on me and yell, "We're *family!*"

So what, I'd think to myself. What was this blind devotion to *family* about? What if your relatives were people you had nothing in common with, except for some genetic

17

material? What if you weren't related to them—would you want to spend even one minute of your time with them? If the answer was no, then I didn't understand the point of this forced camaraderie.

I made a vow to myself early on—when I got old enough to make my own decisions, I would never attend any of these obligatory family gatherings again. No one would make me spend time with people I didn't like; I didn't give a damn if they were related to me or not.

My aunt had never had much interest in me or my brother, so it came as quite a shock when she turned up at our door after Ken had died, crying and distraught. She sat next to me on the couch, patting my arm, saying she wanted a relationship with me, wanted to "be an aunt."

So, for a brief time, I had an aunt. She picked me up at school a couple of times and took me to lunch. One time, she took me back to her home for dinner. That was a fiasco.

Her kids never listened to her, no matter how much she screamed (and she screamed a lot). At the table, my youngest cousin, about nine years old at the time, wouldn't sit still, and my aunt was yelling at her to settle down. She didn't, and ended up knocking over the can of soda next to her plate.

I watched, horrified, as my aunt jumped up, ran over and snatched up the soda can. She then grabbed my cousin by the hair, dragged her over to the sink and proceeded to pour the rest of the soda all over her head, as the child sputtered and howled.

After that, I didn't get any more dinner invitations, and the lunch dates ended as well. I was relieved.

In 1980, my mother and aunt had a bitter falling-out, over what I can't recall. My aunt enumerated resentments that went back all the way back to their childhood. Ugly words were exchanged; among other things, my aunt screeched at my mother, "Your daughter is crazier than all of my kids put together!" Gee, I love you too, Auntie.

They did not speak again. In 1981, my aunt hanged herself in the garage. One of her sons found her. It was a violent end to a very sad life.

My uncle back East had a wife and three kids, whom I've seen twice in my entire life. I do have a treasured memory of staying at his house for three weeks when I was 13. I was there for the two-week Christmas holiday, and my mother had arranged things with school so I could stay an extra week. Quite an adventure for me, since I'd never been away from home for that long. It was also my first time on a plane and my first time seeing snow. I shared a bedroom with my cousin, who was 16; when she wasn't there, I'd try on her clothes. They took me to see all the typical New York sights and made me feel very much at home.

However, that was a one-time visit, never to be repeated. My uncle left his wife of many years for a younger woman, had a disastrous marriage with her and then went back to his ex-wife. She subsequently dumped him, and as far as I know, his kids don't speak to him.

Both my maternal grandparents passed away in the 1980s. I sometimes wish I had some sweet memories of them, some idea of what people are talking about when they speak of their grandparents with affection and reverence, but that simply wasn't my experience. If I'd had even one grandparent as a positive role model, perhaps I'd view the elderly with respect for their wisdom and interest in their stories, rather than with distaste and impatience.

I share blood with these crazy people, folks. Is it any wonder I chose not to procreate?

Awkward Adolescence

"You don't have to suffer to be a poet; adolescence is enough suffering for anyone."
—John Ciardi, American poet, 1916–1986

By the time I was 11 years old, both my parents had remarried. I lived with my mother and M, my stepfather. Rina, who had been with us since before I was born, had been let go (my mother felt she was no longer necessary), and I was quite bereft by her absence. My father had married the stunningly beautiful S, a dancer and actress. I idolized her and loved visiting the two of them on weekends. Ken had graduated high school and gone on to do the hippie thing—dropping out of college, growing his hair long and experimenting with drugs. It was the 1960s, after all.

Relations between my mother and me were not good. We fought like crazy; loud, screaming fights, often ending up with her slapping me. Once she threw a glass of water all over me in my bed. Another time, she flung a dish on the floor at my feet and one of the pieces cut my toe. She hated how free and loose things were at my father's house and she overcompensated by imposing a lot of rigid rules on me, which made me seethe with resentment.

My bedtime was so strictly enforced that if I went to bed 10 minutes late one night, I had to go to bed 10 minutes early the next night. I had to make my bed the minute I got up, before doing anything else. Television was restricted to a brief amount and if I wanted to extend that time for a special program, I had to barter and beg, and cut back the following evening. None of my peers had this level of restriction. When I mentioned it to them, they laughed.

From my early childhood, I remember a lot of fear. Now my primary emotion much of the time was rage.

My mother, in her perpetual quest to control me, came up with unusual punishments. As I mentioned, I was a loner child who loved nothing more than to stay home and read. I used to go to the library and check out 10 books at a time, the full amount allowed. Once when I was nine years old and my mother got angry with me, she told me I couldn't read for a week. To me, this was devastating. When I couldn't escape into my beloved books, I had no idea what to do with myself.

One day during that horrible week, I walked to a nearby park to get out of the house for a while. This particular park had an enclosed children's area, with swings, slide, jungle gym and other fun things in a large sand pit. As I wandered around by myself, kicking at the sand, a toddler detached himself from his mother and came waddling over to me. I can still remember his face, beaming with delight and open trust up at me.

If that were to happen now, I would squat down, beam back at him and make funny faces, and feel the urge to run my finger along his baby-soft cheek. But then, caught up in my own whirlwind of anger, all I felt was resentment at this happy little creature invading my space.

Subtly, I shifted one leg forward and nudged my knee into his chest, and he fell over backward into the sand.

The child was unhurt; the mounds of sand cushioned his fall. But of course, he howled at this mistreatment and his mother came running. She did not say anything to me, but her searching eyes were full of questions as she picked him up. I muttered, "He fell," and turned to walk away.

Even now, all these years later, I can't think of that baby without getting a lump of shame in my throat. Chances are that he forgot about the incident minutes after the fact; however, I'll always remember that I was more than likely the first violator of his baby innocence.

But I was only a child myself, and caught up in an all-too-common vicious cycle of anger and damage. Wounded people turn around and wound others.

My stepfather was a good and decent man, but he never had a chance with me. I resented his presence, resented that my mother (seemingly) cared more about him than about me. He had two children from his first marriage and was very devoted to them, so my mother would throw that in my face constantly (the implication being that my own father wasn't quite so devoted). I got sick to death of M being likened to a saint. I didn't care who he was or what he did; he wasn't my father.

We had moved out of Beverly Hills, where I'd spent my first 11 years, into West Los Angeles, an area called Palms. I had to adjust to a new, much smaller school. There, I met Jean, and we soon discovered that we lived a half-block from one another. By the end of sixth grade, we were inseparable. If she wasn't at my house, I was in her apartment. And if we weren't together, we were on the phone with each other. She introduced me to the popular Gothic horror serial *Dark Shadows* and we parked ourselves in front of the TV every weekday afternoon, swooning over handsome Quentin Collins. We both had huge crushes on teen idol David Cassidy as well.

Eleven days apart in age, we turned 12, then 13. She was tall and thin, with silky-straight long hair, and she developed early and hugely. All I developed was a bigger roll around my belly. I still had the braces and the frizzy hair. We did adolescent girl things like buying matching dresses. Only they didn't really match; hers was size 5, mine was size 13. But she was my best friend and we knew everything about one another.

We could make each other laugh until we peed our pants. She was so envious that I got my period first and couldn't wait to call me and crow about it when she finally got hers. Of course, after a while, we both wondered why the hell we'd wanted the damn thing in the first place.

Boys liked Jean. Boys talked to me because I was friends with Jean. I was the sidekick, the unattractive buddy. I was used to feeling second-best, so this was familiar territory. It still hurt, though. She was very popular in junior high and I tried my best to keep up with her. When she started smoking, I did too. When she cut class, so did I.

When I spent weekends with my father and S, I was able to forget about my home life for a while and enjoy a very different existence. They still lived in Beverly Hills, in a large house above Sunset Boulevard. There was a swimming pool and a pool table, and I had my own huge bedroom and bathroom.

Weekends were party central—they had an open-door policy and many people dropped in, including my father's writer friends and the occasional actor or comic. Food and drink were plentiful, music played, S danced, my father told jokes and made everyone laugh. I hated it when Sunday nights came and my father drove me home. Although a lot of the time, he didn't—he'd ask someone else to do it because he'd had too much to drink. Odd, because the people he asked had usually drunk as much as he.

Sometimes Jean would come with me to my father's house on weekends. She thought Dad and S were the coolest parents ever, as did I. They never embarrassed me in front of her like my mother did with all her inappropriate comments and nosy questions.

Fights with my mother escalated and got uglier, and my shrieking refrain at the end of them became, "I want to live with my father!" She would ask her friends for their advice on how to handle me, and when they came over, I'd get strange looks and little lectures from them. That mortified and infuriated me; I hated how she was airing our dirty laundry to anyone who would listen. And of course, her friends' kids were always better behaved, smarter, nicer, thinner, prettier, got better grades.

I know I was no picnic as a daughter either. I tormented my mother with comparisons to S—her beauty, her grace, her gorgeous clothes. And I was hateful to M. One night, I was on the phone (with Jean, as usual) and he wanted me to get off. I ignored him and kept on talking. He came into my room without knocking, strode over to the bed and pushed the button down on the phone, disconnecting my call. I was beside myself with fury, but there was nothing I could do. So I stopped speaking to him.

At dinner, it was my job to clear the dishes and put away the leftovers. I'd clear everything else off the table and leave his plate. When my mother yelled at me to get the plate, I'd pick it up with the tips of my fingers as if I found it repulsive. Later on when I was going to bed, I'd pass their room and call out, "Good night, Mom." One night, M blew up and said, "Goddammit, if you can't say good night to both of us, don't say it at all." *All right, what-*

ever you say, I thought. The next night, I didn't say good night to either of them.

I know, I know. I was horrible. My anger was all-consuming and I had no healthy outlet for it.

I think my extended silent treatment to M was what finally undid my mother, because shortly thereafter, we had a huge, bitter fight and she screamed, "You want to live with your father? Fine! Go!"

So, as soon as the school year ended, I packed up all my things and moved into the 4300-square-foot house with Dad and S. I was 13 and that summer was possibly the most idyllic I've ever had.

Freed from my mother's rules, I slept until past noon, didn't make my bed, watched as much TV as I pleased, went swimming at midnight, ate anything I wanted. S was very kind to me, talking with me until all hours, taking me shopping, driving me everywhere. I volunteered weekdays at a recreation center for teens at Roxbury Park, hung out there and played pool, answered phones and drew fliers for various activities.

I did not speak to my mother all that summer, although we exchanged a few letters. My best friend Jean, as it happened, had also gone to live with *her* father and stepmother in Carlsbad, but she came to visit me and would stay for several days at a time.

Life was good, that summer of 1971. I didn't have a care in the world.

But that was all about to change.

CAREFREE YOUTH, MY A@#

"Only the good die young."
—Oliver Herford, British-born American writer, 1863–1935

In September 1971, I turned 14 and started ninth grade at Beverly Hills High School. Things started to change after I went back to school; the party-time atmosphere of the summer was over and reality had set in. I was in a new school and knew no one, and I struggled with many of my classes.

And things at home were definitely different. My father, who had always been the life of the party on the weekends, was not the same during the week—he was busy, tense, often withdrawn. My stepmother assumed most of the responsibility for me; she drove me to and from school, ran errands with me, talked with me, counseled me. When I got poor grades my first semester, she was the one, not my father, who came to school and talked with my teachers. Dad would stay out of things until she pushed him to get involved, and then he would jump in, yell at me over whatever I'd done and then withdraw again.

On weekends when he was drinking a fair amount, he was more jovial. During the week, he was someone I didn't know.

I started seeing my mother again for brief visits. It was awkward and uncomfortable for both of us, but she tried and so did I. Still, I wished S were my mother. I felt so much closer to her, although I was beginning to get a sense that she was growing impatient with having to deal with me so much. I don't think taking on all the burdens of being both my mother *and* my father had been on her agenda. Also, things between her and Dad seemed a bit strained.

A frequent visitor during the weekend gatherings was a local cop who patrolled our area. S had met him while walking our beagle, Sheba. He was in his late 20s, handsome and cocky and flirtatious. Something about him made me uncomfortable, but I couldn't quite figure out what it was. Maybe it was the way he looked at me.

One Sunday, we were having a party and he dropped by during a break. S fixed him a plate of food, beef stroganoff over brown rice. He sat on the couch in the den, putting the plate on his knees. I was sitting next to him. He shifted slightly, and a small pile of the rice tumbled off his plate and scattered over his crotch.

"Now look what you made me do," he scolded.

"Me?"

"Yeah, you," he said, eyeing me. "Well?"

I was genuinely perplexed. "Well, what?"

He gestured at the rice all over his lap. "Go ahead, clean me up."

Nice. I was 14 years old, for God's sake.

At the end of April 1972, S went away for a while. My father said she was staying at a friend's beach house by herself, that she needed some time alone. This made me nervous, but I kept quiet. In the meantime, I had a carpool taking me to school in the morning, but S wouldn't be around to pick me up after school, so Dad gave me money for cab fare to come home each day.

On May 1, I arrived home and was surprised to see several cars, including my father's, parked in our large circular driveway. The front door was unlocked and I entered, feeling apprehensive. Some of my dad's friends were there, and their faces turned collectively toward me, staring at me with what looked like pity.

Then my father came forward, took me into his bedroom and said he had something to tell me. I jumped the gun. "You and S are getting a divorce?"

"No."

"Oh. Well, aren't you separated?"

"No, honey," he said, "it's not S. It's Ken."

My brother. Dad didn't have to say anything more; I could tell from the tone of his voice.

"He's dead, isn't he."

"Yes," my father said, and then started to sob. It was a car accident. Five people had been in the vehicle; only the driver survived.

I'd never seen a grown man cry, and seeing my own father do so threw my world upside down. Life felt like a nightmare, one from which I desperately wanted to wake up but couldn't.

Later that day, my mother and M showed up; Mom crying so hard, she could barely walk. She clung to me and said I was her only baby left, begged me to never leave her. The rest of the afternoon and evening was a blur of pain and tears, of the doorbell and phone ringing, of sad faces and murmured words of comfort.

At some point, a family friend showed up with buckets of chicken. It was the perfect gesture, as none of us had eaten anything in hours.

Dad called S at the beach house where she was staying and asked her to please come home. As I recall, she did not come back that night, but the next day. Or perhaps the day after that. It really didn't matter at that point.

Because when my father called to tell her that his son had died, he found out she wasn't alone. Mr. Lecherous Cop was with her. I didn't learn this tidbit until several years later.

I didn't go to school for two days. People came and went; the phone never stopped. When you're an adult and someone close to you dies, you don't have time for the pain at first. There are too many details to be handled, too many harsh realities that won't go away simply because you need time to grieve. But when you're a kid and don't have to deal with any of that, you have nothing but time.

People act different when there has been "A Death." On the morning when I went back to school, I couldn't face going in, so I cut my first class and sat by myself on the front lawn. I knew I'd be reported as absent, so I had to go to the office and tell them I was late. The sour-faced woman behind the desk glared at me and asked why I'd missed first period, and I said I didn't feel well.

She snapped that she had to call my parents and went to the phone. I watched her face as she spoke. "Yes... Uh huh... Oh... I see. I'm sorry. Yes, thank you." She hung up and when she came back over to me, there was a pitying, sickly sweet smile on her face. "Yes, dear, you go on ahead to class," she said in her best tones of false kindness.

I wanted to slap her silly.

Because Ken and I had been eight years apart and the opposite gender, we never had a chance to get close. Still, he was always there, my big brother. As I grew older, perhaps he could have given me insights about our parents. Instead, I felt abandoned once again. *How could you leave me alone with these crazy people?*, I thought. *What will I do now?* My parents were both wrecks, and although S had come home, she was somewhat detached. I was scared. Now the only child, I had to make good. I had to be better.

I had not been raised with any sort of religion, even though my family was Jewish. All the years that Rina lived with us, my parents got Christmas trees and celebrated that holiday to make her feel at home; she was Catholic and deeply religious. My mother tried to introduce Judaism to me later, but I had no interest. I had been to few Bar Mitzvahs and the obligatory Passover Seders, and that was as far as I wanted to go.

I didn't know whether or not I believed in God; I never gave it that much thought.

Ken, however, was deeply spiritual, a seeker, and someone who was willing to trust and believe, to the point of naiveté sometimes. Shortly before he died, he joined a cult that was worshipping a 13-year-old guru. He traveled with this group, played music and lived a Spartan existence. The last time I saw him, he seemed happy and healthy; he'd cut his hair, quit smoking and seemed at peace with himself, albeit a bit fanatical about this "knowledge" with which he claimed to be enlightened. I thought he was a little nuts, but I was 14, what did I know?

After his death, two very distinct groups of his friends came to see us. One group was comprised of his old high school friends, the ones I remembered from when I was little. They gave me warm hugs, cried with me and talked with me for hours, relating all sorts of fun Ken stories.

Then there was the second group, the friends he'd made in the cult. They didn't cry; they didn't share stories. They preached to me, told me my brother was in a better place, that he had "gone home" and other euphemisms, and that I could miss his earthly being, but I should try not to grieve.

I have a clear memory of sitting in our living room with one of them sitting across from me, looking very placid with her hands folded in her lap. "Dear Sister, do not be sad," she said earnestly. "Ken is with his True Father now."

I just stared at her. *I'm not your fucking sister. And Ken's "true father" is sitting right over there, drunk and crying. Get out of my face.*

My anger was deep and profound. And that day, I decided there was no God. There was no reason why someone like Ken should be killed while a loser like me was left to live. No loving God would take a happy young man with his whole life ahead of him, splatter him on the freeway and then leave me to deal with all this crap. I was well and truly alone.

* * *

Summer passed. I turned 15 and went into 10th grade. School was no easier this year and my grades slipped. I fell in with a semi-rough crowd who cut classes, did drugs and had a lot of sex. I was still a virgin, but I smoked cigarettes and pot with my friends. We got the munchies and pigged out at all hours, and my weight escalated.

There was one good thing about the 10th grade: in my English class, the teacher, Mr. Stern, introduced us to the concept of journaling. I had never kept a journal before and took to it immediately, relishing the feel of my words and emotions pouring out of my fingers from the pen onto the lined paper, filling page after page. Then, and in the coming years, it seemed that the ability to release my feelings in this manner kept me from going completely insane.

I had frequent nightmares. In one I can still recall, I was stranded in a small boat, adrift in a large body of water with no land in sight. I was frightened and alone, so I was overjoyed to see Ken's head pop out of the water.

He smiled reassuringly at me and I thought I would now be rescued. I reached out to him and as I did, the smile left his face and he disappeared under the surface of the water once more. I cried and screamed for him to come back, but he didn't.

One morning before school, shortly before the holidays, I was waiting for the carpool to pick me up. My folks kept cartons of cigarettes in a drawer in the living room, and I used to wait until they stocked the drawer and then steal packs, figuring they wouldn't notice. I wasn't sure whether or not the drawer had been refilled lately, so I quietly slid it open. Damn... just two packs left, so I couldn't take one.

"Erica, what are you doing?" S had walked into the room. I froze, my stomach plunging to my feet, my ears buzzing with panic. "I said, what are you doing?"

Just then, the carpool honked outside. "Go to school," she said. "We'll discuss this later."

If you think I was a nervous wreck all that day in school, you would be correct. But I had no idea what was coming.

S picked me up from school, saying that my father was waiting for me at home. The lecture about smoking turned out to be rather anticlimactic. What could he say? He smoked himself.

Just as I was heaving a sigh of relief, he went on to tell me that he and S were splitting up.

She'd been sleeping in the spare bedroom, so it shouldn't have come as a shock, but it still did. The worst part of it was they couldn't afford to get a divorce until they sold the house, and the housing market was lousy at the time. She couldn't afford to move out, so she was going to continue living there, but would go about her business.

As I was reeling over this, Dad told me he had to go out, but said we could talk about this further at another time. He went out the front door, then came back in. "Hey, Erica?"

"Yeah?"

"Do you have any cigarettes? I'm out."

Excuse me? "Um... no," I stammered.

"Oh, some help *you* are," he scoffed, and then left, only to come back in yet again, triumphantly waving a pack of cigarettes in his hand. "I found these under the car seat," he said, and he dug into it, pulling out several and handing them to me. "Here you go. I'm buying more tomorrow."

Yes, it was extremely weird. And it turned out to be the best way he could have handled the situation. He treated me like an adult rather than a child, and in doing so, removed the thrill and forbiddenness of smoking for me. I soon got bored with it and quit before I left high school.

Brief segue regarding the aforementioned carpool. There were three other girls in the carpool: Faith, Judy and Jamie. Faith's and Judy's parents drove us, but when it was Jamie's turn, the driver was a maid named Margaret. Therefore, I never got to meet Janet Leigh or Tony Curtis.

* * *

As far as S was concerned, now that she and Dad were separated, I had no idea where I stood with her—if she still cared about me, if she would still be my confidant and surrogate parent.

She used to tell me directly when I had displeased her somehow, but now she went to Dad instead, bypassing communication with me.

One evening, my girlfriend and I were at the park, waiting for S to pick us up. One of the guys in our crowd was waiting with us, keeping us company. As S drove up, I gave him a hug and a quick kiss good night, and my girlfriend did the same.

S didn't say a word. But the next day, when my father and I were driving my friend back home, Dad blurted out of nowhere, "S said you were necking in public. I don't want you doing that again. You look like a tramp." I was shocked and horribly embarrassed; it hadn't been like that at all. But when I tried to tell him so, he snapped, "I said *no necking!*" End of subject.

Sometimes late at night, I'd awaken and hear them fighting. I'd get up, tiptoe across the room and put my ear to the door, listening.

One night, I heard S yelling about how out of control I was and how my father needed to step up and be a parent.

31

"I'm sick of being her designated parent, when she already has a mother and a father," she said. "I've been doing it for too long, and now I'm done. I resign."

Well, I guess I got my answer about where I stood with her. I slunk back to bed, burrowed under the covers and curled up into a tight ball. I was too numb to cry.

Life went on. I hung out with my friends more and my grades slipped further. I did not date, however. Even though it was the '70s (the pre-AIDS era of promiscuity), I was far too uptight to even consider sex; the idea frightened me. I had some fierce crushes on certain boys, but they were one-sided and went nowhere.

At home, things were increasingly tense. S came and went and lived her life separately from ours. My father threw himself into his work. I withdrew from both of them, and the evenings I was home, I ate frozen dinners and canned soup and watched a lot of TV by myself.

One Saturday night I was supposed to go out, but decided at the last minute that I didn't feel like it and I stayed home. I was comfortably crashed on the living room couch, watching TV with the dog snoring at my side, when the front door opened and my father walked in. With him was a woman I'd never seen before. When I first laid eyes on her, my initial thought, and I kid you not, was, "Oh God, it's come to this. Dad's gotten himself a hooker."

She was dressed in a skin-tight green jumpsuit made of shiny material, very low-cut with unnaturally large breasts bulging out of the plunging neckline. Her makeup looked as if it had been spackled on, she had false eyelashes, her lips and fingernails were painted fire-engine red. Over-teased and over-sprayed black hair surrounded her face. My father was in his 50s, but she looked to be in her early 30s.

The moment was awkward; clearly, they hadn't expected me to be there. My father introduced us and then they left. I shrugged it off and went back to the TV. Have a good time, Dad. Leave her a nice tip.

I had no idea that night, but things were about to change once again. If I thought my life had sucked before, it was a trip to Disneyland compared to what was coming.

MY BODY, MY PRISON

"I think I've lost another 2 ½ pounds, but I think my fa-ther's scale is a little off. By the time school starts, I ought to have lost a noticeable amount of weight. Then maybe I'll be noticed, and people who lose weight receive considera-ble admiration and attention. I think I could use a little of that."
—my journal, July 23, 1973

By summer 1973, my father and S were divorced and Dad and I had moved to a two-bedroom apartment. He was dating Green Jumpsuit Woman (turns out she wasn't ac-tually a hooker after all). B is the initial of her first name; as coincidence would have it, it's also the first letter of bar-racuda. But it was early in their relationship and she hadn't shown her true personality yet, so she was nice to me. I was suspicious of her at first, but gradually grew comfortable with her and her two kids.

My weight was the highest it had ever been and now my size 13/14 clothes, the largest size I'd ever worn, were too tight. I didn't think much about it, although there were painful reminders of my overweight condition.

Earlier that year when we were still living with S at the big house, I'd had a couple of friends over and we were in the den playing records (round black vinyl objects that you played on a thing called a hi-fi). We got a little silly, rough-housing a bit, and I stumbled and sat down hard on the wooden coffee table...and then I fell through it. It splin-tered all around me with a horrible sound and I landed with a loud thunk on the carpet.

S heard the noise and came running, and she saw me sitting, stunned, among the shards of the table. The look on her face transformed from concern to disgust. She rolled her eyes, turned to walk back out and loudly announced, "It's diet time!" My friends burst out laughing. I wanted to disappear.

I loved to eat! Food was a comfort and had been for many years. My mother was a good cook and we ate well.

When I was little, food was always a reward or a bribe. ("Be a good girl when we're shopping and we'll get ice cream.") As I grew into my teens, the cutting remarks became more frequent. "You're not going to eat all that, are you?" "Do you really need that second helping?" "Are you eating *again*?"

But I ignored them all and went on stuffing myself. I could eat a large pizza all by myself, or an entire Sara Lee coffee cake. I'd make Kraft Macaroni & Cheese and eat the whole pot. Pints of ice cream were supposed to be four servings, but I made them one serving.

But that summer, I'd finally had it. My mother suggested I go on Weight Watchers® and I agreed. She said she'd do it with me, so we went to meetings together. This gave us a shared focus and brought us closer. We'd never really had anything in common before.

My starting point was 155 pounds; WW set my goal at 125. I followed the diet faithfully, but the weight loss was frustratingly slow. Still, by the time 11th grade started, I had lost enough weight so that people noticed. The positive attention hit me like a triple espresso.

I turned 16—my birthday present to myself was breaking my diet and eating fried chicken, of all things. I passed on cake and had a hot fudge sundae instead.

Everyone I knew was eagerly going for a driver's license, but I had no desire to learn how to drive. After what happened to my brother, I was too scared. At least now we lived in the "flats" area of Beverly Hills and I had access to the bus just two blocks from our apartment.

I had dropped out of the stoner crowd I'd been hanging with, because I no longer enjoyed their company. They were all about drinking, drugging and screwing and it got old, not to mention scary. Therefore, I spent most of my time alone. At least with no social life, I didn't have to deal with tempting food at every turn. My weight continued to drop and I bought new clothes. I came closer to my goal weight each week.

Just before Thanksgiving, I became terribly ill. My temperature shot up and I developed a sore throat that was so painful, I couldn't eat or drink.

I had never experienced anything like this; it felt as if razor blades were cutting into my throat. It turned out I had both mono and strep throat, so I was put on antibiotics plus codeine for the pain of the strep. I missed two weeks of school and basically lived in my bed, sleeping on and off in a haze of pain and drugs.

Thanksgiving came and went. I remember my dad went to a restaurant owned by a friend of his, and he brought home complete Thanksgiving dinners on china plates for us. But I couldn't touch more than a couple of bites.

My mother came to visit me, as did B, bringing soup and books and games. Although I had gone missing from school for two weeks, my phone did not ring. I suppose I shouldn't have expected otherwise, but it still hurt.

It took a long time to recover and I was very weak. School was a nightmare because I had missed so much. Then I went to my WW meeting and discovered I'd lost eight pounds. I was now below my goal; I weighed 122. You would think I'd be overjoyed, but instead, I felt panic. *Now what do I do?*

Do I stay on the Weight Watcher's plan, even though I've lost all my weight? Do I start eating more? Do I incorporate some treats back into my diet? How much? What if I gain the weight back? What if I went through all that work for nothing?

Today, WW is a very livable plan that incorporates all types of food and a points system. But back then, the plan was much more rigid and completely cut out certain foods, including anything made with sugar. I had no idea how to re-incorporate those foods, or in what amounts. Also, back then, products did not come with nutritional information and calorie counts.

I knew how to diet, but I didn't know how to eat in order to *maintain* my weight; I was flying blind. So... I decided the easiest thing was to keep on dieting.

My weight dropped below 120, then to 115. And then to 110. I lost my periods and I was tired all the time. The compliments on my new body were becoming comments of concern.

But the thinner I got, the better I thought I looked. I didn't want curves and roundness; those were composed of FAT. Fat meant ridicule and shame. In my distorted view, even a small fold of skin was fat.

I loved how my collarbone, ribs and hipbones stood out in sharp relief. My father greeting me with "Hey, skinny," was music to my ears. I stopped buying groceries and preparing healthful meals and snacks; it was much simpler to just not eat.

There was only one problem—I was starving! So eventually, I'd cave and binge on everything I could get my hands on for a day or so. Fueled by shame over my binges, I'd counteract them with days of starving myself.

And so an insidious binge/starve pattern was born. Eating normal meals and the feeling of comfortable fullness became distant memories. I was either ravenously hungry or I was stuffed to the point of sickness; there was no middle ground.

I never purged, as I had a fear of vomiting. That made sense; vomiting was a loss of control and that was unacceptable to me.

My life had been a series of events I had no say-so over, but finally, I'd found something I could control—my own body. So instead of making myself throw up, I started abusing laxatives and diuretics when I felt fat from my binges. Soon my body adjusted to them and I had to increase the dosages.

Food consumed my thoughts day and night. I read women's magazines just to look at the pictures of the pot roasts and cakes and pasta, and I went to the market and walked up and down the aisles, looking at tempting displays but never buying anything other than my usual apples, carrots and instant coffee. Unless I was bingeing.

One time, I grabbed a loaf of French bread and started cramming chunks into my face as I shopped. Before I knew it, I was at the register with my meager groceries, plus a waxed-paper bag that was empty save for the loaf's heel. Embarrassed, I put the bag on the conveyor belt. The checker picked it up, looked at it and then at me, and said in a tone of the utmost disgust, "The whole loaf?!" My face burned with shame.

Another time, I caved in to compulsion and bought a cinnamon coffee cake. I made it to the car and then began tearing into it as I drove, barely paying attention to what I was doing. After several mouthfuls, I became horrified at my manic gorging and without another thought, I opened my window and threw half a cake into the street.

I would go to bed hungry and dream of eating. I'd have nightmares of gaining all my weight back and then some. Sometimes my father came home late at night and I could hear him putting leftovers in the refrigerator. I kept our fridge mostly empty, since he was almost never there anyway and I ate so little. Knowing there was something new and wonderful in there consumed me and I couldn't go back to sleep. Finally, I would give in, get up and go to the kitchen and devour whatever he brought home, at 3:00 A.M., standing at the sink or at the open fridge door.

What was it like to co-exist peacefully with food without thinking about it night and day, without it being my best friend and my worst enemy? I forgot. And for many years, I had no idea.

EVIL WOMAN

"It hurts, thinking that this woman is calling me all kinds of dirty names and wishing me dead, and my father won't tell her where to go. How can he have a relationship with someone who hates his child?"
—my journal, April 30, 1974

In spring 1974, I had all four wisdom teeth pulled. Not an experience I would recommend, especially if the teeth are impacted (two of mine were). Eating was a challenge for a while and my weight dropped to 107. But it was all right, because I was anticipating a three-day weekend vacation with my father, B and her daughter M. I was going to eat anything and everything I wanted.

Early on a Friday morning, the four of us headed out in B's car to La Costa, a fancy-shmancy resort and spa in Carlsbad. M and I shared a room; she was two years my junior. La Costa was extremely plush and great for a romantic getaway or a weekend of pampering, but it held little interest for two teenage girls. I thought it was boring and pretentious, and ridiculously expensive. But whatever; it was where our parents had chosen to go.

On Saturday morning, M and I had plans to have breakfast together and explore the grounds. But when I woke up, I discovered she had already left without me. Not the biggest deal in the world, but when you're 16, everything is a big deal.

When I found her having lunch with her mother, we argued. It wasn't much of an argument, just a little snit, really, but B got very agitated with me, butting in and snapping, "What the hell difference does it make, Erica—just order some lunch now and forget about it."

Fine. I shrugged it off and got some food. Then, B wanted M and me to come with her while she had a day at the spa.

We weren't getting any treatments, mind you. No, we just had to sit around while she got her hair done, a manicure/pedicure and an avocado facial. *Yawn.* Meanwhile, my father had come down with a cold and was back in his hotel room by himself.

After about an hour, I decided I'd had enough of watching B sit there with green mush on her face, so I excused myself and went back to my dad's room. We spent the afternoon playing our favorite card game, Spite and Malice.

Around 5:30, B came back to their room, her hair ratted a foot off her head and a murderous look on her painted face. "Erica, I want to speak to your father." I had no idea what this was about, but I wasn't going to hang around and find out. I went back to my room and found M there, changing her clothes. I asked her what was going on, but she wouldn't speak to me. What the hell? After she'd changed, she left.

I don't remember how long I sat in the room by myself, wondering what was up. When my father arrived, I didn't have to wonder anymore; he was furious with me. Apparently, B was not pleased that I had the audacity to prefer my father's company to hers; plus, she was ticked off that I had argued with her daughter. She and M were in the main dining room waiting for him while he talked to me. Oh, hell. Fine, so I'd listen to the third degree and order room service afterward.

As my father was in mid-lecture, the phone rang and he picked it up. B's voice came screeching out into the room. "Where the fuck are you? Get away from that bitch! We're waiting for you!" The venom in her voice made my blood freeze. I figured she was mad, but this was beyond mad.

Dad insisted he'd come down when he was good and ready. "Goddammit, we have three prime-rib dinners sitting here waiting!" To that, my father replied, "You can take your prime-rib dinners and shove them up your ass." As you can imagine, that was not well received.

"I'm coming up there! You tell that bitch to get ready, because I'm going to kill her!"

Say what?

My father slammed down the phone and I freaked out. "Don't let her in here! She's going to kill me!"

"She's not going to kill anyone," he scoffed as he went to crack the door. Within minutes, B stormed in, pushing the door open so fiercely that it crashed against the wall and slammed back shut. Then she proceeded to get right in my face and call me every ugly name in the lexicon, with all the requisite filthy adjectives.

Along with the name-calling, she said she wished I had died with my brother, and that I should be in a shrink's office every single day with guilt coming out of my ass because I was still alive. That I destroyed people's lives and I should be put away. All this because I hadn't wanted to sit and watch her get lacquered and spackled? Where the hell was this coming from?

My mother had yelled at me many times and criticized me to pieces, but she'd never said things like this. I was paralyzed; I could not speak. I opened my mouth, but nothing came out. I was too scared to defend myself for fear she would attack me physically.

Her tirade was horrible enough, but the worst part it was that my father just sat there. I kept looking at him, waiting for him to jump in, to tell her to knock it off, that she couldn't say things like that to his daughter. But he said nothing; his face was impassive and stony. And so she screamed filth at me until she ran out of expletives, then turned and strode out the door. Outside, she yelled, "Ed, get out here. Get away from that c***." Without a word to me, he left.

A few minutes later, M came back in, crying. She still would not speak to me, which was fine by me. I was so hysterical, I trembled all over and my teeth were chattering. It took an hour for the tremors to subside, but the panic never left me. After M had gone to bed and our lights were out, I lay on the bed fully clothed, muscles rigid, heart banging in my chest. I couldn't move, I couldn't sleep. Every sound I heard, in my mind, was her coming back to kill me. Sweat drenched me and I could smell my own fear.

The next day, the three of them drove home. I was in exile, unwelcome in B's car; my father put me on a plane. I found out from M, who finally spoke to me, that B and Dad had fought all night in their room, and my father had broken two chairs and torn a lamp out of the wall.

Things between my father and me were strained after that weekend. He refused to discuss what had happened, and he spent most of his time after work at B's house now. The only time he came home was when he needed some of his things, or when they'd had a fight.

Sometimes late at night, I'd hear him come in. Then a minute or two later, he'd get on the phone. As I'd done before, I'd leave my bed and go press my ear to the door. He would try keep his voice down, but it was still audible, and I could tell from his end of the conversation that she was talking about me during parts of it. "No, I'm not going to talk louder." "That's right; I don't want her to hear." "No, she is *not* a c***."

Now, those who know me are aware that I have a violent revulsion for that word; I can't speak it, and obviously I can't even type it either. It's silly of me; a word is just a word. But it's a word that resonates with some of my ugliest memories; hearing it is like a fist in my stomach.

In all our years together, my boyfriend has used it once. Not to me, thank God; he was talking about a relentless telemarketer who had called him several times. At the time, I immediately lost it and screamed, "If you *ever* use that word again in my presence, I'm leaving you."

Extreme, I know. But I never heard him say it again.

This whole fiasco did have one unexpected benefit—I grew closer to my mother and M, finally. She was appalled at B's behavior and my father's apathy around it, and she hated that I spent so much time alone. By now, they had bought a house in the San Fernando Valley and I started spending weekends there with them. My living situation from a few years prior had now flip-flopped.

As summer passed and I went into my senior year, my life followed a set pattern. Each weekday, I'd get up early, have a cup of black coffee and an apple or a large carrot, take the bus to school, and come back home at 1:00. I slept all afternoon, woke up and did homework, watched some TV and went to bed. Most of the time I didn't eat anything else, until I got so hungry and weak that my control slipped.

Come Fridays, Mom and M would pick me up that evening and take me back to their house, where I'd stay until Sunday evening. Weekends were active; we'd shop, cook, garden, entertain, see movies. And I'd eat everything in sight. My mother was distressed with my weight and made sure she had all my favorite foods in the house, and she cooked everything I liked. Friday through Sunday was one long binge. Then I would come home Sunday night, my stomach so distended and taut that I wondered if that was what it was like being pregnant. Monday morning, the cycle would begin again.

My weight was now around 105 and my periods were still missing. Unlike many young girls with eating disorders, I did not exercise. I was too exhausted and weak most of the time, and simply doing day-to-day necessary activities was a huge effort. In fact, I used to beg off Phys Ed as often as I dared, claiming I had cramps. Ironic, since I didn't even have periods.

Eventually, my father was able to arrange reconciliation between B and me. However, she had revealed her true colors to me and this was to be the first time of many that she did so. She could keep the sweet façade up only so long before the next explosion. Then I'd be in exile once again.

As high school graduation approached, it became clear that my father wanted me to move out that summer so he could move in with B. He said he would pay for it, and suggested that I move to the Valley so I could live closer to Mom and M. Why not, I thought. I would no longer have any ties to Beverly Hills once I was out of school. On weekends that spring, my mother and I went apartment hunting, and she looked at other places for me during the week. Together we found a one-bedroom unit in Canoga Park. The name of the street? Independence Avenue.

It was settled; right after graduation, I was moving into my own place. Not that it would feel that different, really—my father spent so much time away that I might as well have been living alone anyway. I looked forward to a fresh start. Maybe I could conquer this crazy binge-starve syndrome too.

Dark Days

"Elvis Presley is dead. Just like that, no warning, he's gone. No more suffering. Some people have all the luck. There's no one in this world who wants to die more than I do."
—my journal, August 16, 1977

My first apartment on Independence Ave. cost $159 a month. It had gold shag carpeting, bubble-gum pink kitchen appliances, high-beam ceilings that leaked when it rained and dreadfully ugly black linoleum in the bathroom. But it was mine. I put a cardboard box in front of the living room couch until I could afford to get a coffee table, the first piece of furniture I bought with my own money.

Because my father had essentially hustled me out so he could go shack up with B, I guess he felt guilty, because he offered to pay my rent and bills if I went to school. However, I didn't want to go. Who needs college, right? Another few years of cramming my brain with useless crap that I wouldn't remember. Hey, I was 17; I already knew everything I needed to know. Dad said if I wasn't going to attend school, I had to work.

So I got my first job at a burger joint near my apartment. After the better part of a year spent smelling like grease and onions and having mustard permanently embedded under my fingernails, fending off lecherous bosses and dealing with the fast-food-eating public, I changed my tune.

I remember the day I had my epiphany. It was the lunch rush and a trio of construction workers came in from a nearby site. They were dirty and disgusting, and they deliberately gave me a lot of trouble as I took their order, asking several questions, pretending they didn't hear the answers and asking again, ordering things and then changing their minds, making me cross things out so many times that I had to start over. The line piled up behind them and I got flustered, and they laughed at me. They got their food and sat down to eat in the dining room. I forgot about them until they got up to leave and one of them called out, "Hey,

43

honey? I think you need to do some cleaning up here." Looking over to where they'd been sitting, I didn't need my glasses to see they'd left a disaster area.

The manager sent me to the table to take care of the mess. Not only had they left all their used food wrappers and napkins, but they had taken bits of meat, bun and soggy fries and smashed them into the table. Then they'd opened up ketchup packets and smeared the contents on the table, the chairs and the nearby window. Cigarette butts and ashes topped off the detritus. Also, they'd ground the mess into the floor underneath with their dirty work boots.

It took a half-hour to clean all that, and I did so with angry tears dripping. As I scrubbed and mopped, it hit me: "If I don't go back to school, this is the only kind of work I'll be able to get for the rest of my life." After that, I was more than ready to go to college. So, you scumbag jerks, wherever you may be now, thank you!

* * *

California State University, Northridge was a large, daunting campus and I had no idea what I wanted to major in. That first semester, I took a full-time (12-unit) load of general education classes. The amount of reading and homework required was a shock; much more than high school, and I struggled a bit. My grades were so-so.

Before the second semester began, my father called. We did not speak very often, so hearing his voice on the phone always made me tense up—it was never good news. Sure enough, he gave me two orders: choose a major and get a part-time job. When I protested, saying that I didn't think I could handle full-time school plus work, he said, for the first time of many to come, "Well, you could always tell me to go to hell." In other words, I could do it his way, or I could manage completely on my own without him.

So I found a job, cashiering and stocking in a building-supply warehouse near school. The hours were flexible and several college students worked there, so I was able to work my schedule around classes. I had no idea which major to choose or in which direction I wanted to go, but Dad insisted, so I chose Graphic Arts. Why? Because my brother had been an artist. I figured I should be as well.

I was now taking 12 units and working 25 hours a week. My eating disorders ramped up; now I was going on uncontrollable compulsive binges along with the stuffing and starving regimen. I was tired all the time, depressed and filled with anger that I crammed down with food or detached from by oversleeping. Many times I cut class because I simply could not get out of bed. I had days where all function ceased; I'd stay in bed all day, not dressing, staring at the TV for hours, not answering the phone.

Relations with my father and with B were rocky at best. B would call me, act very sweet and engage me in conversation. Then, within the next 24 hours, I'd get an angry phone call from my father, accusing me of insulting her somehow. She'd take innocent things I said and convolute them, and no amount of pleading and protesting on my part could get Dad to believe me. We'd have periods of not speaking to one another, make a grudging peace and then repeat the cycle. I got so used to being accused of things that never happened that I likened the feeling to being in prison for crimes I didn't commit.

After I barely made it through that second semester, stressed out from my job and making mediocre grades, my father found out that, although I'd been taking what was considered a full class load, 12 units per semester would take me five years to graduate, not four. He hit the roof and told me I was going to take 15 units from now on.

I freaked out. I told him I absolutely could not handle five college courses and 25 hours of work. I had spoken to a school counselor who told me that these days, very few kids graduated in four years, because many of them worked part-time and it was too difficult to take so many classes. He kindly offered his time if Dad wanted to come to school to talk with him, but Dad wouldn't hear of it, even though I begged him to *please*, just meet the guy, hear him out. He knew best and I was going to take 15 units, period. Either that or I could always tell him to go to hell.

During the summer, my depression worsened. I worked more hours because I was off school, and other than that, I was for all intents and purposes non-functional. Fall loomed in front of me and I felt like I couldn't face it. I knew three moods that summer: deep depression, intense fear and blinding rage.

One morning, I woke up feeling not the usual turmoil, but an eerie, detached calm. I was due at work, but I didn't go and I did not get dressed. Instead, I pulled a stunt I'd seen in the old movies and TV shows—I blew out all the pilot lights in the stove and the heater, closed the windows and turned up the gas. I opened the oven door, put a pillow on it, sat on the floor and rested my head. Then I drifted off to sleep, thinking that was that.

Well, it always worked in the movies. In reality, I woke up two hours later with a raging headache in a stinking apartment, and burst into tears. *Fuck,* I thought, *I can't even die right.* As timing would have it, my mother had chosen that morning to run errands and she dropped by the hardware store to say hello. My co-workers told her that I hadn't shown up and I wasn't answering my phone. Within minutes, she was pounding on my apartment door.

It was not a good day. After opening all the windows and wrapping me in a blanket, my mother called my father, and he and B came over. Why he had to bring *her* was beyond my comprehension. I huddled on the couch, shaking all over, while they argued and talked about me as if I weren't there. My father was cold and angry at first, then started crying, which baffled me. B and Mom sniped at each other and nearly came to blows. My mother, bless her heart and her melodrama, cried, "I've already lost one child; I don't want to lose the other." B sneered, "Oh, knock it off, E—what did you ever do for the other one when he was alive, anyway?" My mother went paper-white. I then found my voice and screamed at B that I hated her and wished I were dead just so I wouldn't have to hear her filthy mouth ever again.

Definitely not a good day.

Mom called the store and told them I was very ill with food poisoning, so I didn't lose my job. My father chose a local shrink and had me start going twice a week. However, he did not ease up on the edict of 15 units plus 25 hours of work. It didn't matter what the school counselors or my mother said. Even when the shrink told him he should back off, that fell on deaf ears. I had no choice.

* * *

That following year is a blur. If I wasn't at school, I was at work, or vice versa. If not either of those places, I was home or in the library studying, or in my car en route to any of the above places. I did not have a spare minute to call my own and I often pulled all-nighters because I had so much reading and studying to do. I slogged through one day and the next and marked time toward the weekend. I had promised that I would not attempt suicide again, and I did not. But I thought about it all the time.

The obsession with my weight and eating continued. I got on the scale several times a day. If I binged, I'd torture myself by getting on the scale to see how many pounds of bloat I'd incurred. I'd weigh myself after each visit to the restroom to see if I'd lost a couple of ounces. At my thinnest, I was 103, but it fluctuated wildly because of my eating patterns.

My doctor tried putting me on antidepressants, but in those days, there were no SSRIs (selective serotonin reuptake inhibitors) such as Prozac and Effexor. If you had bipolar disorder (or manic-depression, as it was called then), you took Lithium. If you had a psychosis, you took powerful drugs such as Thorazine that left you with the energy and personality of a lump of Malt-O-Meal. And if you were depressed, there were drugs called tricyclics. I took one called Parnate for seven weeks. Along with depression, I now suffered from dizziness, ringing in my ears, insomnia and an ever-present bitter taste in my mouth. No, thank you.

During this year, the doctor also had me keeping a journal, which he read twice a week at our appointments. Therefore, I had a written record of all that went down and how I felt, which I referred to as research for this book. I had been writing for years, so it was an exercise that came easily to me. Finding the time for it, of course, was a challenge. But it was the only place, besides his office, where I could express myself.

My father and B got married that year. I found out about the wedding from a third party; I was not invited.

The temptation to succumb to depression and stay home in bed was constant and powerful. During one particularly bad funk, I didn't go to school for two weeks, right before midterms. Of course, after I snapped out of it and realized how badly I screwed up, I was sick with panic. One day back at school, I was so overwhelmed with how behind I was, I leaned up against the wall in the hallway, sank down and buried my head in my arms.

One of my teachers saw me and approached, squatting down to ask if I was all right. She took me to her office, talked with me and told me I needed to go to all my teachers and speak to them. Tell them that I was having problems, and ask how I could make up for the lost time and the midterms. She gave me a project for her own class, a fairly easy one. I took her advice and went to each class to speak to the instructor. Luckily for me, all of them were compassionate and gave me makeup assignments that were quite manageable.

Carla Green was that teacher's name; I found out the following year that she had passed away of leukemia. I never forgot her.

I managed to keep the part-time job at Builder's Discount this whole time, even though I was moody and temperamental and would get into it with customers. The store had an unusual policy—no exchanges or refunds, everything as is, and no advice on what to buy. The hard-core contractors who knew exactly what they wanted loved us, because we were so cheap. The average Joe who wanted it all—low prices *and* full service/advice/option to return or exchange—was not always too happy with us. I was constantly hungry and tired and my anger was perpetually simmering below the surface, so when someone gave me a hard time, I gave it right back.

How I didn't get fired, I'll never know. Looking back, I'm very grateful for that job, as I was able to change my hours each semester to accommodate my classes and they took me on full-time each summer.

Sophomore year ended; I got a couple of Ds, but I passed everything. I developed stomach problems; I was in pain and nauseated nearly all the time. The nausea made me anxious, and the anxiety would fuel the sick feelings. In August 1979, my mother took me to her doctor and he decided to put me in the hospital for a battery of tests, including an endoscopy. You haven't lived until you've been sedated and had a tube stuck down your throat into your stomach.

Unfortunately, I was still on my father's insurance and when he found out I was in the hospital under my mother's doctor's care, he was furious. It didn't matter that I was in perfectly capable hands; he wanted the control and the say-so. He called me at the hospital and told me that I was to pack my things and he'd send a cab, and they'd transport me to *his* doctor and *his* hospital.

I was sick, weak and worried about what could be wrong with me, and I felt safe and cared for where I was. "No," I said to him. "I'm staying here. I don't want to be moved. I don't feel well and I'm scared."

After a pause, he said in that cold voice I knew so well: "If you don't go to my doctor, I will cut you off my insurance plan." That was my cue to kowtow and obey him.

Something in me snapped; I didn't care anymore. Screw the consequences. "Go ahead," I said.

He was taken aback. "Go ahead?"

"Yeah," I said wearily. "Do it. I don't care."

"OK, babe," he said. "OK." And he hung up on me. That was the last time we spoke to each other for five-and-a-half years.

Luck was with me for once; my stepfather had a good friend who was one of the bigwigs at his HMO, and he was able to pull some strings and get me transferred immediately onto his and my mother's insurance plan, because I was under 23. (The health insurance system wasn't the fiasco it is now.) After all the tests, it was determined that I had a lot of inflammation in my stomach, a kind of pre-ulcer condition, caused by stress. With two prescriptions (Valium for anxiety, Compazine for nausea), I went home.

My father went on paying the school bills and my rent during my junior year, even though we did not speak. It was a business arrangement; I'd submit school receipts to his business manager's office and get reimbursed. And once a month, I received a check from that office, made out to my landlord for rent. When they increased my rent, I informed the office of new amount, but then heard from an administrative assistant, saying my father refused to pay the increase. So I had to give the landlord two checks: my father's plus one of my own to make up the difference.

In summer 1980, with just two semesters to go before I graduated, I received a letter from him. Businesslike and to the point, it stated that he was "sick of playing banker to a JAP [Jewish American Princess]" and as of now, I was cut off. I should have been finished with school by now anyway, so how I managed my final year was my problem.

Strangely, I didn't panic. I was just numb.

My mother had a cousin who was also in television. He was quite successful and very wealthy; he and my father had started their careers as writing partners in the late '40s–early '50s. When I told Mom what Dad had done, she suggested that I should go see our cousin and ask for help, since he had done many things for her and M and she knew he would do whatever he could for me.

So I pocketed my pride and made an appointment with him, and in his plush Century City office, I explained the situation. He spoke little, and when I wound down, he said, "Your education is the most important thing you have and you must finish school." Then he had his assistant cut me a check. When I looked at it, I started to cry. Not only was it enough to cover my tuition and supplies for the next year, but there was enough left over so that, if I budgeted carefully, I could also pay my rent and all my bills and not have to work. For the first time, I could focus 100% on school. No strings attached, no ultimatums, no more dreading the phone lest it be my father with another edict.

The relief, the sense of freedom, was profound.

Functional, Yes. Happy? No

"I got into bed at 9:00, knowing full well I was very tired and needed extra sleep, but I just lay there taut and the sleepy feeling wouldn't come. I couldn't shut off thoughts of work, and lots of other thoughts I didn't like—such as that my whole life is work, that I have nothing else, that when I'm not at work, I lie around like a vegetable, that time is going on and on and on and I'm wasting my entire youth. I'll turn around and find I'm 30 with no memories of my 20s (just like now I'm almost 25 and have nothing to treasure from my late teens and early 20s). And I'll still be a goddamn virgin!"
—my journal, February 18, 1982

My senior year at CSUN was amazing; what a difference it made when I didn't have to go to work. I was fully focused and well-rested, and I enjoyed my classes, even made a couple of friends. I graduated on the Dean's List because my final grades had been so good. For the time being, I stuffed down my anger and sadness over my father. I figured I no longer had one and that was that.

The eating issues were still with me, but they had become so ingrained, I viewed them as part of who I was and accepted them. I didn't see any way out of the patterns. Each day was a challenge and a question mark. Would I stick to my plan today? What unexpected occurrences would throw me off and trigger a binge? How could I avoid tempting food?

My depressions came and went, but I found myself with no sense of myself or inner strength. As one of my many shrinks over the years said, I was completely "other-directed" and my daily frame of mind depended upon externals. If all went well and according to plan, if everyone around me cooperated, then my mood was stable and good. However, life seldom cooperated that thoroughly, and the smallest of unexpected incidents could send me into either a rage or a deep funk. Plus, my daily mood was dictated according to what the scale read.

* * *

Something interesting happened during my senior year—I heard from my stepsister M, B's daughter. She had moved to the Valley and was living about ten minutes from me. We got together and ended up spending a fair amount of time with each other for a while.

I learned quite a lot from her. Apparently, after I was out of the picture, she became the family scapegoat. Nothing she did was right and her mother was always threatening to throw her out. Eventually, that's exactly what she did. M was working full-time as a supermarket checker, making decent money. She was able to afford her own apartment and I visited often.

M had told B that she was in contact with me, which infuriated B. My name was mud in that household and no one was to speak of me. According to M, my father had called her a few times, lowering his voice as if he didn't want to be heard. "How is Erica?" "How is her health?" "Is she still in school?" "Is she dating?" "Is she happy?" Needless to say, this was a shock and an eye-opener.

It was also rather enlightening to hear M say that all my father's decisions regarding me had been prompted by her mother. The battle lines had been drawn early and clearly— he had to choose between me and her. On the one hand, there was his troubled teenage daughter who would be moving on with her life anyway; on the other, a young companion and regular sex. He made the wrong choice, out of his own needs and weaknesses. I could fault him for weakness, but as far as malice was concerned, B was the champion there, not my father.

In May 1981, I graduated. Soon thereafter, my best friend and I both got our first real jobs in a graphics office. I started as general office help and driver, picking up and delivering jobs, but after a while, the boss discovered I was excellent with typography (I knew all the terms, how to recognize fonts, how to read type specs, etc.) and that I had a sharp eye for errors. Within a couple of months, I was retired from running errands and was proofreading full time. My career had been born.

* * *

As I went through my 20s, working and doing little else, the spanking thing niggled at the back of my mind. The days of working at the hardware store had been rife with spanking comments and threats, all of which made me blush and squirm. The office manager at my first job called me "brat" and, as usual, my stomach lurched. One of the typesetters had made some funny errors and I was teasing him about them. He glared at me and said, "How would you like paddle marks on your bottom?" I couldn't answer; my throat had closed. As always, I kept the feelings to myself, thinking there was something freakishly wrong with me. But I couldn't stop those feelings.

I dated here and there, but never anything serious. I was attracted to men, but they scared me; I did not trust them. I had many secret crushes and fantasies, but had no idea how to make anything real out of them. Still a virgin, I grew obsessed with having sex and finding out what all the fuss was about already. However, during that era, it was highly unusual to be a virgin into your 20s, and I discovered that when men were faced with the prospect of being my first, they ran in the other direction. My next-door neighbor at the time summed it up nicely, saying, "Virgins are a drag. You're so worried about whether you're pleasing or hurting them, you don't get any pleasure yourself." I fervently hoped that not all men shared his view.

In December 1983, I was invited to an office Christmas party that a former employer was having. I didn't really feel like going, but I wanted to see some old friends, so I decided to suit up and show up.

Once there, I had to admit it was nice. They'd gone all out with a dance floor, music and catering. I chatted with some former coworkers and clients, and then I met Bob.

He was six-foot five, handsome with brown hair, blue eyes, mustache and dimples. Nice suit. *And*…unattached. The woman he'd come with was just a good friend.

We talked and flirted a bit, but when the dancing started, I lost him. All the young women (and some of the older ones) wanted to dance with him and I was much too shy and self-conscious to ask.

Dejected, I hung out, wishing I could get down on the dance floor, that I could be free and sexy and loose like some of those other girls were. Instead, I just sat there and I got cold, so I went to get my jacket. And then there he was, appearing at my side out of nowhere. "What's up with the jacket? You're not leaving, are you?" I said no, I'm just cold. He then said that perhaps if I danced, I would warm up, and he grabbed my hand. Oh, crap.

I was stuck now, so I bravely marched out to the floor with him. But then the fast song ended and Michael Jackson's "Human Nature" came on. *Oh well,* I thought, figuring that was that. Until he pulled me into his arms and we slow-danced. Good thing he was leading and holding me close, because my legs suddenly felt very shaky.

After that dance, he moved off and went on to someone else, but that was all right. I was feeling all mushy and giddy, just from that one stupid dance. *Good grief, Erica. Are you 26 or 14?*

The shot of confidence stayed with me. Later, when I was ready to leave, I went looking for him. He was sitting a dance out, having a drink and looking unbearably sexy— his jacket was off, his tie loosened, his sleeves rolled up. I said I was leaving and asked him if he would walk me to my car. He obliged.

At my car, he faced me. I was wearing one of my favorite necklaces, a crystal pendant with the initial E etched into the back. The clasp on this necklace never stays behind my neck; it always slips down. Earlier in the evening when we were talking, he'd reached out and adjusted the chain so the clasp moved back up. On the dance floor, he did that a second time. Now here we were in the parking lot and he did it a third time. "That's three times," he said. "Now you get a wish." I knew what I'd wish for, but I didn't have the nerve to voice it.

He fished in his wallet for one of his business cards but couldn't find one, so he handed me a scrap of paper and asked for my number. Said it was nice to meet me, gave me a hug and he was off. Yeah, right. Chances were, that suit would go to the cleaners and that bit of paper would be lost without another thought.

I couldn't stop thinking about him. I had no phone number, but I had a first and last name, and I knew he lived in Van Nuys. After a couple of days went by and I didn't hear from him, I thought, *Oh, what the hell.* I looked in the directory and found just one Bob C. in Van Nuys. So I addressed a holiday card to him, writing inside, "This is the girl at the Xmas party whose necklace you kept fixing. You said I had a wish coming. So here's my wish: I'd really like to see you again. By the way, if you're not the same Bob C. who was at the party, Merry Christmas anyway!" And before I could talk myself out of it, I mailed it. Mind you, this took all the nerve I had. I was not known for making bold moves in those days.

He called.

I lost my virginity to him on December 30. (Finally, my #1 New Year's resolution didn't have to be "GET LAID.") This time, I played it smart and didn't tell him I was a virgin until we were in bed together about to do the deed. He was rather nonplussed at first, but he rallied, made the best of it and was kind and complimentary, marveling that I could look as I did and yet make it to this age without any "male input" (his words). So my first time was more clinical than romantic, but I guess it could have been worse.

I do remember feeling disillusioned the next morning, however. He was pleasant, but rather hands-off. There was no sign of what had happened between us the night before. After all the romance novels I'd read, I expected more passion and intimacy, and was confused. But I found out later that it wasn't me, it was him. He admitted to loving sex, but not liking the touchy-feely stuff. Not my type, for sure. However, I don't regret that he was my first. We had sex a couple more times after that and then things died off.

My weight was fairly stable now. I was still on the thin side but not quite as skinny as I'd been during my college years. Periods had returned (oh, happy day), and after the second time Bob and I had sex, I was late. For birth control,

I had wrestled with a device called the *Today* sponge, and afterward when I went to remove it, the blasted thing was pushed up so far I couldn't find it. After a bit of panic and thinking I was going to have to make an embarrassing trip to the ER, success—my finger hooked onto the elastic loop and I was able to pull it out. And after that, no period, but then it finally came and I nearly fainted with relief. *Fuck this,* I thought. Is *this* what you have to deal with when you're having sex? I knew I didn't want children; I was not mother material. Besides, I'd sooner jump off a bridge than be pregnant, what with my obsession over weight.

So I had a tubal ligation. Snip, snip—no babies! The doctor thought I was insane and tried to talk me out of it, but I insisted, and I never regretted it for one second. I felt better, knowing I'd never have to worry about pregnancy. Of course, shortly thereafter, AIDS came into the news. So much for the days of carefree sex; not that I was having all that much of it anyway. After Bob, I didn't have sex again until I was in my 30s.

* * *

Toward the end of 1984, I got a phone call from someone to whom I hadn't spoken for many years—my brother's boyhood best friend. He and his family had lived two doors down from us when I was growing up. We caught up; he was married and had a baby son, and he would love for me to come over and meet them. Then he casually dropped a bombshell.

He was in touch with my father, who was in the process of divorcing B. We hadn't spoken since summer 1979; I had just assumed we wouldn't speak again and eventually I'd hear about his passing. Now here was a blast from my past, telling me that my father wanted to see me.

I had to think about it. Did I really want to see him after all we'd been through? Just because he'd finally unloaded Vampira didn't mean that the past 11 years were magically erased. I had my mother and stepfather, and my father had been out of my life for many years; why stir the pot? It would have been simpler to say no and go on with my life.

But I didn't. I guess when all was said and done, I wanted a father too.

My brother's friend arranged for my father and me to meet at his house. I remember little about that night, except that both Dad and I dressed up, and when he first saw me, his eyes welled and he said, "You look beautiful."

It would be tidy and pleasant to say that we had a blessed reunion, all was forgiven and forgotten and our relationship was golden from that point on. However, this isn't a movie script.

Dad was not willing to talk about the past; whenever I brought it up, he shut down. We'd get together for dinner and sort of dance around one another, making small talk. He didn't want to talk about much of anything, it seemed. What he *did* want to do was buy me things.

For my 28th birthday, he bought me a complete new stereo system. For Christmas, he bought me a VCR (they were fairly new then and quite expensive). He gave me checks and gift certificates frequently. My reactions to these gifts were mixed; while I enjoyed them, I had a faint resentment, feeling like I was being bought. The old wounds and unresolved issues still lurked, and money and electronics merely glossed over them. As was my pattern, I stuffed the feelings down where I didn't have to deal with them. And when his offers escalated (a piano?!), I turned them down. Eventually, they stopped.

* * *

I was still leading a very isolated life, going to work, coming home, spending most weekends alone. My therapist at the time (yes, I've had several) was a big advocate of support systems and had been encouraging me for some time to investigate 12-step programs. She said I was too tightly wound and controlled, and that I needed to learn to let go and practice acceptance. Easier said than done, certainly. I had shared with her many times my feelings of being invisible, that I didn't matter and I would pass through this life without anyone knowing I was here. She said that most people live that way; few of us get to experience being the center of attention and I needed to "accept my periphery." On the other hand, though, if I went to meetings and shared, I would get some of the validation and acknowledgment I so craved.

I knew I had a lot of pent-up rage; I struggled to keep it tamped down, but it found its way to the surface anyway. A local community college had a seminar on anger, so I signed up for it. We worked in groups and I kept fairly quiet in mine. But then we also had to spend some one-on-one time with a counselor, performing exercises.

My counselor was a young man named Roger, and he had me kneeling on the carpet with large cushions around me. Handing me a tennis racket, he instructed me to beat on the pillows with it. Well, that sounded like a ridiculous thing to do.

Thud. I gave a nearby cushion a half-hearted thump. "Come on, harder," he urged. I whacked it again, feeling foolish. "Come on, Erica," Roger snapped. "I know you've got more in you than that. Go on! Who are you mad at? Who would you like to pound on? I know you have somebody you want to slug with that racket. Do it!"

I hunkered down, gripped the racket in both hands and began to whale on the cushion. At first it was just going through the motions, but then the rage burst forth, and I was pounding and pounding, crying and screaming. When Roger finally stopped me and I released the racket, one of my palms was blistered and bleeding. It would be difficult to figure out who was more shocked: him or me.

My mother was a confusing presence in my life at that time; she tried to help me, but she pushed and criticized so much, it just made me angrier and changed nothing. She wanted me to be more social, to date, to get more hobbies, more friends, etc. Despite my pleading with her and finally ordering her not to, she'd set me up on blind dates with so-and-so's son or nephew. Once, she even gave my phone number to a woman at the beauty parlor getting her hair done at the same time. This woman was a perfect stranger, but hey, she had a son who was a doctor, and single. Mom couldn't understand why I was apoplectic over that one.

One summer, my mother's longtime friend's daughter was getting married. There was to be a plush wedding, and Mom was fussing at me about it, asking what I was going to wear. Because I rarely went anywhere, I didn't have a dress that would suit the occasion, so reluctantly, I agreed to go out and buy something new. Then she said, "Do me a favor—get something that drapes softly around you, so people won't see how scrawny you are."

That's when it dawned on me: My mother wanted things for me because of how they reflected on her. If I had a great career or interesting hobbies, that gave *her* bragging rights. If I looked good, she was proud and wanted to show me off to her friends. But if I didn't look good, she was embarrassed by me.

I decided to spare her; I told her I wasn't buying a new dress and I wasn't going to the wedding, either. She screamed and raged at me, but I did not change my mind. We didn't speak for over a month.

However, she was right about one thing—I really needed some more people and some support in my life. Out of desperation and loneliness, I finally looked into 12-step meetings and started experimenting with local ones. I didn't feel like a good fit for AA, as I wasn't an alcoholic, but I certainly qualified for Al-Anon, ACA (Adult Children of Alcoholics) and EA (Emotions Anonymous, for those who have emotional issues but don't abuse substances).

My early meetings took place in churches and school-rooms, with groups that varied in size and age. EA meetings were non-smoking, but they had the requisite tables set up with instant coffee and cocoa in Styrofoam cups, sweets and literature. I especially liked the Wednesday night meeting room because it had a fireplace.

Of course, at first, I completely balked at all that business about Higher Powers and God. I was an agnostic; how the hell was this going to work for me? Still, I kept going, because somehow, the program and the people had grabbed me regardless. I liked some of the basic principles: Powerless over people, places and things. The only thing we can control is our own actions. Acceptance—of ourselves, our feelings, our foibles. Practicing humility (which is not thinking less of yourself, but rather, thinking of yourself less). Accountability. Plus, I found many of the people to be warm and welcoming (OK, some of them were a little nutty, but so was I).

I also struggled with the concept of give-and-take, of friendship. Having learned early from my mother and father that nothing I did would be good enough, I chose to do exactly that—nothing. I would not give, because giving was for saps who would get sucked hollow by the takers. Neither would I take; accepting favors and kindness from others would render me vulnerable and beholden, and I found that to be unacceptable.

Don't think twice, if you're nice, they'll make you cry.[1]

However, I wanted to be liked, and quickly discovered that my wry humor was well received. My pitches often made the entire room crack up and that was validating. However, that became another point of obsession—how would I make everyone laugh tonight? How could I put a humorous spin on whatever was bothering me, so people would like it?

One evening, I was in a great deal of emotional pain, but couldn't bring myself to raise my hand. *No one wants to hear me unless I'm funny,* I thought. Still, I couldn't stand the idea of going back home without unburdening myself. So, five minutes before the meeting ended, I timidly raised my hand.

The leader beamed at me and said, "Oh, good! Come on, Erica, make us laugh." And my face crumpled.

"I'm sorry," I blubbered. "I just can't be funny tonight. I'm so sorry!"

Afterward, people crowded around to hug me. The meeting leader apologized to me over and over. But it was all right. Now I knew that it wasn't my job to provide comedy. All I had to do was show up and be myself, whoever I happened to be at that moment.

Still, the semi-religious undertone bothered me. "Sought through prayer and meditation..."? Prayer to whom? Some simply said it was a power greater than our-

---

[1] "They'll Make You Cry," The Beau Brummels, ©1965, Ron Elliott.

selves without naming it. Can't get any vaguer than that, can you? But, being a perfectionist, I was frustrated because I couldn't come up with my own concept.

One day, I visited a senior member of a local group so we could talk. I didn't mince words, blurting, "I can't get with this God shit!" She wasn't offended; all she did was laugh. "Forget about it," she said. "The only thing you need to know about God is that you aren't."

For whatever reason, that resonated. *Oh. Okay, that's simple enough.* She also said that the beauty of the 12-step program was that you could take what you need and leave the rest. Armed with this information, I forged ahead.

No, I wasn't a model 12-stepper. I didn't practice the steps in order. I didn't take the written moral inventory or do the official amends or many of the other traditional things that were suggested. I didn't sponsor anyone and, although it was common practice for members to give each other their phone numbers and be available for calls, I wasn't comfortable with that. But I showed up faithfully to meetings twice a week, I spoke at nearly all of them and I slowly built up a circle of friends. I loved how I could share the most outrageous, shameful behavior and the reaction would be appreciative laughter and "been there, done that." Maybe, just maybe, I wasn't such a freak after all.

* * *

As I'd mentioned earlier, I did not exercise, since I was too tired most of the time. The one exception was when I was punishing myself for overeating—spurred by guilt, I would do penance with bursts of compulsive, vigorous exercise. Naturally, this would result in crippling muscle soreness and my good intentions would disappear until the next binge. Therefore, my physical activity was sporadic at best and I wasn't reaping any health benefits from it.

One summer workday in 1987, I had made a compulsive dash down the street to the doughnut shop on the corner. Fueled with desire to return to my cubicle and chow down in private, I started to run, but my foot slipped on the curb and I went down, my ankle twisting. The pain made me scream, but I couldn't just sit there in the middle of a busy street, so I got to my feet and hobbled back to my office. Once there, I looked at my left ankle—it had immediately and enormously swelled and was rapidly turning various colors.

After work, I went to the ER. My ankle was not broken, but it had sustained a very bad sprain—a Grade III with torn ligaments. I had a brace on my ankle and needed crutches, which I had never used before. Much to my shock, I did not have the upper-body strength to bear my own weight on crutches. As a result, I developed painful tendinitis in my forearms and wrists. Simple gestures such as turning a faucet handle could elicit shrieks. My lowest moment was the night I woke up needing to pee. I couldn't walk on my swollen ankle, and when I picked up the crutches, shards of white-hot pain shot up my forearms. In tears, I crawled on my hands and knees to the bathroom.

That was a wake-up call for me; I realized my body, even though it was thin, was in deplorable shape and I needed to do something about it. But more than that, I had to change my attitude about exercise. Instead of thinking of it as a punishment, I tried considering as a gift I gave myself; the gift of health and fitness. I would work out because I wanted to, because it was good for me, not because I was flagellating myself over a binge.

Instead of overdoing it, I started out slowly, doing one workout a week, then two, then three. I began with aerobics classes and then added weights and machines. At first I joined a workout studio and bought classes, but then I graduated to gym memberships. Little by little, my spaghetti arms and stick legs took on some shape, and I gained some strength and stamina.

I won't lie and tell you I came to love exercise. If I could take a daily pill that would tone my heart and my body without doing any huffing and puffing, my inner couch potato would take over and I'd never get off my butt. But altering my attitude about it helped a great deal, and once working out became a habit, I knew it would be with me for life.

It seemed I was ending my 20s on many positive notes. I had a decent job. I had taken steps to improve my health and well-being. I was making friends and had a place to go where I felt like I belonged. And my father and I had reconciled, at least on the surface.

But I was still unhappy. My days still revolved around my obsessions with food and my weight. I was still at the mercy of my moods—depression, anger, fear. I was an emotional chameleon; if the people around me were in good moods, then so was I, but as soon as I encountered any negativity, I took it on myself.

I was a high-functioning person. I worked long hours, went to the gym 4–5 times a week, went to meetings, ran errands and kept my place clean. I had a circle of friends and a social life. I was a runner, always on the go; if I stopped for a moment, feelings would catch up with me and that would be intolerable, so I would go to sleep out of sheer exhaustion and then enjoy that escape for 12–15 hours at a time.

Even though I had the alcoholic gene, I also had far too strong a need for control to ever succumb to the lure of drugs or drink. I had smoked pot briefly in my teens and early 20s, but one episode with horrible paranoia ended that. I had been smoking with my neighbors and was suddenly convinced that they had poisoned me. Somehow, through the panic, I'd had the presence of mind to know this was not reality and I'd gone back to my apartment to wait it out. As I sat alone, my teeth chattering with fear, fighting the urge to run out the door screaming, I thought, *If I get through this without ending up in a straitjacket, I will never smoke pot again.* And I never did; I was 24 and that was the last time I touched the stuff.

So, despite seeming reasonably healthy on the outside, I felt like a prisoner of my own body and mind, with no sense of who I was. Some days were decent; many others weren't. None of them contained any real joy.

My father once wrote: "Life—an entrance, an exit, and a whole lot of bullshit in between." Was that the best I could hope for?

HEARTBREAKS AND BREAKTHROUGHS

"I need to accept and forgive myself for being the way I am...who did I have to learn from? How can one learn positives with negative role models? I have just as much to UNlearn as I have to learn. And it PISSES ME OFF!"
—my journal, June 17, 1989

In 1988, my father called me at work one day. I was surprised to get a call from him there and asked if something was wrong. "No," he said. "I just want to tell you that I've quit drinking and joined AA." Very matter-of-fact, in the same neutral tone of voice one would discuss the weather. A year after that, his lifelong best friend died of emphysema, and my father quit smoking, a habit he'd had since he was about 12 years old. He was doing all the right things, making many positive changes, and I applauded him for it. I know he was reaching out and doing the best he could. But things still weren't right between us.

* * *

My dealings with the opposite sex were still dysfunctional. I was definitely attracted to men, but I didn't trust them and I feared getting close to them. Therefore, I developed a familiar and insidious pattern of crushing on men who were unavailable to me for one reason or another. That kept me safe—frustrated and empty, but safe and in control, and control was of paramount importance.

I had missed out on so many of the basics one experiences in their teens and 20s—dating, first loves, proms, learning how to forge relationships and communicate effectively with the opposite sex. In my early 30s, I had the mentality and experience of an adolescent in that area. I hungered for touch, for affection—the hugs at meetings just didn't cut it. But I had no clue how to bring that into my life in a healthy manner. Sometimes the yearning was so strong, I would book a full-body massage just to feel a man's hands on me.

The years 1988–91 were spent endlessly obsessing over a young man I worked with. Chuck was 10 years my junior, six-foot-four, with a manly build and boyish face. He had a girlfriend—of course she was young, cute and perky. I hated her. Not that she ever did anything to me, but she was living the life of a normal 18-year-old and I was so jealous I could croak.

We flirted, Chuck and I. We bantered and teased, danced around each other at the office. He used to come into my cubicle and massage my neck and shoulders. In today's lawsuit-happy office atmosphere, I suppose such personal touching would be considered inappropriate, but back then, it wasn't that big a deal, not in the casual types of offices in which I worked.

His hands were strong and sensual, and his touch would leave me trembling and discombobulated, wondering what the hell was going on with me. *Oh, for God's sake, knock it off,* I thought. *He's a kid. A big, dumb, goofy kid. A big, dumb, goofy, funny, sexy... ack. Shut* up, *Erica.*

The crush had plenty of fun moments, but it caused me a lot of pain as well. Other-directed as I was, my daily mood at work was determined by how Chuck treated me, what kind of mood he was in, if he was flirtatious or indifferent. The highest points and conversely, the lowest points, were often my interactions with him.

Christmas 1988, our office had had a good year and our boss arranged to have our holiday party at his country club. It was going to be quite fancy: a nice dinner, live band, dancing, very dressy. And of course, we could all bring dates.

Everyone else was looking forward to the party; I was dreading it. I knew no one I could bring, and there was no freaking way I was going to go solo when everyone else was paired. If I had to sit around all evening with a fake smile pasted on my face, watching Chuck and Cutie-Pie together, I'd throw myself under a train.

I ended up asking a friend at EA to be my date. We had gotten to be buddies at the meetings and I told him all he had to do was show up in a suit, have a nice free dinner and maybe dance with me once or twice. I'm embarrassed to admit this, but it didn't hurt that he was a very handsome guy and I felt that being seen with him would somehow validate my existence. Pathetic, I know. But at least I went. In years past, I would have come up with some excuse to get out of it.

Why was it such a big deal? Simple. It was the first time that I'd ever brought a date, a real date, to any sort of event. I was 31 years old. Most women that age had been going to similar functions with dates for roughly half their lives.

Interestingly, that night Chuck asked me to dance, even with his girlfriend there. And when our fast dance ended and a slow song started up, he pulled me into his arms and danced with me to that one as well. Did I feel any glee over that? *Nahh*, not much. It's not like I relived those dances countless times in the following weeks. I still remember the songs: the fast dance was "All Shook Up"; "The Christmas Song (Chestnuts Roasting)" was the slow one.

Chuck knew about my feelings and he used that to his advantage, teasing and provoking me at times. His comments and gestures would get me flustered and blushing and that fed into his ego, so he'd continue. It was like being back in school, when boys teased me and I had no idea how to react to it.

Better late than never, I suppose; I got to sharpen my bantering skills and had my own victories. One morning, while I was buried in work and not in the mood for any nonsense, Chuck came wandering into my office, stuffing his face with a large custard-filled doughnut. There he stood, alarmingly close, watching me. I turned around in my chair and snapped, "Well? What have you got to say for yourself?"

He grinned at me engagingly and answered, "Mmmmmm… this is good. Want a bite?" I shook my head and said no, thank you. He gouged his finger into the pastry and pulled it back out coated with custard. Then he waved that finger right in front of my lips. "Want some cream?"

That did it. I'd show him.

I grabbed his hand in both my own and proceeded to put on quite the show of licking his finger clean, slowly and deliberately, my eyes fixed on his. I finished by plunging his finger deep into my mouth to suck off the remnants of the custard, then pulled it out, letting go of his hand and smiling sweetly at him. "Thanks. You're right, that's good."

I wish I'd had a camera at that moment. He just stood there staring down at his finger, then said in a strangled voice, "Wow. I really like the way you did that." Then he walked out—rather stiffly, I might add, if you'll pardon the expression.

But I digress. My point was that I spent way too much time ruminating over men who weren't right for me, thus preventing myself from being open to a real relationship. I was too scared, and this was how I dealt with it. Ultimately, it left me feeling empty a lot of the time.

* * *

My 33rd birthday came and went, and my father forgot it. I was very angry, unreasonably so. After the fact, he left me contrite messages on my answering machine and he sent me three belated birthday cards, one with a check in it. I knew he felt bad, and really, anyone can forget a birthday. Still, I was consumed with resentment. I didn't know where this overreaction was coming from, but soon thereafter, awareness hit full force.

I had started attending a Saturday morning EA meeting in a local hospital. The room we met in was off of a cafeteria, so we could hang out there afterward, have lunch and chat. It was a large, nurturing group and I felt very comfortable there.

One of the members started bringing her 11-year-old daughter with her. This was a little disconcerting to some of us, because we discussed adult subjects and emotions at times and it didn't seem appropriate to have a child there. But there was nothing in the literature or rules that forbade it, so we allowed it. She was a shy little girl, all skinny elbows and knees, brown hair, and glasses with the same type of thick, ugly brown frames I wore at that age.

One morning, she raised her hand to speak. Rather than try to resurrect what she said and how I reacted to it, I'm going to let my journal entry for that day, back in October 1990, do the talking—angry all-caps speak intact.

She shared a long, painful story, the type I often hear in Al-Anon from adult children remembering the past, but I've never heard it straight from the real thing, an 11-year-old child. The gist of it was the weekend she spent with her father, and how he'd gotten drunk and been negligent and irresponsible. [Her mother] couldn't take it—she left the room in tears. Half the room was crying. Me, I went completely to pieces. For the past two weeks, I'd been struggling with my resistance to calling my father. After he forgot my birthday, he left two messages on my machine, sent me those cards and a check, and aside from a polite thank-you note, I didn't respond. I knew I was relieved, in a way, that he'd forgotten so I wouldn't have to do the usual dinner bit, and I didn't want to call him because he'd suggest getting together, and all this resistance was mixed up with guilt and confusion as to why I was resisting—what was the big deal? So I spun my wheels over it and took no action, using the excuse that I've got too many other things to deal with right now.

But sitting there listening to [the little girl], I was 1/3 my age. I was 11 years old, visiting my father on weekends, adoring the soggy drunk who was the life of the party, basking in his intermittent attention...and always riding home with someone else because he was too drunk, or couldn't be bothered. ("Take the kid home, will you—I'm a little loaded.") I sat there and cried, tears rolling down my face, and I couldn't stop, even after [she] was through—I had to leave the room and go get Kleenex. I HATED HIM! Right then, I hated him. I hated his selfishness, his emotional abandonment and manipulation. I HATED being a fucked-up adult because he was a fucked-up father. And for once, I got past the logical-adult guilt trip: "He did the best he could." "Come on, he's a sick old man, give him a break." "It wasn't that bad—you weren't physically or sexually abused, you were well provided for. It could have been worse." FUCK THAT! *He was unloving, ungiving, undependable, incapable of giving any kind of nurturing or support, critical... and all I ever wanted from him was his love and acceptance. And I NEVER GOT IT! Yes—someday I will be able to say he was incapable of giving it, and forgive him... but for now, I HAVEN'T dealt with the fact that I DIDN'T GET WHAT I NEEDED, AND I HATE HIM FOR IT! And I need to FEEL it! That self-centered son-of-a-bitch—he has one kid left in this world and he can't even keep track of her birthday! DAMN him! All my defective patterns with men, the never-ending attractions to the un-available, the fear of rejection if I seek the attainable... it all started with him. There it all was, coming up in great gushes at the meeting.*

A friend came out after me and as soon as she approached me, my anger spewed forth. I kept my voice down, but the words were harsh and came from a place that had been so deeply buried, I hadn't been consciously aware of it. "I hate him, that son-of-a-bitch! Fucking drunken bastard! I hate him! How could he treat me like that? Why do people have kids when they don't want them, when they don't have a fucking clue what they're doing?"

I was sobbing so hard, it made my friend cry. She was 20 years older than I, and had two grown kids. She'd had three; one son had committed suicide when he was 20. Although the questions I was blurting were rhetorical, she was offering her own answers: "Because we don't know any better; because we try our best and think we're doing a better job than our parents did." But I couldn't hear her. I was riding the waves of rage, allowing myself to fully feel them for the first time in years.

Later that day, I recounted the story to my therapist. More tears, a lot of screaming—I actually made *her* cry too. I didn't want to deal with all this shit; I didn't want to hate him. I thought I was done with that in my 20s. But I guess I had stuffed down a whole lot more than I thought and it had to come out.

I knew I needed to talk to my father about all this. But I wasn't ready.

* * *

My friends and I liked to hang out at a restaurant called Good Earth, near my apartment. The food was excellent, not too expensive, and the atmosphere was quiet and comfortable so one could sit and talk for hours, drinking their spicy blend of iced tea.

Toward the end of 1990, a handsome and charismatic waiter there began flirting with me. He was tall and blond, with mischievous hazel eyes. I'd usually go to this restaurant about once a week, so I started requesting his station.

The sexual tension crackled. One time, I left the table to use the restroom; when I came back, my friend said, "Boy, is he hot for you!" She went on to tell me that as I'd walked away, he'd stood by our table, openly staring. Then he'd smiled and said, "I guess it's true what they say—behind every great woman is a great behind."

The flirting progressed to his slipping me provocative notes on napkins, and one night, his phone number. My girlfriend and I had occupied his table for hours, so we pooled our singles (eight in all, I think) and tied them together into a neat bundle, using a straw wrapper. Then I wrote my own phone number on the wrapper and left the money on the table.

We had a rather intense affair for the next six weeks or so. Remember, I was quite naïve. He had pursued me so thoroughly and sweetly, using lines that most women my age (33 at the time) would recognize as BS, but I took them at face value. Yes, I actually bought the "I've never met anyone quite like you" and "My feelings for you are so intense, they scare me" lines. (I cringe now; God, I was dumb.) And once I became completely open and available to him, he grew bored. Long story short, he dumped me right before the holidays. No explanation, just backed off and acted like none of it had ever happened.

Of course, I was a wreck over it, tormenting myself over what I could have done wrong, plotting on how I could rekindle his interest and crying copious tears. I remember sharing about him at an EA meeting, and one of the men there hugged me afterward and said, "Oh, honey—you didn't really buy into that 'you're special' line, did you? All guys use that line. *I've* used that line."

Rather cynical, that; the implication being that any time a man tells a woman she's special, he doesn't mean it. I got upset and said, "OK, then maybe you can tell me something—why do you guys say stuff like that when you don't mean it?" He shrugged, gave me a sad look and answered, "Because at the time, some of us think we *do* mean it." (sigh) Whatever. My hunger for attention and affection had clouded my judgment once again. Okay, so this guy didn't have a girlfriend, wasn't married, etc., but he was emotionally unavailable nonetheless.

Funny side note about him, which I remembered after rereading old journals: in the few weeks we were together, he must have threatened me with spanking at least two dozen times. The outgoing message on his answering machine was quite clever; you'd hear a woman's breathy voice whispering, "Hi, this is Tiffany," and she'd go on crooning until his voice broke in with, "Tiffany, get off the extension. Tiffany, that's enough." Then he said, "Leave your name and number, and I'll call you back as soon as I'm done spanking Tiffany."

Imagine the heart attack I had when I first heard that message! I think he may have been one of us, but I didn't get the chance to find out. He did have handcuffs—yes, I saw them. But he never used them on me. The kinkiest thing he ever did was put a blindfold on me. Oh, well.

THE TRANSITION BEGINS

"When I get input from the opposite sex, I come alive, feel beautiful, sexy, confident. When I don't get any input, I wither, feel colorless, lifeless, ugly and inferior to other women. DAMN it! How, I don't know, but I want to feel sexy and beautiful on my own, from within! This is my goal... self-confidence, love for me, an appreciation of me—I want my personal power back where it belongs, with ME."
—my journal, November 15, 1991

The year 1991 was not a good one for me. I began it with depression over Waiter Guy. Then I found out that Chuck was quitting, and not only was he leaving the company, but he was leaving the state. He had broken up with his girlfriend and wanted to make a fresh start elsewhere.

Guess what—after four years of foreplay, we finally slept together. Admittedly, it was anticlimactic. He was sexy and a great kisser and good with his hands, but he was still just 23; very quick, and he knew nothing about giving a woman an orgasm. And he had to smoke pot beforehand.

Still, I don't regret it. It made his remaining weeks of work a lot of fun, even though they were bittersweet. I'd be hunched over some tedious job and he'd suddenly swoop up behind me, lean down and murmur in my ear, "We... were... *naked!*" Then there was the time he was hanging around, looking like he wanted to say something but couldn't quite get it out. Finally, he dropped his voice and said in a rushed whisper, "That was the best blowjob I've ever had in my life and I wanted to thankyouverymuch," and dashed out of the room, embarrassed.

I had to laugh—best in his life? At 23, just how many had he received? But here's what he didn't know: before we hooked up, I was so freaked out about my pitiful lack of sexual experience that I bought a book about "how to drive a man wild in bed," and carefully read and reread the chapter about oral technique. I guess I was a quick study.

When he left in February, I cried and cried. I was inconsolable for a long time. He had been a great source of fun and support at a very difficult job (not to mention a lot of lively sexual tension), and my days without him felt empty and sad.

Over the holidays (excellent timing), I had received notice that my apartment was going condo and I had to move in six months. That was a huge blow, not only because I loved my place, but because I hated change and upheaval, and moving is one of the biggest changes one can experience. When the time came to start packing and hauling, I injured my back during the process and it took the better part of the year to fully heal, so I dealt with a lot of pain and inconvenience. Once I got into my new apartment, I discovered I had the Neighbors from Hell. Last but not least, my therapist of several years, whom I loved and trusted, broke the news that she was retiring.

Nope, not a good year at all.

In the beginning of the year as I dealt with these issues, I found my nerves were perpetually raw and at the surface, ready to be touched off. I had very little patience (not that I had that much to begin with) and certain things I had pushed aside were now stubbornly coming back to the fore. One of them was my relationship with my father.

Ever since I'd had that meltdown at the EA meeting, I had been avoiding him, putting off making dinner plans with him, afraid of what seeing him might touch off. I decided to write him a letter.

I was direct. I told him of my resentment and anger, of the difficult times I'd been going through lately and how he had no idea because he never cared enough to ask. How things between us had never been aired and discussed, and he tried to smooth them over by giving me money and gifts. That I was sick of our get-togethers where we talked about his work, trivia and little else.

At this point, I figured I had nothing to lose. He'd been out of my life for several years and I'd adjusted to the idea that he would remain out of my life for good. If this letter angered him and he bowed out again, no great loss for me. At least I'd had my say and I felt clean and clear, finally.

Before I could lose my nerve, I addressed the letter and mailed it.

When a reply came in the mail, I felt a bit sick with apprehension. I expected to open it and find a defensive and angry rebuttal. Much to my shock, my father's letter began by saying that despite all the bullshit in his life, he was a lucky man; most fathers never received so much honesty from a daughter.

He then went on to apologize, and to say he was sorry for all I was going through. He wrote that he too would like to be closer, that we did need to talk about things, but he wasn't sure if he could handle that. Would I please have patience and bear with him, and he'd do the best he knew how? He ended by saying he loved me.

I would have never imagined I'd get communication like this from my father, not in a million years. Maybe he could change after all. Perhaps I could, too. It was a start.

Little by little, over time, we talked. I remember odds and ends of conversations about my mother, about his second wife S, about wife #3, B. One night, I shared a nightmare with him, one I'd had shortly after the fiasco in La Costa and then had again a few more times over the years.

In it, B and I were in a hotel room. She had locked the door with an ornate, old-fashioned key and then dropped it down into her cleavage (once anything went in *there*, it was irretrievable). She then advanced menacingly on me, her red-painted fingernails like talons, reaching out to claw me. I kept backing up and she kept moving forward, until I was up against the wall with nowhere to go. Frantically, my eyes darted around the room and I saw my father off in the corner, sitting in a chair, silently and passively observing. I screamed and begged for him to help me, but he said nothing, didn't move, didn't blink. And as those nails started to tear at my face and chest, I woke up, terrified and crying.

My father's eyes flooded with tears when I told him this story, and when I said I could forgive everyone else in my life but I would always hate her, he whispered, "Don't hate her. Hate me. I allowed it."

A few days later, I received mail from him; a letter sharing his anguish over my dream, saying he wished he could turn back the clock and change things. I still have it, and it still makes me cry. No, I never forgave her. But I reached a point where I could pity her. Despite all she put me through, I had prevailed, and while she lost everything, I gained a father.

* * *

Sometimes in the midst of the worst insanity, there are moments of clarity. Because of the back injury, I had to drastically alter my workouts. At this point, I was exercising obsessively, four to five times a week. Also, because of the stresses of moving, of dealing with losses and grief, I was bingeing more. Result: my weight drifted upward. I felt like I had no control over anything in my life: my job, my home, my health, my eating, my relationships, my counselor retiring. It was a time of tremendous upheaval and resulting anxiety attacks.

I was still in the habit of weighing myself daily, and I gave the scale the power to make or break my day. If the number at my feet was not to my liking, it set the tone for my mood. And you know what? It was getting pretty damn tiresome.

One morning, I stepped on the scale after taking a diuretic, hoping to see a lower number, but I didn't. I swore and yelled at the scale, felt the "fat panic" surging and suddenly, I was sick to death of the whole syndrome that I'd been caught up in since I was 15 years old.

Without taking time to think about it, I jumped on the scale until it cracked. Then I picked it up and dropped it onto the bathroom tiles with a satisfying crash for good measure. On my way out to the car, I hurled the now-useless scale into the dumpster and slammed the lid shut. Goodbye, you piece of dreck. Good riddance.

Aside from the small postage scale I use to measure food portions, that was the last time there was a scale in my home. I wish I could say I was rid of the food/body obsession, but at least I had freed myself from the numbers game. Baby steps, as they say.

* * *

In the processing of rereading old journals from my early 30s, the one theme that runs throughout is struggle. Struggling with a job where I was doing the work of at least two and dealing with difficult personalities. Struggling at home with noisy neighbors. Struggling with bad relationships and crushing on one unavailable man after another. But more than anything, struggling with myself.

Each day had a degree of white-knuckling and pushing myself to get through. The combination of depression and mild OCD, and the resulting desperate need for control, had me so completely enmeshed, I couldn't imagine breaking out of it, no matter how much therapy I had.

A journal excerpt from May 27, 1993:

"When I got into bed last night, I was so tired, my body just ached for sleep, but I couldn't relax—I was lying there waiting to hear noise from [my neighbor's] bedroom. As I lay there, my heart banging away in my ears, I just got sick of it. So fucking sick of the struggle to control everything and everyone around me. All I could think was, 'I want peace, I just want peace.' I'm so sick of caring and worrying about neighbors and what's going on at work and who's doing what to whom and why and how it affects me. I just want the ability to live my life day to day as it comes and let others live theirs, and let them be around me without focusing on them! There is always going to be a neighbor I can hear. There are always going to be ups and downs at work. There will always be unexpected, unplanned things. There will always be change. And I'm so TIRED of caring and fixating and obsessing and stressing about it all…Do I need medication, am I chemically imbalanced, or what? I'm not looking for a magic answer, a magic pill, a diagnosis that will solve all my problems and overhaul my whole life. But I can't help but wonder if my struggles with the outside world would be a little more ma-

nageable if I didn't feel like I was at war with myself, with my own body and mind. What are my answers?"

This was the first time I began to consider medication again. I knew that antidepressants were better now than they had been when I took them long ago. However, my resistance was still present. I didn't want to be one of *those people*—people who needed medication. Didn't that make me crazy? Different? Weird? All the things I had fought against being all my life? Why couldn't I simply be strong enough to snap myself out of all this dysfunctional behavior and thinking? Meds were for the weak, I thought.

But maybe, just maybe, life could be better with them, a tiny bit easier. Perhaps the first step to breaking out of my self-imposed prison was to surrender to the need for medication, for a little extra assistance to smooth out the kinks in my wiring. Without them, I had my pride intact, but we all know what pride is worth.

When my therapist retired in 1991, she referred me to a colleague. I liked Susan immediately; she was a few years older than I, warm and kind, with a soothing demeanor that always settled my nerves no matter how bad I felt. She witnessed a lot of tears and pain, screaming rage, my absolute worst, and through it all, she staunchly believed in me.

In September 1993, Susan gently suggested that if I wanted, she could give me the name of a psychiatrist who specialized in depression and medication. By that point, I was willing. I had just turned 36 and felt like life was passing me by. There had to be something better than this. She gave me a number and before I could talk myself out of it, I called and made an appointment.

Dr. K had several forms to fill out and asked a lot of questions. I figured he'd heard it all and none of what I had to say made him blink. He told me about the SSRIs and how they worked, explaining that the results were not instantaneous and one had to try them for at least a few weeks. He also warned about possible side effects, the most common being nausea and vomiting. Swell. Just what a person with emetophobia (fear of throwing up) wants to hear. Nevertheless, I took the week's worth of Prozac samples and the prescription he gave me and left.

The next morning, I took the Prozac with me to work, so I could take it after I had some breakfast. By midmorning, I was convinced that if I took this damn pill, I'd end up retching violently in the restroom. I nearly bailed, but then decided to call a dear friend whom I knew had been on Prozac for some time. With her on the phone with me, I swallowed the capsule. That was October 30, 1993.

While I never did experience the dreaded nausea, I had to deal with some other side effects. My sleep was adversely affected; I had relentless insomnia. When I did doze off, it was fitful and brief, and I would awaken around 1:00–2:00 A.M., unable to get back to sleep. Plus, my heart palpitated. I would feel completely exhausted, and yet it was like I had an engine running inside of me that I couldn't shut off.

I told the doctor about these symptoms when I had my first follow-up visit a week later. He asked, "Is this bad enough to discontinue the medication?" After a moment of hesitation, I said no. If I started over with something else, there was no guarantee it would be any better.

And so I continued, somehow getting through nearly three weeks of this. Then came the night when I dropped off into solid, deep sleep, and stayed asleep for 12 hours. Hallelujah! After that, my sleep was normal once again.

Around the holidays, I noted in my journal that I hadn't wept for five weeks. For me, this was quite a record, since I had perpetually leaky tear ducts. I felt a little bit more stable, slightly more even-keeled. Since my system had adjusted to the beginner dose, my doctor upped it. Ooops, too much. My hands trembled like I had Parkinson's disease. He knocked the amount back down a bit and the shakes subsided, thankfully. My body once again adjusted and my side effects passed.

After six months on the Prozac, I went back to the meds doctor. While Prozac was helping with my depression and negativity, it was doing nothing for the anxiety or the obsessive/compulsive behavior. Changes and unexpected occurrences still brought on panic and extreme irritability.

Dr. K told me about Buspar, an anti-anxiety medication. Unlike tranquilizers such as Xanax, Buspar was long-acting and affected serotonin (like the SSRIs). Studies had proven that for many people, the combination of Prozac and Buspar worked better on OCD and anxiety better than any other existing drugs for those conditions, with fewer side effects. I read the article he gave me, and it sounded fascinating and promising.

But... *two* medications? Just how crazy was I, anyway? Needing one psychotropic medication was bad enough, I thought. Still, I left his office with sample boxes and a new prescription.

The next day, I called Susan. She was encouraging; yes, she'd heard of Buspar and the studies, and she had another patient on those two meds. So I decided to try the Prozac/Buspar cocktail.

Fortunately, I didn't suffer side effects this time, aside from some mild drowsiness for a couple of weeks. The anxiety wasn't miraculously erased, but I could feel the sharp edges dulling. I no longer felt the compulsion to check and double-check everything, such as the bathroom heater or the curling iron, even though I knew perfectly well I'd turned them off.

* * *

The same year I began the meds, there were many transitions at my job, mostly in the form of downsizing. The economy was lousy, our industry was changing and my boss was a cheapskate; those factors combined made for a rather challenging workplace.

I had been with this company for over seven years. For most of that time, I had my own room, a private area where I could close a door, concentrate and focus, retreat when I was in a bad mood (which was often) and mind my own business. No matter how crazy things were around me, I had my little haven. The only people I had to deal with were my co-workers—I had no contact with the clients, which was fine by me. When I had downtime, I could sit and write, read, work a crossword puzzle, make phone calls without being overheard. It was a loner's paradise.

However, that all changed.

My room was at the back of the shop, along with the typesetters' room. Up front, there was a reception area, a conference room, several cubicles, a front desk area where the office manager sat, the darkroom and the job packaging area. We used to have a part-time camera operator who did all of the darkroom work. When he left, they did not replace him. Instead, the office manager (who had started out as the camera operator) resumed those duties. So, whenever he was in the darkroom, guess who had to come up front and sit at his desk, and do his work as well as her own? That's right; little old me.

At first, I bounced back and forth between the two stations. When I was at the manager's desk, I had no privacy; I truly was front and center. I may be an attention whore, but this was one time where I did not want to be a central figure. I had to answer phones. When jobs had questions, I had to call clients. I had to write up and schedule work. I had to supervise the typesetters. I had to greet clients who came in. Oh, and I still had to do all the proofreading too.

There was no more hiding; I was fully exposed. If I was having a bad day, I had to suck it up. Sitting alone in my room and allowing tears to drip on my work unseen was no longer an option. But still, I had the knowledge ever-present in the back of my mind that my room was still there and I could go back to it from time to time when there wasn't camera work to be done.

Then that changed as well; the day came where I was told I was being permanently relocated to the front desk. It wasn't a matter of choice; it was a done deal and I had to consider that area my own from that day forward.

Probably needless to say, I hated it. I am not a people person; I hated customer service. I do not multitask well; I prefer to focus on one thing at a time. I don't hide my feelings easily; if I'm in a lousy mood, my face reflects it. This new position completely went against my personality and work style. But I had to do it, if I wanted to keep my job. Learning how to handle it was imperative.

Looking back, I realize that without the medications, I wouldn't have been able to do this. Not for even one day. As it was, it damn near sent me to the loony bin, it was so stressful for me. I struggled mightily and there were days when I ran into the restroom and burst into tears or cussed out my boss in the privacy of a stall. I made a ton of mistakes. But somehow, I kept going. I improved, I got into a rhythm. I still didn't like it, but I could function, one day at a time. I gained credibility and my co-workers no longer challenged my decisions.

Eventually, my confidence grew to the point where I felt emboldened enough to ask for a raise. I hadn't gotten one in three years, and now, more than ever, I felt I deserved one, since I was wearing so many hats. I could sit back passively and wait to be recognized, but that would be an interminable wait in this company.

Rather than make the request impulsively, I crafted a letter to my boss, stating all the new responsibilities I'd taken on over the past year and how I felt a merit raise was in order. After perfecting it, I put it in an envelope and left it on my boss's desk.

He didn't get back to me for a while, but then came the morning when he took me into the conference room for a talk, which ended up lasting 45 minutes. No, I did not get the raise. It wasn't much of a surprise; my boss gave his usual excuses about how the money simply wasn't there to give. (Meanwhile, he still lived in a ritzy gated community and belonged to his ritzy golf clubhouse, but whatever.)

However, I got something else I wanted; he told me I was doing a great job. That I had changed and improved, and I was a much more vital part of the company now. And here was the icing on the cake: I was more likable these days, more fun to be around.

How do I express just how much of a miracle this was? This was a man who would sooner relinquish a testicle than give kudos. I once argued with him about how he never gave us any praise and his reply was, "I pay you; what more do you want?" So to hear those accolades from him was truly something rare. Sure, I would have liked the money; part of me wanted to say, "Thanks, that's nice—now cough up some cash, cheapskate."

Still, his words were a testament to the medications and how I was changing with them. My efforts plus pharmaceuticals were paying off. I wanted to continue, to keep moving forward. If I could conquer this job, I could do so with other obstacles and challenges too.

However, for the first time, I didn't just want to exist to conquer things. There had to be more to life than that.

I wanted some fun and fulfillment. And maybe, just maybe, that wasn't too much to ask for.

Part II: Living

"The depth of your despair will, in turn, be the height of your joy."
—my favorite "12-step-ism." Source unknown.

Playing Catch-up

"Am I going to have sex ever again in this century??"
—my journal, May 18, 1994

One of the first things to kick into gear after a few months on meds was my long-dormant libido. Oh, I'd had sexual feelings, but they were of the one-sided, obsessive variety. From what others have told me, I put out a vibe of desperation and anxiety, of neediness and hunger, and at the same time, I came off as controlled and uptight. Not an attractive combination, and therefore, men weren't responsive to me. So you can imagine my shock when I found myself receiving a barrage of male attention.

Much of it was at my gym, as I spent a lot of time there in those days. I'd been at this particular gym for several years and there had been a couple of flirtations here and there in the past, but nothing like what was going on now. Workouts that used to be about an hour-and-a-half stretched into three hours, because I spent as much time socializing as I did exercising.

There were about four different men chatting me up; none of them were available, so it was banter that was never intended to go anywhere. At first, that confused me. I may have been 36 years old, but emotionally and experience-wise, I was still a rather naïve teenager. I didn't understand flirting just for sake of doing so; I thought it had to lead somewhere.

One man in particular was so flirtatious and complimentary, I thought for certain that he was interested in me. Imagine my chagrin when I finally got up the nerve to ask him if he'd like to go out sometime, and he said, "Oh… I'm really flattered and I'd love to, but I can't; I'm married." I was so embarrassed, and annoyed as well. "What was all that flirting about, then?" I asked.

He just smiled at me as if I were a backward child. "I'm married; I'm not *dead*." Interesting. I learned a lot that day.

So this was good "practice" for me. That was Susan's interpretation—that all my interactions with men were practice. For what, I had no idea.

I hadn't had sex since 1991 and the last time was the pits. I was still reeling from the losses of Chuck and Waiter Guy, and a guy pal suggested we try a friends-with-benefits arrangement. Why not, I thought. Ack. Good buddies don't necessarily translate into good lovers. When he arrived at my apartment and I asked if he'd like to open the bottle of wine I'd bought, his answer was, "Why, is your arm broken?" When the time came to go to the bedroom, he dashed in ahead of me, yanked off all his clothes and flopped onto my bed, looking at me expectantly. Sheeesh... is it too much to ask for a little seduction? And his idea of nookie sweet-talk? Running his hand up my leg and saying, "You shaved, didn't you? Nice—smooth as a baby's ass." Be still, my heart. Needless to say, that was a one-timer. The fact that the poor bastard's weenie was about two inches long didn't help, either. The need to ask "Is it in?" is not a good thing.

Getting back to the gym—believe it or not, mine had valet parking. I never used it; there was plenty of parking a little farther away. I couldn't quite get the concept of paying good money to attend a nice gym, ostensibly to exercise, and yet being unwilling to walk a few extra steps. So I'd park my car and walk through the valet area. The valet, a very handsome young man, would call out greetings to me each day. "Hi, Gorgeous!" "Hi, Sunshine!" *Sunshine?* Who, me?

When I'd walk out later in the evening after finishing my workout, he wasn't as busy. He started calling me over to chat with him. A customer would come out and he'd have to fetch a car, but he'd point at me and say, "Don't you go anywhere," and dash off. So I'd stand by and wait for him to come back, and we'd resume our conversation. Sometimes, if it was a cold or rainy night, I'd bring him coffee or a hot chocolate.

He was 22 years old and quite the wild boy. Why he was paying so much attention to me, I had no clue. (Told you, I was very naïve.) I just knew I liked it, very much. I looked forward to seeing him, to our talks and banter. We had nothing in common, but he was sharp as a tack and conversation was easy.

One very slow night, we talked for a long time. He was teasing me about how "buttoned-up" I was, how I thought about things too much and couldn't be spontaneous. "When was the last time you felt like doing something and you didn't think about it, you just did it?" he asked. What could I say? That was a foreign concept to me.

But, standing there in that parking lot in the dark with this gorgeous young hunk, I was hit by an urge and my heart started pounding with nerves. *Come on, Erica. Live a little.* Before I could think myself out of it, I blurted, "OK, fine. You know what I want to do before I leave?"

"No, what?" he smirked.

"I want to kiss you," I replied.

Much to my satisfaction, he looked taken aback for a moment. "*Kiss* me?" he said. "Yup, right now, right here in this parking lot," I said.

He recovered quickly and glanced around the immediate vicinity. No one there; no one coming. And he stepped up close and laid one on me. Yes, we're talking tongue.

You know that old romantic-novel cliché about a kiss making knees buckle? It really does happen. I hadn't been kissed in over three years, and it gave me such a head rush, I got giddy. I couldn't remember where I'd parked my car and I stumbled around the lot looking for it. He laughed at me, calling out, "My God, what did I *do* to you?" He had no idea.

Once, we made out while he had me pinned up against my car, my legs wrapped around his waist. Another couple of times, we fooled around in my car. I know... so high school, right? But remember, I had never done this sort of thing when I really *was* in high school. He was a biter, and I went to work with large welts/bruises that no amount of makeup could cover. Most people reach a certain age and disdain hickeys. I loved them. They announced to the world, "Look! Erica got some!" Well, technically, I didn't, because he and I never had intercourse. But if other people thought we had, I wasn't about to set them straight.

* * *

A few months before my 37th birthday, a new employee was hired, a typesetter named Mike. He was in his late 20s, rode a motorcycle, and came off as impossibly macho to me. He was good-looking and smart, but I didn't like his crude humor or his "I'm-all-that" attitude. I figured he wasn't going to last long anyway, since he made a lot of mistakes in the beginning.

But he persevered and remained. Little by little, I saw glimpses of another side of him; a side that was funny and sweet. It was as if he had two personalities: the one he showed around his male peers and the one he allowed to slip out when it was just him and me. It baffled me and drove me nuts on more than one occasion. There were times when, in the presence of his office cronies, he would say things that made me want to either slap him or leave the room in tears. Then he would turn around and be so endearing, I'd forget about the other side.

Slowly, I learned to overcome my hypersensitivity with him and toss back my own wisecracks. Like the day I came to work dressed up in a sexy all-black outfit. Several others complimented me; Mike asked if I was going to a funeral. I retorted, "Yes—yours."

We became buddies. Work-wise, although he was sharp as hell and knew his stuff, he was careless and made mistakes. I got into the habit of covering for him whenever I could, sticking up for him when our boss would take me aside and bluster about what a screw-up Mike was. I said he had potential, that we were extremely busy and needed him. I wasn't used to our boss listening to me, but now that I had this new position and I had a better overall picture of the shop's goings-on, I suppose I had more credibility. So, grudgingly, he kept giving Mike another chance.

My birthday came. This office wasn't much for acknowledging birthdays; we'd get a group card and that's about it. So I got my card and a fat-free muffin with a candle in it. Mike had known it was my birthday, but he forgot. I was hurt; after all that covering for him and all that crap he said about how I was his best friend there, he couldn't be bothered to remember to say "happy birthday"? Later that afternoon, I got a floral delivery from a friend. Mike saw it and said, "Oh yeah, right, it's your birthday!" *Screw you,* I thought.

A couple of days later, I found a bag from a bookstore on my desk, with a Post-it note on top: "Happy birthday—sorry it's late. Mike." I looked in the bag, thinking it would be some sort of trivia or humor book, or puzzles, perhaps. It was a hardcover book of classic love poems. Huh? And inside was a bookmark with a cat on it; Mike knew I loved cats. What on earth…? I was floored; I didn't know what to say.

When he came into my room to bring me some work, I held up the book and said, "You're certainly full of surprises!" He asked if I liked it; I said of course I did, it's beautiful. He hugged me and said, "You deserve it." To this day, I still don't know what to make of that gift. From someone like Mike, I would have sooner expected a book of dirty limericks; this came completely out of left field.

At this point, I'll bet readers think they know where this is headed. Nope—nothing happened between Mike and me, except friendship. However, he came into my life when I was in a state of transition and he was the catalyst for some memorable experiences.

In the graphics/typesetting industry, the state of the workload was cyclical and oftentimes either feast or famine. We'd been extremely, crazily busy, but then things died off and we entered a slow period, right after my birthday. There was a lot of down time and, during the next couple of weeks, Mike and I spent a lot of time talking and getting to know each other. We fell into a comfortable and easy banter—he said he found me "intriguing." Yeah, whatever. That's me, Ms. Intrigue.

He found out I'd never been on a motorcycle, and of course, it became his mission to get me to ride on his. He didn't know I was scared to death at the prospect and I didn't want to admit it. So I would put him off whenever he brought it up.

The banter got edgy at times. I'll always wonder if he was "one of us"; he made spanking-related comments often. One morning I brought him a corrected job and I was teasing him about a typo. He didn't turn to look at me, just shook his head and said, "You're lucky that I didn't have breakfast this morning and I'm feeling weak."

"Oh, yeah?" I sneered. "What would you do?"

Without taking his eyes off his computer screen, he dropped his voice and growled, "I'd put you over my knee and spank the hell out of you."

Well, now. I was glad he wasn't looking at me, so he couldn't see my face flushing crimson.

As I grew to trust him, I shared more. One day, I told him how I'd always thought I was different and weird, that no matter where I went, I felt like I was trespassing. And how I'd wished I could simply be more "mainstream" and fit in better.

I'd shared this feeling with others over the years, and always got one of two reactions: Either denial ("You're *not* different!") or judgment ("Well, maybe you should try to change, then"). Not from Mike. He looked at me, made a "what are you babbling about" face, then he said:

"Erica, I don't think you can help but be different, so maybe you shouldn't worry about it."

Yes, it's simplistic. But I guess I was ready to hear it. In other words, *stop fretting about who you're not, Erica.* I think that was the day I first began to embrace my otherness, rather than rejecting it. After all, since when is being like everyone else such a great thing, anyway? And why do we take so damn long to learn that?

Mike's birthday was in mid-October and fell on a Friday. He had a girlfriend and a group of friends, and they were going out for dinner that night. He asked me if I'd like to join them; his friends wanted to meet me. Of course, my instinctive reaction was "No, I don't want to; it's something new and I don't like new things." But the New-and-Improving Erica was thinking "no" first and then trying her damndest to say "yes" anyway. So I accepted the invitation.

On that Friday, work was dead and we were down to a skeleton crew. Our boss hadn't come in and my supervisor didn't have camera work, so he was watching the front and I was able to go back into my old room. In the early afternoon, Mike wandered into my room and we started talking again. He told me all about his girlfriend and asked me if I'd ever been in a serious relationship. I had to say no, and he said I was too picky. I snapped, "That's not it—there's a lot about me you don't know." To which he replied, "So tell me."

And so I did. I talked and talked and talked. I told him about depression and eating disorders, about feeling like I lost 20 years of my life to them. About isolation, fear of just about everything, lack of trust. Of not experiencing so many of the normal rite-of-passage things of youth. About self-hatred and the suicide attempt at 19. Finally, I told him about therapy and starting medication, and how I now found myself taking baby steps to catch up with where my life should be; that most things normal for others were a major deal/ordeal for me.

He didn't say a word, just sat quietly and watched my face. I wound down, then blurted, "*Why* am I telling you all this?" "Because I'm listening," he said. "We all have our secrets."

"Yeah? So what about you? Tell me some of yours," I challenged him.

Now it was my turn to sit and listen, while he told me his own horror story. His family emigrated here when he was a child and they lived in the projects of South-Central Los Angeles. For those who are unaware of the area, let's just say it's a hellhole and leave it at that. His father was old-school macho; when Mike got beaten up at school one day and came home crying, his father made him go back out, find the kid and keep fighting until he was the victor. "If someone hurts you, you hurt them worse. Men don't cry. Men don't show their feelings—if you have a problem, you suck it up and deal with it yourself."

By the time he was 12, he was in a local gang. And by the time he was 16, he'd seen friends die and had nearly been killed himself—he'd been beaten senseless and left in the street. At 17, he joined the army—more violence. He thought about committing suicide, but his will to survive was too strong and he knew he could make a better life for himself if he hung in there. And so here he was.

I asked how many people knew this story. He said his girlfriend, his roommate/best friend and now me. And he hoped I wouldn't reject him.

I nearly wept. I wanted to cradle him like a child. I wanted to find his father and punch his lights out. We talked a little longer and then he had to go do some work. The rest of the day passed and at closing, he and I were the only ones left, so we prepared to lock up and leave, but then ended up hanging out and talking more. He said that he couldn't wait for me to meet his friends; they'd love me, and because they were young and lots of fun, perhaps they could help me recapture some of the years I lost. *That* did it—I wept then.

When I was ready to leave, I told him I'd see him at the restaurant, and he said, "No, you can't go yet. It's my birthday, and there's something I want." He went to get his things and came back to me, grinning, holding two helmets. "You're going to take a bike ride with me. I brought an extra helmet for you." Oh, God.

Taking a deep breath and wiping my eyes, I bravely went down to the parking lot with him, dumped my stuff in my car and put on the helmet. "So what do I do?"

"Keep your feet on the pegs, move with me, hold on tight and *don't* scream in my ear," he teased, as I got on behind him. And off we went. I admit I let out one yelp when he accelerated down the driveway, but then I clamped my mouth shut and hung on tighter.

WOW. My first motorcycle ride, at age 37, was unbelievably exhilarating. I finally understood the appeal of these machines. Mike did not baby me; he sped up, whizzed along, zipped around corners. My first words when we got back were, "Got a cigarette?"

So, it had been quite a day already, what with all this revealing conversation and the ride. But it wasn't over yet.

* * *

91

When I showed up at the Japanese restaurant later, Mike, his girlfriend and his buddies were already there. A seat between two of his single friends had been conveniently left open and I sat there. On my left was Mike's best friend and roommate Doug, whom I liked immediately. He was 26, charming, quick-witted and so damn boyishly cute. I was taken aback at the sudden surge of attraction. *Get a grip, Erica. What's up with you and these young guys?*

This group was sharp, but although I was nervous, I think I held my own pretty well. The food was a challenge; there were no utensils and I'd never used chopsticks before. Yes, another "never." I couldn't get the hang of the damn things, and Mike was laughing at me because I was stabbing at my scallops and shrimp with the tips, trying to spear them so I could actually eat something. His friend Phil on my right tried very patiently to show me how to hold them, but I fumbled and bumbled and ended up bumping his arm and making him spill his sake. Doug, after observing for a while, cut to the chase—he simply picked up my chopsticks and began feeding me. Not surprisingly, I liked that much better.

After dinner, they all went to shoot pool and I joined them. But I declined the invitation to the coffeehouse later—it was late and I was beyond exhausted. And I'd had an incredible amount of stimuli for one day.

Back at work Monday morning, Mike teased me, saying I'd made quite an impression on his friends, and that both Doug and Phil wanted to go out with me. Phil was very nice and, at 32, closer to my age...but I wasn't drawn to him as I was with Doug. Both men started calling me at work each day—between the two of them and Mike, I was reeling with all this unfamiliar attention.

Mike was getting a huge kick out of all this and made an effort to include me in the group gatherings, including inviting me to Phil's place one night where they were all playing cards, and over to his and Doug's apartment when they were preparing to move. He kept being a mixer, teasing me and pushing me to go for it with both of them. I did go out with Phil a couple of times—one lunch and one dinner. I enjoyed his company and told myself he was a better fit for me.

After Doug and Mike moved into their new apartment, Doug invited me over to see the place and to watch one of his favorite movies. So on a Wednesday evening, I went over there. The apartment was nice, but it was a classic "bachelor pad." They didn't even own a refrigerator; all they ever ate was take-out! I watched them eat delivery fried chicken dinners—the plastic utensils had been left out, so they ate with their fingers and slurped the macaroni salad directly from the little cups. "Christ, you guys," I said, "don't you have any silverware?" "Yeah, but none of it is clean." I decided to leave that alone.

We watched the movie, and when it was over, Mike disappeared quietly into his room, putting on some soft music before he left. Subtle, Mike. It worked. All that business of telling myself that Doug was too young for me and I should focus on developing something with Phil? Shot to hell, with one kiss. And when he suggested we "take this off the couch," I knew I was about to end my long drought. I was nervous beforehand; told him it had been a very long time. He didn't seem to be too concerned about that; told me I was beautiful and seduced me sweetly. My initial self-consciousness melted away under his hands.

In the next few hours, we talked, laughed, played, snuggled, kissed and kissed and kissed, and made love four times. Ah, the stamina of youth. Mike eventually got bored in his room and came back out, and he stood outside Doug's closed door, hollering, "Are you *still* at it? Aren't you done yet? What are you *doing* in there? What's all that giggling about? Huh?" We laughed and ignored him, and he finally went off to bed.

More time passed as we lay entwined and getting to know each other. Finally at 2:00 A.M., I wrenched myself from Doug and got ready to go home. I had to go to work in a few hours and I wasn't about to do the Walk of Shame into the office, wearing yesterday's clothes, sporting smeared makeup and "just got fucked" hair.

At work the next day, Phil dropped by to surprise me. I looked like hell and felt very awkward with him, knowing there was no way now that I could date him anymore. Not after sex with Doug.

The next few weeks are a blur. Doug called me every day. Shortly thereafter, I went back to his place and this time, spent the night, and we fell into a pattern of my visiting once a week or so. We'd hang out with Mike and his girlfriend, or with their buddies, for a while, but then we'd always slip off to his bedroom.

The sex was unbelievable. I suppose, under normal circumstances, he would be the more inexperienced one and I'd be the older, wiser "teacher"—but we all know I was hardly normal. He took the sexual reins; publicly, he was mild-mannered, sweet and boyish, but in the bedroom, he was a tiger and there was nothing boyish about him. He was creative and inexhaustible, and I followed his lead. Before him, I'd never orgasmed from a man, only from a vibrator. So I was shocked and pleased to discover just how wildly orgasmic I was.

He wanted sex before we slept and when we first woke up. At first I felt self-conscious about the latter (bedhead! morning breath!), but I came to love it with him. We gave each other full-body massages; he had amazing hands.

Nothing kinky, though; the closest we came to kink was playing around with one of those flavored lotions from the adult toy store. (By the way, if you've never tried one of those lotions, keep it that way. They are a big fat sticky *mess*—we both felt like we'd been rolling in strawberry jam.) But you know what? At that point, I was having one hell of an awakening and all I wanted was sex and more sex with him. I didn't care what flavor it was. I had a lot of catching up to do. And there was certainly plenty of variety anyway; we did it in every position, in every room, on the bed, on the couch, on the carpet…

Besides the firsts with sex, there were several other mini-firsts for me. Once, when I was having a dreadful day at work, he sent me flowers there to cheer me up. No one had ever done that for me before and I went to pieces over it. In retrospect, it probably threw him a bit when I called him to say thank you and started bawling on the phone.

When he came to my place and spent the night, I woke up with him the next morning and realized this was the first time that a man had spent the night in my bed. My previous lovers had always left after sex. I watched him tromping around my bedroom in his goofy plaid boxers with his wet hair in his eyes, and I couldn't stop giggling with sheer delight until he stopped, looked at me and said, *"What???"* "Nothing—you're just so damn cute!" He pulled a mock-disgusted face and went into the bathroom.

Looking back, I realize what an unlikely pairing we were. We had two things going for us: 1) mind-blowing sex, and 2) we made each other laugh often. Other than that, we had very little in common. Our tastes—food, music, books—were different. Our life references didn't match, due to the age difference. I recall one time when we were talking about TV shows we'd liked as kids and he was shocked that I'd never seen *Sesame Street*.

"How could you not have seen *Sesame Street*?" he spluttered. "Everyone has seen *Sesame Street*!" "I haven't," I replied. He wouldn't let it go. "But how? I grew up with it; I watched it every day!" I sighed. "Um, honey? That's because when *Sesame Street* first came on the air, you were a year old. I was already 12." "Oh…yeah," he said, somewhat sheepishly. I just smiled and asked if he'd like some water to wash down his foot.

And while our age difference was only 11 years, it appeared to be more. I mean, I looked like what I was—a woman in her late 30s. Doug, on the other hand, didn't look a day over 18. I certainly looked like his *much* older sister, if not his mother. I took him with me to the holiday party at my boss's house. My supervisor told me that his date, after meeting Doug, had commented, "Does he shave yet?" Well, *meow* to you too.

So, given these factors, it would have been smart to keep it simple, enjoy a fun and casual sex-buddy relationship, right? But no. I had to go and fall in love with him.

We were invited to a Christmas gathering at his mother and stepfather's house. I was rather nervous about it, as I hadn't met his family before, and it was going to feel a little weird meeting his mom (since she was all of 13 years my senior). I came to his place a few hours early, ostensibly to help him wrap presents. But I was so edgy, he decided to relieve my tension a bit. So there I was in post-sex bliss, and I felt this overwhelming surge of affection and appreciation for him. Before I could think better of it, I did the unthinkable—I said the "L" word.

I didn't expect him to say it back and he didn't. All he did was hold me very close, not saying a word. But I also didn't expect that would be the beginning of our downhill slide.

The holidays passed and I felt him backing off. I had hoped to spend New Year's Eve with him, as I'd always fantasized about spending that night with a man, having a romantically wonderful time. However, Mike and the gang had other ideas; they wanted to shlep to San Bernardino to some all-night carnival. That sounded about as appealing to me as a raging stomach virus, but I knew Doug would want to go, so I told him to go ahead and I spent the eve alone. After the fact, he told me that the event had been, in his word, "chintzy." I told him I'd missed him; he did not say it back.

The daily phone calls dwindled, then stopped altogether. We still got together once a week and he was sweet and attentive as ever, but once the night was over, we'd go our separate ways and I wouldn't hear from him for another week. A couple of times, Mike came into work and asked me if I was going to so-and-so's birthday party or to the such-and-such gathering, something or another that involved his gang. And I would be forced to say I knew nothing about it, embarrassing us both.

Then came the Monday morning when Mike told me that on Saturday, Doug had been in a bad accident on the freeway. He was OK, but his car was totaled. And I had to hear this from someone else? I called him at work, told him I'd just heard and I was so sorry, and then asked, "Why didn't you tell me?" "Didn't want you to worry, and there was nothing you could do anyway," he replied.

My father and I were having regular dinners out by then, and he had asked if I'd like to bring Doug to one of them. When I broached the subject to Doug, he became clearly uncomfortable, gave me a bunch of excuses and then finally admitted he thought it would be awkward. I didn't push it, but I did say, "But I met *your* family." He shrugged and said, "That's different." How so, I wanted to ask. But I didn't.

We straggled along through January and February, with me in complete denial. The writing was on the wall, but whenever we got together and the sex was still so phenomenal, I forgot everything else. But come March, he ended it.

I knew it was coming when he suggested getting together at my place instead of his, and mentioned that he wouldn't be spending the night. Still, nothing prepared me for when he lowered the boom. He said he'd been feeling guilty, knowing what he "needed to do," but he didn't want to do it. That he didn't have the same feelings for me that I had for him, and it would be kinder in the long run to end things now, rather than wait until he met someone else. Really? Kinder? According to whom?

The initial conversation, after that bombshell, went something like this:

"How *do* you feel about me?"

"I like you and I care about you."

"Do you enjoy my company?"

"Yes."

"Do you still find me attractive, still like making love with me?"

"Yes."

"Do you like it when I go out with you and your friends?"

"Yes."

"But you think we should stop seeing each other."

"I think it would be a good idea."

It made no damn sense to me and the pain was excruciating. I couldn't stop crying. We were lying on my bed side by side, and he rolled over on top of me, clinging to me and burying his face in my chest. He said he hoped we could continue being friends and that I'd still hang out with him and the gang. I said no, that's impossible. He actually seemed surprised at that and said he didn't want to lose me as a friend. I wept, "It can't be all your way, Doug. You can't tell me you want me in your life, but you're going to keep me at arm's length. I can't do that—I love you." What the hell, I could say it now all I wanted, since I had nothing to lose.

When he lifted his head to look at me, his face was wet, his eyes red. "Why are *you* crying?" I asked. "Because I'm hurting you, and I don't want to." Then *don't*, stupid! I didn't say that out loud, of course.

I had to tell him to leave. He was looking at me so intently, like he was trying to memorize my face, and I couldn't stand it; my eyes were swelling, my nose was beet red and my makeup was halfway down my face. It took nearly a half-hour to actually get him out the door; he wouldn't let go of me. Ridiculous, right—he was the one doing the severing, after all! So what was this clingy stuff about? But finally, he was gone.

I can look back now and realize just how melodramatic this all was, and how completely extreme my reactions were. But at the time, I wanted to die. I wanted to go to sleep and never awaken. And yet, after a sleepless night of sobbing my heart out, I had to get up in the morning, get dressed and go to work. Be an adult. Oh, and see Mike, who of course would know.

Being dumped hurts like hell. In a way, it feels worse than a death. When a loved one dies, they leave everyone; when someone dumps you, they just leave *you*. Much more personal, and you're left feeling like a failure. And you know they're still out there, moving on with life while you're stuck in pain. I went on auto-pilot for a while, my old stomping grounds. I went through the day-to-day motions, showed up where I needed to be. But I cried all the time and I looked like a zombie. I tried my best to maintain composure at work, but I've never been able to hide my feelings worth a damn.

I missed his silliness and his goofy laugh. I missed his growling kitty noises. And oh *God*, would I ever have sex like that again? It seemed unlikely. My body hungered for him.

A week later, my boss called me into the conference room and told me that while he sympathized with what I was going through, he hoped that I could deal with it—and quickly—because my depression was affecting his business. I looked bad and I sounded bad on the phone. For the first time since the breakup, I felt an emotion other than misery—*anger*. I said I was sorry if my pain was bothering people, but I was a human being, not a robot. He then got pissed off, dropped the phony caring act and said that if I didn't want to help myself, then fine, but if I didn't pull myself together, he'd have to send me home for a few days. (Unpaid, of course.)

I went stone cold. *OK, you heartless son-of-a-bitch,* I thought. If he wanted professional, I would damn well give him professional. I swore to myself that I'd be strong at work, even if it killed me. And somehow, I was. I would take breaks and go cry in the bathroom. But in the public eye, I held it together.

Life went on, as it always does. I moved through the stages of loss: shock and denial, depression and anger, and finally, acceptance. Mike and I remained close, but he was a constant reminder of Doug and it was painful and awkward. And then a little over a month later, he too was gone; he'd screwed up at work one too many times and they fired him. Full circle, I thought in my melodramatic mode. Mike came into my life, Mike brought Doug into my life, Doug exited, and now Mike was exiting too.

Did it hurt? Hell, yes. Would I have rather not known them? Hell, *NO*. As they say in 12-step, it was AFGE.

Another Fucking Growth Experience, that is.

SEX IS GREAT, BUT...

"[A man I met] said he could tell by the way I was talking that I was, or could be, into role-playing. I said, what does THAT mean? He said, 'You know...being dominated.' I said I really couldn't say, since I've never experienced it, and he answered, 'Yeah, but you've fantasized about it.' (Shit—have I ever.)"
—my journal, March 13, 1996

A couple of notes to close out the Doug episode. First, after a few months, both Mike and Doug came back into my life, briefly. They were no longer roommates; Mike had temporarily moved back in with his parents while he went back to school, and Doug had moved into an apartment across the street from them. I tried hanging out with their little group again, but it wasn't the same.

However, Doug and I had sex twice more, the final time on my 38th birthday. I was very glad for those times; not just because they were spectacular, but because I hated that his last memory of me was bawling my eyes out and looking like a boiled lobster with a runny nose. Now I could feel I'd closed this chapter on a positive note.

Also, inadvertently through Doug, I discovered an unexpected and most welcome side effect of my medications. On Valentine's Day, he'd brought me a two-pound box of See's candy, my favorite chocolates. While I was thrilled with the gesture, I felt a familiar panic; I had to get rid of them. I couldn't keep them in the house, because I would compulsively binge on them. I could tell myself I wouldn't, but past experience had shown otherwise; will power couldn't override the compulsion. So I planned to bring them into work and let the vultures there gobble them up.

But I didn't have to do that, as it turned out. The chocolates stayed in my refrigerator, day after day. A few times, I opened the box and took one. Two, tops. Then put it back. This was new... I waited for the terrible urge to strike, but it did not. And after some thinking and researching, I realized that my antidepressant/anti-anxiety cocktail had lifted one of the worst symptoms of my eating disorder. After all these years, I could now keep chocolate in the house, even See's. And cookies. And cereal, and bread. And all my other previous binge foods. It was a miracle.

* * *

It was now fall of 1995. I had been through many changes in recent months, including leaving my dead-end job and starting a new one. I now had a much longer commute, and I worried about my 13-year-old car that was breaking down constantly. My father matter-of-factly offered up a solution during one of our dinners: He said, "Go buy yourself a new car." Right, Dad. Just like that? With what money? I said that I couldn't afford car payments, and he gruffly replied that I wouldn't have car payments.

It took a moment for the light bulb to flicker on. "Are you saying what I think you're saying?"

"Yeah. Go pick out a new car. Tell me what it costs and I'll send you a check."

I was speechless; I couldn't believe he was offering this. And while I'd turned down some extravagant offers from years ago, this was different. I needed a new car, badly. So I accepted it, thanking him profusely. He said I didn't need to thank him, that he should have given me this when I was 16. To which I replied, "No, you shouldn't. I wouldn't have appreciated it then."

So here I was, with a brand-new job and a brand-new car. The job turned out to be a nightmare, but more on that later. I didn't have much time or energy for a dating life, and I'd decided that this falling-in-love business was for the birds anyway and I just wanted to get laid now and then. So, years before the term "Friends with Benefits" was coined, that's what I sought. Around that time, I discovered the "Alternatives" section in a local free paper, the *L.A. Weekly*.

Back then, the Internet hadn't taken off quite so much and old-fashioned paper personals ads were still the norm. In the *Weekly*, there were the regular ads, and then there were the "alternative" ads. These were for the folks who weren't seeking moonlight walks on the beach, marriage and kids and happily-ever-after; they wanted something other than the traditional relationship.

There were quite a few with kinky references in them, but I wasn't ready for those yet. So I selected one that sounded intelligent and interesting, casual and non-committal, and called the 900 number, $2.99 a minute. After punching in the mailbox code and listening to the gentleman's outgoing message, I left an introduction and my phone number.

He called soon after that and we had several phone chats. I liked how he sounded; bright, laid back, funny and warm. He didn't push to meet immediately, just seemed to be content with talking and getting to know one another a bit, which made me feel comfortable.

Because he had an unusual name, I'm going to use his initial, B. We met on Halloween night; he had me come to Old Town Pasadena to his workplace. Remember, it was a paper ad, no pictures, so this was the first time we were laying eyes on one another. He was thin, blond-haired and blue-eyed, clean-shaven, and had very thick glasses and a sweet smile. A co-worker was there with her two small children, preparing to go trick-or-treating. When we started to walk out the door, both kids broke away from their mother, ran to B and threw their arms around his knees. I took that as a good sign; how bad can a guy be if small children like him, right?

We had coffee and walked through the streets of Old Town, people-watching and looking at the various costumes. It was a cold night and I had no jacket, so he offered me his. "Won't you be cold?" I asked. "I'm from Michigan," he scoffed. "This is a heat wave." Ah, he was a gentleman, too. Nice.

He escorted me back to my car, and when I gave him a hug, he asked for a kiss. It turned out to be one hell of a kiss that sent me home beaming. Perhaps there was Sex After Doug, after all.

So B and I became lovers. We fell into a casual, semi-regular routine—every two or three weeks, I'd go to his place or he'd come to mine. Since my work was on the way to his apartment, sometimes I'd go there straight from the office on Fridays, bringing my overnight bag. B turned out to be one extremely sexual man. Upon his or my arrival, we'd go straight to bed and wouldn't come out for hours, until hunger drove us to seek food.

He had an insatiable mouth, loved to kiss and caress and massage, and wanted sex all the time, even when I had my period. In between bouts in bed, we'd go to dinner, see a movie on occasion, and he insisted on paying. We were both night owls, so sometimes we'd stay up watching videos, have intense sex and then get up to go out to eat at 2:00 or 3:00 A.M.

I'd never met anyone quite like him and I haven't since. He was the most mild-mannered and even-keeled person I'd ever known; I can honestly say that in the year we were together, we never exchanged a single cross word and I never heard one leave his lips.

He was calm and relaxed, and being around him soothed me. I was dealing with tremendous stress at work, and he'd tease me and say that by the time he was done with me, I'd not only be stress-free, but "at a stress deficit." He was so easy to be with, never demanded anything from me. We were both free to see other people. As affectionate as he was, he didn't use traditional pet names; never called me "honey" or "sweetie" or anything like that. Sometimes he'd call me "kiddo," which was a bit strange, considering he was six years my junior.

Sexually, we knew each other well, but I found that I knew very little about him. I knew the basics, like where he worked, where he grew up, what kind of music he liked, etc. But after we'd been seeing each other a few months, I met a friend of his who came to my workplace to apply for a job. I chatted with him while we waited for my boss and he said, "So how long have you known Dr. A?" "Doctor?" I repeated stupidly. His friend told me that B had a PhD from Cal Tech Institute, a school well known for having brainiac students. Well, this was news! B was very modest about himself, but this was ridiculous. When I asked, "How come you didn't tell me you had a doctorate?", he shrugged, smiled and replied, "You didn't ask!"

In many ways, this was the perfect relationship, exactly what I needed at the time, no pressure. And yet… and yet. I was restless. I wanted something more. I wanted him to be dominant. That certain *thing*, whatever the hell it was that had been within me for as long as I could remember, was demanding attention.

So I provoked him, tried to spur him to action. Once at his place, he was doing laundry and he wanted me to get off the bed so he could remove the sheets. I playfully refused and stayed where I was. Much to my thrill, he picked me up bodily, carried me out of the room and dumped me on the couch. But that was the only toppy thing he ever did.

Another time we were in a restaurant seated side by side, and I had dropped my hand into his lap and was teasing him. He squirmed and fidgeted, clearly flustered, and said I was bad to do this to him in public. *Aha*, I thought. "Yeah?" I taunted, not stopping. "What're you going to do about it?" He answered, "I don't know!" Oh, crap. Not the answer I had hoped for.

One day in February 1996, I was shopping at Mrs. Gooch's market (which later became Whole Foods) on my way home from work. I was tired, looked and felt like hell and it was pouring rain, and I wanted to get this over with, so I'm sure I had my "stay away from me" face on. While I was paying, I saw a young man talking with some of the store employees near the doorway, and I overheard him saying something about misplacing his car keys. As I walked out, he turned away from them and fell into step with me, following me into the parking lot. "Hi, I'm Ken," he said, sticking out his hand.

I couldn't help smiling at him and I shook his hand. It was wet and cold outside, but he was in shorts and a t-shirt. "Aren't you cold?" I asked. "Nah. You on your way to the gym? You're in leggings," he said. I answered no, I was going home, then said I hoped he found his car keys and started to fish in my purse for my own.

"Hey, I hope this doesn't sound too forward, but would you like to go for coffee sometime?"

I froze and stared at him. *I can't believe it. I'm being picked up in the parking lot of Mrs. Gooch's. This kind of thing does not happen to me.* "How do I know you're not some serial rapist?"

He assured me I was quite safe with him, then added he knew a lot of the workers here—would I like to ask them about him? I said no. This was so ridiculous—we were both dripping rain, for God's sake. He asked if I was married or had a boyfriend. I told him I was seeing someone, but it was open.

"I knew it!" he blurted. "All the good-looking women are taken! Here, open this door and let me slam my head in it." He grabbed at my door handle.

I laughed. This guy was growing on me, rapidly. Before I could think myself out of it, I found a piece of paper in my purse and wrote my name and phone number on it. Perhaps letting a perfect stranger pick me up in a store parking lot wasn't the most prudent move. But that encounter turned out to be rather pivotal.

Ken did call, and we met for coffee and chat. And for a brief period, I had two men in my life. They were polar opposites; while B was wiry, fair-skinned with silky blond hair, Ken was muscular with olive skin and dark curls. B's temperament was calm and even; Ken's was intense and moody. B was cocoa—warm, sweet and soothing—while Ken was a jolt of highly caffeinated coffee. And I was wildly attracted to them both. However, Ken had a fascinating edge over B.

Ken threatened to spank me. Repeatedly. In phone conversations and in person. Even though I didn't tell him so, he intuited that his words along those lines turned me on and he stepped it up. He'd call me at work and purr into the phone that I'd been a very bad girl. If I teased him, I'd hear, "Keep it up and I'll put you over my knee." I'd get so flustered and excited, I could barely speak. I was dying to tell him that I really wanted him to do it, but I couldn't. I just hoped that he knew, and he certainly seemed to. "I know just what you need." "I know how to take care of you." "Your day will come, just wait." And I'd squirm and tremble, wondering how this would play out, *if* it would play out.

A little over a month after we met, we made a Saturday dinner date, and when he asked if I'd stay the night afterward, I said yes. There had been a lot of making out up until this point, but no more. The day before our date, he called my office. When I answered, he didn't say hello, just, "I want you to know that you're in a lot of trouble."

I damn near had a heart attack, but I managed to conceal that minor inconvenience and tossed back, "Thank you for sharing that—I'm going to tremble for the rest of the day." Unfazed, his voice cool and smooth, he started to tell me what he was going to do to me, but I couldn't handle it—I had work to do and I needed to focus. "I don't have time for this nonsense. Did you call for any other reason besides to babble your idle threats?"

"Idle? I'll show you idle! Now get back to work." Easy for him to say. Oh, I couldn't wait until the next night.

Well... I guess it wasn't my time yet.

We went to dinner with a friend of his, and then out for coffee. I was restless and fidgety, impatient to get back to his place, but he was yammering away with people at the café. I gave him some noise about all his yapping on the way to the car. "Just wait until I get you home," he said.

Finally, we were there. Once inside, I waited for him to make a move, but he didn't. After all this waiting, I couldn't stand the tease, so I yawned. "Well, I guess it was all talk after all. Guess I'll be going," and I got up and headed for the door, opening it. Before I could walk out, he was suddenly at my side with a steel grip on my upper arm. "Get back in here," he growled.

(OK, I know what you're thinking. This is the part where I should have been really, *really* scared. But I wasn't.)

Kicking the door shut, he scooped me up in his arms and carried me into his bedroom. Clothes flew off, and then he pushed me onto the bed, face down. *This is it,* I thought. He gave me a few slaps on my bottom, but before I could register anything, he rolled me onto my back. And slapped me full in the face.

I reacted viscerally, recoiling and shrieking, "Don't *do* that!" Instantly, he was hovering over me, wringing his hands, apologizing profusely. "I'm sorry! I'm sorry! I've never done this before; I didn't know what I was supposed to do."

Never done this before?? What happened to "I know just what you need," etc.? I suppose this was my first exposure to the scene version of one of life's lessons: People can talk a good game, but actually knowing what they're talking about, that's a different story. I know this now, but I sure didn't know it then and it was a shock.

We ended up having sex anyway, but it was awkward and mechanical, and I felt quite wretched the next morning. Ken acted like nothing had happened, took a shower and dressed, offered me coffee. He was chipper and cheery, clearly a morning person, and I just wanted to crawl away and go home. Fortunately, it was Easter Sunday and he had a brunch to go to, so the discomfort wasn't prolonged.

I felt embarrassed and ashamed, but worse than that, I was disappointed. Here I thought I was finally going to experience what I'd been fantasizing about for as long as I could remember, and this was how it ended up. After all the buildup and anticipation, the frustration was all but unbearable. And I couldn't talk about it with anyone. How could I? It was my nasty little secret.

Going back to work the next day sucked. I still felt like hiding, but that wasn't an option. It was hot that Monday and I wore a sleeveless shirt, not realizing that I had finger bruises on my right arm. My boss commented on them, concerned, and I was mortified. As the day progressed, I felt like this secret was going to burst out of my chest like an alien and if I didn't tell someone, I'd go mad. I called my therapist and left a message, asking her if I could have a phone session when I got home. Upon my arrival, I found a return message from her, telling me when to call.

I was so shaky, I felt sick. But I knew I had to do this—I had to get it all off my chest, out of my head. So I called Susan and with little preamble, I told her everything in a big tumbling torrent. The years of the desire and the fantasies, the endless fixation and how I felt stigmatized and apart because of it. Meeting Ken and my encounter with him. And how, despite how poorly it had gone, it left me craving more. What the hell was wrong with me?

Finally, I wound down, grateful this was on the phone because I couldn't have looked her in the face. When she spoke, her voice was incredulous. "That's it? This is the big, terrible secret you had to tell me? Erica, do you have *any* idea how many women out there have thoughts like this?"

Come again? This was not the reaction I expected. After so many years of thinking I was a freak, here I was confessing it to my shrink—and she was telling me I was normal? That hundreds, thousands of others shared this with me? My brain struggled to wrap around this concept, and tears of relief gushed as we discussed it. Not only did this person whom I respected and trusted tell me that my desires were okay, she encouraged me to explore them further, safely. I wasn't sure how I was going to do that, but it was nice to have someone grant me permission to do so.

Ken disappeared after our night together; after I waited for what I thought was a reasonable amount of time, I contacted him and said I wanted to talk. We got together, and he gave me a song-and-dance about how he thought he could handle the fact that I'm seeing someone else, but he couldn't, he was too insecure. Yeah, whatever. How convenient that he figured that out *after* he fucked me. I got the "can we be friends" speech, and what the hell, I agreed with it, after I gave him a piece of my mind for his poor communication skills.

A couple of weeks later, I heard from him again—he wanted a booty call. I turned him down. That was the last of Ken. But I don't regret knowing him; he was an important catalyst in my awakening.

One day around this time, I was indulging in one of my guilty pleasures: reading *Cosmopolitan* magazine. In the Classified Ads pages, I saw the header "**Fun – Fantasy – Romance**." And directly beneath that was something like **OVER THE KNEE ROMANCE**; I forget the exact verbiage. But of course, I had to read the ad, since that heading had my nerves firing.

It was for some company named Shadow Lane and they were offering an "introductory package" for $15. I had no idea what that was, but the ad sounded classy and non-sleazy, and I was intrigued. I made out a check and sent it to the listed P.O. Box post-haste.

Interesting how I'd been reading *Cosmo* for a long time, but never noticed that ad before. Coincidence? Yeah, probably. But as the old saying goes: "When the student is ready, the teacher will appear."

I guess, at long last, I was ready.

BIRTH OF A SPANKO

"I realized that I can't deny or bury this particular side of my sexuality anymore; I need to explore it. And I need to put out an effort to find someone safe and trustworthy to explore with. So...I'm answering ads in the L.A. Weekly *again."*
—my journal, April 29, 1996

I had no idea what to expect from Shadow Lane, so I was quite curious when a large manila envelope arrived, postmarked from them. I was in such a hurry, I sat right down on the carpet, tore open the envelope and dumped the contents in front of me. And there I sat for the next hour or so, looking at a treasure trove of spanking material. Brochures and video catalogs. The latest version of their full-color magazine, *Stand Corrected,* and another magazine called *Scene One* with nothing but personals. Letters and testimonials, party reports. Lots of pictures, with attractive men and women. More important than attractive, they looked... well, normal. Not one of them looked like the freak I'd imagined myself to be. How validating this was! Nothing looked scary or intimidating. These people were clearly having fun.

As I waded through all these goodies, my eye fell on a handsome man with sandy blond hair and a mustache, and I remember saying out loud, "Holy crap, who is *that*?" I kept seeing him, too—he was in the videos, in the brochures and in the party photos. Hell, if spanking men looked like this guy, I wanted to get into this group for sure.

Yes, of course. That man turned out to be the one and only Keith Jones.

Besides being reassurance that I was most certainly not alone in this spanking thing, the Shadow Lane material turned out to be a wealth of information. In *Stand Corrected* was possibly the best, most thorough article ever written about spanking and all its facets. Called "The Politics of Playing," it was written by Eve Howard and, with text and photos, covered a whopping 20 pages. Everything

110

from scene terminology to clothing to safe words to spanking etiquette was discussed, and I would suggest this article as a mini-Bible to everyone into spanking, from newbies on. Sexual or non-sexual? Switching? Marks, tears, implements, to drink or not to drink when playing? All included and explained. It was timely indeed that I was reading this at the beginning of my journey.

Once again, I began perusing the "Alternatives" section of the *L.A. Weekly*, this time looking specifically for ads that sounded like they had to do with spanking. However, at the time, they had some ridiculous censorship in place and the "s" word couldn't be used, so reading between the lines was necessary.

The first ad I answered sounded interesting, and the man returned my message. He insisted that I come over the hill to the Westside to meet him in a bar on a Saturday night. Not my first choice, but he didn't ask for my input.

So I drove there and met him; he wasn't very friendly or forthcoming, our conversation was stilted and he didn't offer to buy me something to drink. The day after, he left me a message, saying he didn't think we had chemistry, and admonishing me for not "dressing up more" when meeting someone for the first time. Excuse me? I'd dressed casually, but neatly. How rude.

Fortunately, despite my inexperience, even then I could tell the difference between dominance and being a jackass. I promptly forgot about him and went on to the next ad that held promise. Besides, if these ads didn't work out, B was still a regular fixture in my life. He saw other people, and he was fine with my doing so too. If I was able to find a man with whom I could explore this side of myself, that was great. If not, I still had B. Win-win, really.

I answered another ad; once again, nothing about spanking, but it mentioned tying and teasing, dominating, and asked if I was "curious about being submissive." If so, then I should explore with a safe, trustworthy, tall and cute man. I liked the description and I liked his voice on the outgoing message. He turned out to be a bit elusive and we played phone tag for two weeks, but then finally settled on a Wednesday evening to meet for coffee. He even called me at work to confirm it, so I knew it was a go.

I got there early, sitting in front of the window so that I could watch for him as he approached. All I knew was that he was tall, wore glasses and was in gray slacks and sneakers. I kept my fingers crossed and tried very hard not to get my hopes up too high.

I saw the gray slacks first. And then there he was, walking in the door and looking at me questioningly. Holy moly, was he ever good-looking! Very tall (about six-foot-four), fit, thick head of prematurely salt-and-pepper hair (he was only 35), dark eyes, nice smile. "You're Paul, aren't you," I said, smiling, and we shook hands.

After he got coffee, we sat on the stools and made opening chit-chat for a while. I was nervous and I guess he was too—his left leg bounced up and down rapidly the whole time. Then he looked at me and said, "Well, have we made enough small talk?" and we both laughed. This sort of meeting *is* awkward as hell; how do you segue into talking about the subject at hand?

I asked if we'd both passed the first hurdle, and at his puzzled look, I continued, "You know, that first moment you lay eyes on the other person—do you go 'ahhhh' or 'ugh'? Are you pleased or disappointed?" He replied that I certainly had nothing to worry about, and for all he knew, I'd taken one look at him and wanted to go home. "No," I assured him, "actually, I thought you were kind of cute." What the hell; what did I have to lose?

It was crowded in Starbucks and he suggested we go for a walk; I thought that was a perfect idea. As we walked, he asked several questions: what did I want, what was I seeking? What were my fantasies?

Grateful for the darkness that hid my scarlet cheeks, I told him how I wanted to be overcome, dominated, spanked. He told me, briefly, about some experiences with other women who answered his ad, what he liked, etc. He was more into control and teasing, he liked abduction scenes, physically restraining…all things about which I had no clue, but I was fascinated. Then he admitted he'd never really spanked a woman before, but he'd be up for giving it a try. If it was fun, then great, and if it wasn't, then we'd say goodbye, no hard feelings. That simple, huh?

Now that this really might be happening, the nervousness ratcheted up. I was so aroused that my legs trembled, but I was terrified. Of what? The vulnerability, the risk of doing something so personal with someone I barely knew. But I got a very good vibe from this guy and I was wildly attracted to him. And at the time, it didn't even occur to me to be concerned that he had no spanking experience. After all, I didn't either.

Meanwhile, Paul just kept looking at me, mildly amused at my discomfort and vacillation, and asked if I'd like to think about it and then call him. Yes, that sounded good. We talked a little more and then parted company. But not before I cemented my image as a blithering ass by once again blurting that I thought he was cute. At least this time, he answered, "You're kinda cute yourself."

By the next day, I was so consumed with thoughts of him that I could barely work, and I knew what I had to do—I called him that night and suggested the following Monday for our get-together, since it was a holiday (Memorial Day). He said that might work, but he wasn't sure what time—he asked if he could call me Monday morning and I said yes. Now it was just a matter of getting through Friday, Saturday and Sunday.

But no amount of reading, looking at pictures, fantasizing or anything else could fully prepare me for just how amazing Monday turned out to be.

FANTASY: GOOD; REALITY: OUT OF THIS WORLD

"I keep reliving Monday afternoon over and over in my head, and each time I do I feel my heart pounding and my senses being aroused. In a way, I still can't believe it—was that woman ME? That wild woman, yelling and fighting, doing kinky things with a stranger—I don't even know his last name, for crying out loud! I wish, I wish I could talk about this with someone..."
—my journal, May 29, 1996

Paul came to my apartment at 5:00 on May 27, 1996—Memorial Day. And yes, it turned out to be a day quite worth commemorating.

We talked beforehand and he asked more questions, all of which seemed valid. Fortified with the information from Eve's article, I had some idea of how a pre-spanking negotiation should go, and he was observing all the etiquette. We discussed a safe word; I had heard of "mercy," but that felt unnatural to me, so I told him that if he heard me yell the word "enough," that meant stop for real. What could he do, he asked, and what was not allowed? Was I OK with my clothes being removed? My arms/wrists pinned?

He enjoyed the idea of role-playing; did I have a particular scenario in mind? As many of my readers already know, I came up with the idea of being a noisy neighbor, playing my stereo too loud, and he'd come to my door and request that I turn it down. I'd be rude to him and we'd go from there.

Once we got into character, Paul never wavered from his; he was a natural. With a calm and powerful presence, he started out polite, but then grew annoyed with my curt refusal to be more considerate. When he turned the stereo down himself, I tried to turn it back up and he grabbed my hand. My heart was banging away, but I managed to snap, "Let go! Get out of here—I don't need this!" To which he quietly replied, "I'm not going anywhere. And I know just what you *do* need." Then he gripped both my arms and half-dragged, half-carried me into my bedroom. I found

114

that I didn't have to fake the struggle; I fought him every inch of the way, but he was so strong.

He sat on the edge of my bed and yanked me face down across one leg. I was soon rendered somewhat immobile by his one hand snatching both my wrists and pinning them behind my back, and his other leg clamped down over mine. With his free hand, he didn't bother with the "spanking over layers" niceties; he yanked down my leggings and panties and started smacking my bare bottom.

How does one explain the rush? After all the years of fantasizing and wondering, my biggest fear was that the reality of spanking would fall pathetically short of what I had built up in my head. But from the first smack, I knew that reality had indeed surpassed anything I'd ever dreamed of. And the sheer joy of that realization fueled me. I screamed, thrashed around, fought him with all I had, even though I loved what he was doing. It seemed natural and right to pretend I didn't want it, even though we both knew I did; it added to the excitement and forbiddenness of it. He had to work hard to keep me down, and we both started sweating.

And oh, that voice of his. He never raised it, didn't say anything ugly or abusive. He simply spoke to me in a measured tone, taunting me, telling me I had this coming and I wanted it and liked it, he could tell. "I do NOT! Stop it!" I'd shriek, and he'd croon, "Stop? No-o-o, I don't think so." When I started to lose some of my fire and gasped out, "OK, I'm sorry," he came back with, "Not sorry enough."

I have no idea how long it went on; probably wasn't all that long, in retrospect. I wanted to keep going, but even in my state of wild abandon, a kernel of common sense remained and I figured that if this noise continued, my neighbors would get concerned. So, reluctantly, I hollered, "Enough!" He stopped immediately.

In the story I wrote (*First Spanking*), posted in many forums and in my spanking fiction book, the scene ended there. Here, for the first time ever, I am going to reveal the rest of it. Why did I not include this before? For the purposes of a spanking story, the second portion of the scene wasn't pertinent. And perhaps I was a bit embarrassed about it, had a lot of confused feelings around it, and I didn't wish to be judged. But here it is.

After we both caught our breath, he took off the rest of my clothes and rolled me onto my back, pinning my wrists over my head. Then he began to tickle me relentlessly. Once again, I thrashed and fought, but it didn't faze him. I'm horribly ticklish, so my reactions were real. His fingers, nimbly flying across my belly and thighs, wandered between my legs, feeling me. "I'll bet you want to do something for me, don't you?" he teased.

"NO! I don't want to do anything for you!" I writhed and squirmed under him.

"Oh, I bet you do." He straddled me, still holding my wrists, and with his free hand, freed his cock from his pants and put it to my mouth. I wanted him to. I believe I would have done just about anything for him at that moment. And yes, we had discussed this, too, beforehand. I knew it was coming, so to speak.

He thrust deep for a few minutes, murmuring, "My, aren't you talented." Then he pulled out of my mouth, glared down and me and growled, "Don't you move." Letting go of me, he took off his pants, then fished in his pocket and removed a condom. Yes, that's right. He was into play rape as well and I knew it. I'd given him the green light on that as well.

After he put the condom on, he pinned me back down again. There was nothing I wanted more at that moment than for him to fuck me, but I played the game and struggled against him, pulling and twisting away. "No! I won't let you! You're not doing this!" And then I heard him say, "You know, you're right." He was out of character, and I opened my eyes and looked at him.

He'd lost his erection. Completely. Neither one of us knew why, because he had been as aroused as I. But there it was. Or rather, there it wasn't.

We did our best to revive it, but it was gone, and we both ended up laughing. As per my original story, *that* was the point where we lay on the bed together, the comforter soaked beneath us. I didn't fully comprehend what had just happened or how I was feeling about it; my senses were on overload. I was lying on my bed naked with a virtual stranger... and I felt completely OK about it. More than OK.

We talked a bit; he asked me how it was for me, how I felt about it. We both agreed that we'd had fun. For me, that was the understatement of the century.

We dressed, he gave me a hug and said he'd call me, and then he was gone. I was dazed and disoriented, and feeling a type of euphoria unlike any other I'd known, not even after the best of orgasms. Everything I did was in slow motion, as if moving too quickly would shatter the bubble of bliss.

Floating into the bathroom, I removed my clothes once again and wrapped my hair in a towel, preparing to shower. My bottom stung and smarted, and I was compelled to look at it in the mirror; little did I know that I was following a basic spanko instinct. The reflection made me gasp, then grin with delight—I was marked. There were no bruises, but both cheeks were streaked with red and purple, and I could even make out a faint handprint on one of them. I stared and stared, blushing from forehead to chest, giggling like a teenager. This was what *he'd* seen, that tall and handsome stranger. How utterly delicious. How *naughty*.

The next day, I noticed that both my wrists were bruised from his grip. I recalled how sickened I'd felt when I discovered the bruises Ken had left on my arm; this felt completely different. These bruises turned me on and I couldn't take my eyes off them.

In the days that followed, the intense euphoria slowly faded and then was replaced by frustration and insecurity; he didn't call. I swore to myself I wouldn't break down and call him, but I did, two weeks later.

The conversation was brief and uncomfortable, since he was on his way out and was already ten minutes late. He did say that he'd been out of town a great deal and he'd been thinking about me—could he call me next week? I said of course, and then he added, "How are you doing, are you OK?" "Paul, you're late," I said. "Go on. I'm fine. We'll talk next week." Then I hung up the phone, dropped onto my ottoman and wept. I felt so isolated; I had Susan, my therapist, but other than her, there was no one with whom I could share about this. So I wrote.

June 9: *"This man came into my life, tapped into a deep, dark, hidden part of my soul and released it, brought it to the surface, made me feel things I'd never felt before, only in my imagination—and now he's probably not coming back. And I'm obsessing over him. I want him to come back to do more wild and wonderful things with me, free me even further. HOW can I feel this way about someone I hardly know? Just how the hell am I supposed to feel, anyway? I'm so confused."*

Of course, now I know this emotional turmoil was all quite normal. But then, I thought I was going mad.

He didn't call the following week, and I kept obsessing, talking about him with my shrink and writing about the endless whirlwind of feelings.

June 14: *"He never did call me this week—could I have been totally wrong about the guy? I mean, could he actually not call at all? Susan said I needed to do a reality check—even though I got caught up emotionally, HE didn't. This was a one-time thing; he saw me once, had a good time, probably thinks I'm nice, but no emotional attachment. And of course, he has no clue as to what I'm feeling on my end—why should he? She asked me what I really wanted—him, or the activity? That's a hard question; of course, I loved what we did. But it wouldn't have been good if HE hadn't been so good! So strong, so big, so powerful; that calm, deliberate voice. And yet so respectful, sensitive, observant of all boundaries, and so damned SEXY. Susan said I could still hear from him, but for now, I need to move on, pick up the* Weekly *and try it again. DAMN IT, DAMN IT, DAMN IT! How could I get a taste of something so incredibly wonderful and then have it jerked away?"*

Oh, the drama. I might as well have been back in high school, freaking out because the boy of my dreams wasn't calling to ask me to the prom. Not that I ever went to any damn prom, but that's beside the point.

Then, surprise, surprise—I came home late on Sunday night, June 16, and there was a message from Paul. He'd been very busy all week, but he didn't want me to think he was blowing me off; please call him back when I had a chance. By this time, I was convinced that he was going to tell me regretfully that he didn't want to get together again, and I prepared myself for that.

I called him the next evening and he told me once again how busy he'd been, he'd had an out-of-town guest, he'd tweaked his back, blah blah blah. *Go on, go on, say it,* I thought, *get it over with.* "So anyway...I've been thinking about you and the time we got together...it was fun. I'd be willing to do it again."

"Huh? You *would?*" I sputtered, completely thrown off balance.

"Yeah—that is, if *you're* up for it." Gee, you think?

The following Thursday evening, there he was once again in my living room. We sat and talked, had a glass of wine. He asked what was "on tonight's program," and I answered, "You made the call, you made the drive, so you tell me—what's your pleasure?"

He then told me about a fantasy role-play that he liked: I'd be in the shower and he'd be an intruder who sneaks in, surprises me in the shower, grabs me and drags me out dripping wet to the bedroom, where he does what he pleases with me. It had nothing to do with spanking, but I admit, it sounded exciting anyway. And as I'd mentioned, I would have done just about anything with him. I said yes.

I put a bath towel on my bed first; I did have to sleep there that night, after all, and I didn't want to do so on soggy blankets and sheets. Then I went into the bathroom, shed my clothes and stepped into the shower, where I closed my eyes and waited.

He slipped in so quietly that I didn't hear him over the water, and when he slid open the shower door and grabbed me, I screamed in earnest. Holding me firmly, he turned off the water and then dragged me across the floor out of the bathroom and into my room, where he threw me on the bed and then pinned me down.

"Please," I begged. "My wallet is on the table. Take it and please GO!" "I'm not interested in your wallet," he murmured. "Then take whatever you want, just go!" "*This* is what I want," he said, leaning down to lick my breasts and nuzzle my neck. When I fought him, he flipped me over and spanked me hard. But not as long this time. Soon I was on my back again, steeling myself for my intruder to have his way with me. And then, once again, he lost it.

It was embarrassing. I tried to make light of it, saying, "Well, I must admit I've never had this effect on a man before!" I felt naked and cold all of a sudden, and I wrapped the towel around myself. He said he couldn't understand it, he'd been so ready; I told him it was OK, don't worry about it.

We talked a while, but it felt awkward and I sensed there was something he wasn't saying. He did his best to assure me that I'd done nothing wrong, that I was "very attractive and very pleasing."

That's nice. Thanks. Now where's the "but"?

Finally, it came out; he was in a relationship, a vanilla one. He really liked her, but he couldn't share any of this kink stuff with her. So he snuck around, placing ads, thinking he could meet women for some "anonymous kicks" and get it out of his system...but it turned out not to be as easy as he'd thought. He couldn't reconcile his feelings for her vs. his darker desires and acting them out with other women, and he was conflicted and guilty.

Of course, I had no idea at the time, but I was going to hear a story like this one many times over in the coming years. I listened quietly; I was such a novice in this arena, I had no idea what to say. Then it turned out there were *two* "buts."

I wasn't his type, physically. There were two types of women he found especially attractive: very thin, waifish women and Asians. Well, I certainly wasn't Asian. Ironically, he probably would have liked me a lot more during the worst of my anorexic days, when I was a good 15–20 pounds thinner. But now, thanks to my recovery, I had filled out a little, put on some muscle and flesh. While I was still thin, I sure as hell wasn't waifish.

Long story short, he just wasn't that into me.

What could I say? Either the attraction was there or it wasn't; I knew this well. Between that and the aforementioned conflict with his relationship, I knew this was the last time I'd be seeing this man. It felt sad, but I'd already gone through my tears and angst and now I felt resigned.

I have no regrets about anything I did with Paul, and I'm grateful he was my first. Let me be clear: I am not advocating this level of edgy play for newbies. Nor am I saying that I fantasize about rape; I do not. But I am stressing that everything was pre-discussed and completely consensual. He was smart, sexy, considerate, and did his best to give me what I needed. My spanking journey began with him. At first, I thought I had fallen in love with him, which was ridiculous—I knew almost nothing about him, and he made sure it stayed that way. No…I fell in love with what he gave me, with what he awakened in me. And I wanted more, more, more!

So the next morning, I picked up another *L.A. Weekly*, and saw an ad that I knew was talking about spanking, even though the word wasn't used. I answered it and he called back; we talked for an hour and met for coffee the following week. I didn't have the fierce attraction to him that I'd had with Paul, but I liked him.

I saw this man, whom I will simply call J, only twice as well, but his impression was indelible. He introduced me to: 1) being spanked outdoors, and 2) the delicious way that fear of being caught could enhance a scene.

He was different from Paul; much bolder, more outspoken about what he wanted. When I was standing at the sugar/creamer area at the coffeehouse, he came up behind me, leaned down and whispered in my ear, "Take your time—I like the view." The pink sweetener packet trembled in my fingers.

We talked, finished our drinks, and he suggested a walk. I figured he too wanted to talk a bit more privately, but he had other things in mind.

We walked past the shopping center down the dark, residential streets south of Ventura Boulevard. He held my hand and kept looking at the different houses, commenting about how the lights were too bright, there were cars parked in the driveway, etc. I grew more nervous as we walked further, wondering what this was about. He picked up on my anxiety and teased me, taking his time, not telling me what he was doing or where we were going.

Finally, he stopped in front of a house that was set far back from the street, had a large driveway/basketball court in front and a long stone wall along the side. There were no lights on anywhere, and he led me over to the wall and told me to face it and put my hands up on it. At that moment, I felt like I was going to pass out, throw up or have a spontaneous orgasm (or perhaps all three), but I obeyed him.

He was very close behind me, running his hands over my bottom and legs, up and down my back, whispering that I was sexy and beautiful. When his palm struck, I jerked, but held my position. I was in tight jeans, so he spanked me over those, and not very long, but enough to make me feel it. When a car drove by, he stopped immediately, gathering me to him, murmuring, "It's OK, it's OK… come on, let's go," and leading me back to the street. My legs were shaking so badly that I didn't think they'd hold me, and I was trembling and laughing and nearly crying from sheer excitement and adrenaline.

We talked for a long time at my car, and J asked a lot of questions, said my reactions were wonderful, that I was a trouper and very adventurous. (Huh? *Me??*) He asked if I'd like to do this again; I said absolutely, and we agreed to meet again that coming Friday.

Then he said, "There's one more thing I'd like to do." *Good lord, what?* I thought. "I'd like to kiss you." I couldn't help laughing. How absurd was this—he'd just taken me down a dark street and spanked me up against a wall in front of someone's home, but now he was asking permission to kiss me?

I said yes, by the way.

On Friday, we met at a different Starbucks. He had requested I wear a skirt this time, and I had, with black lace panties and thigh-high stockings. Coffees consumed, we went to his car and he drove up into the hills south of the boulevard, cruising the dark streets and looking for something, I had no idea what.

I'd had a long day and was getting sleepy, so I took off my shoes, put my feet up on the dashboard and yawned, "I think I'll crawl in the back and take a little nap. Wake me up when it's time."

"Awfully cocky, aren't you? Is someone getting a little antsy?" he teased, still driving around, showing no intention of stopping anywhere. He'd point out extremely well-lit places and say, "How about there?" This man clearly knew how to draw out the anticipation.

Finally, we found a block that had been closed to traffic due to construction, with the street filled with cones and equipment. This was it. We parked, I put my shoes back on, and he told me to take my panties off and leave them in the car. He led me over to a large tree in front of a darkened house set far back from the sidewalk. Facing the tree, I leaned my head into my arms and he stood behind me, lifting my skirt up over my hips, exposing me completely. I stood and shivered, waiting.

The spanking was very hard and it was difficult for me to remain quiet. I was terrified we'd be seen, and the terror fueled my arousal. My flesh tingled and burned, and waves of pleasure shot through me at the same time. When it was over, he steadied me and carefully led me back to the car, helping me back in, where I collapsed onto the seat. I could feel heat and throbbing inside my dress, and I closed my eyes, feeling the A/C and listening to the relaxing music he'd put on. Once again, he asked me questions, gave me feedback and was very sweet to me.

I was marked even more this time, and bruised too. And I loved it.

He called me the next week to ask how I was. Told me he was going on vacation for a few days, but he'd call me when he came back and we could arrange for our next session. Would I like to move things indoors this time, he asked; I replied yes. He said he couldn't wait to see me.

And then I didn't hear from him again.

Time passed, and I waited and wondered. Unlike Paul, J had shown a great interest in me, paid me many compliments and made it clear he wanted to continue playing with me. So I was bewildered by the disappearance. After a couple of weeks, I called him and left a message. He did not return it.

This time, instead of being heartbroken, I was pissed off. What was with these guys? How could they engage in such intimate acts and then just shut it off and move on? I was so naïve then... *Screw this,* I thought. I was sick of answering these ads, of passively waiting and hoping I'd find the right one by chance.

I decided to place my own ad. I could ask for exactly what I wanted and this time, I'd be in control.

Spanking Smorgasbord... and Enter John

"I met John. I've been with him twice. To encapsulate, we met Friday night at 8:30 and talked until 4:00 A.M. Then yesterday, he came over play at 2:30 and stayed until 9:30. There is definitely a connection here—not just the obvious commonality, but a personal one as well."
—my journal, September 3, 1996

Placing a basic ad in the *L.A. Weekly* was free. But if you wanted a bold headline, you had to pay for that. I went for the headline. I didn't want this ad to blend in with all the others; I wanted it to pop and stand out. Attention whore, that's me! Since I couldn't use the word *spanking*, my headline read: **OVER YOUR KNEE**. I wish I had saved a copy of it so I could quote it here, but I remember bits and pieces of it. Particularly the end, where I said, *"No implements, just a firm hand that can be gentle as well."* No implements? Still can't believe I ever wrote that, but I did. Paddles and belts and the like sounded harsh and scary to me at the time.

I then had to record the outgoing message for my personal voicemail box, so I took pains with that, trying to make a good impression with my voice, since that plus a few written words was all I had. The first Friday in August, my ad appeared, and it would be listed for the next three weeks.

To my shock, the replies came pouring in. Twenty, then 30, 40. By the end of the first week, 80. I'd listen carefully to each call. Many of them were instant discards; the men were too far away, they didn't leave me any information (just a name and a phone number), the messages were somewhat rude, they wanted me to spank *them*, etc. But there were those who sounded good as well, so I kept a running list of names, numbers and brief descriptions so I'd remember which was which.

The next couple of weeks were an odyssey of phone conversations and coffee dates; many different experiences. I talked with one man for hours; he was very generous with his experience, told me a lot of information and we agreed to meet, but when we did, I liked him, but didn't feel like playing with him. He loaned me magazines and a Shadow Lane video, so I saw my very first spanking video, *Party Brats*, with the aforementioned Keith Jones in it.

I met a few more men for coffee; same kind of deal. They were nice, but the desire to play with them wasn't there. Then I met Richard, with whom there was instant and mutual chemistry. We talked at an outdoor table at Starbucks, and when the preliminary chitchat died down, I said, "So, what do you think?" He replied, "I think I want to be alone with you." My legs shook under the table; in case you haven't figured it out, my legs often served as an indicator of arousal and attraction for me with their trembling.

I did play with him; had sex with him, too. Twice, at his place. When I was leaving around midnight, I said, "Thanks, I had fun," and he teased, "Yeah, I think the whole neighborhood knows that." What can I say...I'm quite vocal about my pleasure.

Then there was Charlie, whom I was supposed to meet after work on a Thursday. When he called me at work to confirm, he told me that he had a "requirement." I asked what, and was told I had to wear four-inch black high heels. I thought he was kidding, so I flippantly said, "Sorry, I'm not wearing anything like that today."

"So go home and change, then." *Huh?*

"Uh... I don't even own a pair of four-inch heels, in any color."

"Buy some."

I kept waiting for him to tell me he was kidding, but he didn't. When he said we'd have to reschedule so I could get what was required, I flat-out said NO, I don't think so.

"Well then, I guess you don't want to meet me. Tell you what—you have my number. You think about it, and if you change your mind, call me." And he hung up.

Oh, I've got your number all right, pal. My first experience with what I came to call an Über-Dom; a top who takes himself and his fetish way too seriously, and demands instead of asking. Even then, as new as I was to this game, I could sense there was a difference between a dominant

126

confidence and sheer arrogance, and I wanted nothing to do with the latter.

Onward. The next guy, Steve, sounded great and we set up a date to meet, but we ended up misunderstanding the location and missed each other. He then accused me of standing him up on purpose so that I'd "get in trouble." I'm sure there are some women out there who would pull a stunt like that with a top, but I'm not one of them. I didn't hear from him again, even though I kept insisting it had been an honest mistake.

The calls kept coming, and I kept screening, chatting and meeting. In the midst of the various communications, I got a surprise: My second spanker, J, called. He'd seen my ad and said he "knew it was me." He couldn't believe it had been over a month-and-a-half since we talked; I assured him it was. I also reminded him that he hadn't called when he said he would, and hadn't returned my call. He made with the excuses, sounding flustered, then finally admitted he'd gotten busy with other women who had answered his ad. He wanted to get together with me again and tried his best to convince me to say yes.

A few weeks ago, I would have killed for this call, but things were different now. Now I had choices; I didn't have to be any man's afterthought. So I politely told him I was sorry, but I had a lot of other men to meet. I wasn't trying to be mean, but you know, all he had to do was keep in touch, just a little. I don't ask for that much.

One gentleman, N, was farther away than I wanted, but he had such an amazing voice, deep and rich, and he described spanking so deliciously, I just had to call him back. The conversation was off, somehow; he sounded very bossy and cocky, and kept insisting we meet halfway somewhere and I wouldn't be disappointed. So I let myself be convinced to meet him for lunch, but later in the week, I changed my mind and cancelled. Why should I drive for over an hour, when I was getting plenty of local respondents and I was getting a bad vibe from this guy anyway?

On that following Friday after work, I was home changing for the gym, and N called—said he was in the Valley, and would I like to meet? *Oh, what the hell,* I thought. Forgetting about the gym, I changed into a sundress and drove to meet him at a coffee shop at the corner of Laurel Canyon and Ventura.

I knew it was a mistake from the minute I saw him. The icky vibe I'd picked up on the phone grew a whole lot more powerful in person. I didn't find him physically attractive in the least; his hair was so stiff with mousse, it looked like a bird's nest, and his penetrating stare made me nervous rather than aroused. We sat and talked for a while and then he suggested we go somewhere and play. I didn't want to, but I allowed him to talk me into it. Somehow, I knew I'd be safe, but I wouldn't like it. And I didn't.

He drove us to a nearby hiking trail, parked the car and then led me by the hand onto the trails, searching for a private area. It was broad daylight and I didn't like this at all, but he pulled me along none-too-gently and kept looking. However, everywhere we went, there were people. So he took me back to his car, drove to the far end of the parking lot, and let the passenger seat all the way down. I was told to lie on my stomach on the seat, and then he went at it, no warm-up.

It was horrible. Not only did he hit much too hard, but he kept barking orders at me. I had to repeat phrases back to him, call him Sir, say "thank you for spanking me," count the strokes. When I didn't obey him, he slapped my thighs and pinched me with his fingernails. There was nothing fun or sexy about this; he was a brute and a bully.

When he was done, he had me turn around in the seat, and next thing I know, he was trying to push my head into his lap, where I saw that he'd taken his cock out of his shorts. No way! Unlike Paul, who had asked beforehand if this was OK, N was being completely non-consensual and I didn't like it. "I'd love to fuck your brains out right now," he hissed. I told him no and pulled away. "Well, will you at least touch it?" he pleaded, holding it out to me like some sort of prize. "Look, eight inches of happiness just for you."

Yeah, right, I thought. *If you're eight inches, I'm 36D.* But I didn't dare say that out loud. I just continued to shake my head and pull away, and he gave up. Thank God. He drove me back to my car and that was that. I couldn't wait to get home and take a shower. I was horribly marked and sore, too.

Lesson learned, and a very important one too: *Trust my instincts.* I knew I didn't want to play with him, but I did it anyway. I was not going to allow that to happen again. It didn't matter how persuasive the man was—if the answer was no, it was no. Period.

Fortunately, the next day I met with another Steve, and he was lovely. After we had iced mochas and some fun conversation, he took me to his office and spanked me there; another first for me, playing in someone's workplace. Noticing how badly marked I was, he was gentle and sensual with me, and I was grateful. Playing with him definitely removed the bad taste from my experience with N.

By now, I had heard from over 150 men, and I still had another week to go on my ad. I'd met 10 men from the ad in person, played with three and had sex with one. It had been one hell of a ride so far, and it wasn't over.

* * *

One of the callers sounded wonderful in his message, but I was having a hard time reaching him; every time I called his number, I got a machine. But finally, on Thursday night, August 29, I found him at home. We had immediate phone chemistry; he sounded smart, warm, open, and—if his self-description was accurate—gorgeous!

Before I knew it, we'd talked for two hours, and agreed to meet at Starbucks the following evening at 8:30. After hanging up the phone, I fist-pumped and skipped around my living room, jubilantly hollering to no one, "Yes! Yes!" This one sounded more promising than any of them had, and he was local too. I couldn't wait to meet him.

His name? John.

The next night, I went into the Sherman Oaks Starbucks, wearing a flowered, tight-fitting sundress and heels, looking for a man in black jeans reading a book. And there he was; I was right on time, so he must have been early. I liked that. Mischievously, I walked right into his space. "Interesting reading?"

Looking up at me, he smiled. "I'm sorry," he said. "You look nice, but I'm meeting someone."

"You are?"

"Yes—a *much* older woman."

And that, ladies and gentlemen, was that. I was immediately smitten.

We talked inside Starbucks until they closed…and we never bought any coffee. Then we went for a walk. It was Friday night, so things were hopping around us. When he led me down the alley behind the shops, I went willingly. And when he pulled me against him, lifted my dress and smacked me a few times, I wanted more. There might very well have been more, but then we heard the *jingle jingle jingle* of dog tags and realized a man was approaching us, walking his dog. Mortified, I buried my face in John's chest, and stifling his laughter, he yanked my dress back down and held me until the man had passed.

We then went back to his vehicle. He had an older-model Ford Bronco with bench seats, so he spanked me again in the front seat. But he interspersed the spanking with caresses and backrubs, and I was confused. I didn't understand how this sensual stuff figured into spanking, and because I couldn't figure out where this was going or predict what he was going to do next, I got frustrated.

It turned out that was his exact intention—keep me guessing, make me wonder, and see if I trusted him enough to continue. Somehow, I did, but I told him he made me a little nervous and confused. To which he answered, "As well as you should be, my dear."

The play went from sensual to more sexual, and he brought me to orgasm with his fingers. Yes, I wanted it; I was both excited and soothed by his presence. Underneath the teasing and playing with my head, there was a clear tone of sweetness, of concern for my feelings. I didn't get the sense that I was dealing with some sort of mind-fucking sadistic brute; far from it. We talked some more and he admitted he was confused too. He wanted to play with me, but had "vanilla" thoughts of me as well.

130

At 4:00 A.M., I was ready to drop dead with exhaustion, so we had to say good night. He suggested going back to my place, but I wasn't ready for that. I had never bothered putting my panties back on, and they sat in a sodden heap on the dashboard. John picked them up and pocketed them. "If you want these back, you'll have to see me again."

He didn't need to do that; I would have seen him anyway. But that made it extra hot. So we agreed to meet again on Monday, since we were both off work for Labor Day.

The next night, B came over. That was surreal indeed, being with him after the night with John. But I enjoyed him as much as ever, even though I was seeking other outlets. We stayed in bed until Sunday afternoon at 3:30, when we finally emerged and he dressed and left.

The second time with John was even more intense than the first. He showed up at my door not only with the promised panties (laundered, yet), but also with one perfect rose. Not the typical red, but an unusual peach color, which he said reminded him of my skin. Who was this man? Was he a wonderfully smooth and exciting playmate, or was he a hopeless and traditional romantic? Or both? I was thrilled by him and frightened of him at the same time. Why frightened? Because I didn't know what I was feeling. Hormones? Fulfillment of my deepest fantasies? Or was it something more?

Seven hours flew by that Monday with playing, talking and cuddling. We did not have sex. He asked if he could take me out on a real dinner date the following Friday, and I said yes. Something was happening here, and as much as my protective side was crying, "No, no, I don't want to date any of these guys, I just want to play, no strings attached," another part of me overrode the nagging voice. How far could it go, anyway? I was seeing someone else and so was he. He knew I was still calling on other messages from my ad; he referred to the men as my "tele-boys."

Yet we talked every night that week. And midweek, I received in the mail a poem he'd written to me. I am choosing to keep the contents of the poem between John and me, but it was signed:

Erica—For you, effusions of our brief time to-gether, valued beyond understanding. John

I did not know what to make of this. But it made me smile. And I knew, even this early, that I had something a lot more than a simple play partner here.

We talked every night until Friday, when he picked me up for dinner and took me to a beautiful French seafood place called The Seashell. I had joked with him about the restaurant earlier, saying he'd better be careful, because I might order a lobster. When the server came to take our order, I found out that John had reserved a lobster for me in advance, to ensure they wouldn't run out. I was torn; I *love* lobster, but oh my God, so expensive! I was kidding! I would never have ordered that on my own. But he calmly insisted, and yes, the lobster was delicious.

When the server took the vase of flowers off our table, we realized the place was closing. Back at my place, we talked and played until 1:00 A.M., and then he carried me into my bedroom. Now what? Was I ready for this?

Obviously, he was. He went back into the living room, turned off the CD player and the lights, and then I heard him in the bathroom, brushing his teeth. The fearful part of me thought, "Please go," but the part that cried out, "No, no, please stay," was stronger.

But once again, we did not have sex. Instead, we lay entwined, talking until 4:00 in the morning, and then slept. In the morning when we awoke, we stayed there for another three hours. I liked that we weren't jumping right into sex, even though I was tremendously attracted to him. What we were doing seemed much more intimate.

September progressed. I met up with another man, David, who was into stockings and garters. I confessed that I didn't have any, and he said, "If I bought you some, would you wear them?" This was new, but I certainly liked it better than Charlie's ordering me to buy four-inch heels, so I agreed to it. He and I played once; he was a nice guy, but it turned out he was much more into bondage than spanking, so I had my first experience being tied up. It did nothing for me. The best moment of the evening was when he put me in handcuffs, but didn't realize how tiny my wrists are. As he focused on tying my legs down, I wriggled out of the cuffs and threw a pillow at his head.

It was also my first time wearing a garter belt and stockings. I stood in his bathroom changing into them, fumbling nervously with the garters until I finally gave up, came out and asked him to fasten them for me.

My birthday was approaching, and friends and family wanted to celebrate with me. On Friday, September 20, John and I had a dinner date, and then I was going to see B on Saturday night. In a case of spectacularly rotten timing, I woke up sick on that Thursday, but I went to work anyway.

Good thing I did, because mid-morning, my boss called me up front to the counter. Upon arriving, I gasped and clapped my hands over my mouth. There was a huge vase filled with an immense arrangement of peach roses, ferns and baby's breath. I knew who it was from even before I looked at the card.

Friday, I felt a little better and was eager for my date with John. He wouldn't tell me where we were going for dinner and we drove to Hollywood, exiting the freeway and driving uphill on a winding road. At the top was Yamashiro, a landmark Japanese restaurant I'd never been to, but I'd certainly heard of. So gorgeous; what an amazing view. And of course, he'd reserved a table by the window.

I'd never had a man take me out for my birthday before, and John gave me the fantasy date of my life. The food was marvelous, the service perfect, and he had a large shopping bag out of which he kept pulling surprise after surprise. I hadn't expected anything—the roses and this dinner were plenty—so I was overwhelmed with these treats. And he'd written another poem for me.

That night was the first time I told him I loved him. I didn't need him to say it back. I wanted it to come from him when he was ready, not as an automatic reply to my saying it. He did squeeze me tight in response. And, unlike Doug before him, he didn't back off.

The next evening was my birthday dinner with B, but for the first time, I found I couldn't switch gears. I had just been wined and dined and swept off my feet by John, and now here I was with B and I couldn't focus on him. Plus, I was quite sick by this point. So after dinner, I begged off from the rest of the evening and went home.

Same kind of thing happened when John went away for a weekend of camping with some buddies and I had a dinner/play date with Steve, the nice guy I'd met after the bad scene with N. But as the date neared, I realized I couldn't do it, and I cancelled. Why? Because John had admitted to me that he felt a little jealous, although he supported my going. He didn't tell me not to go and yet, I didn't want to do anything that would cause him discomfort. What was happening here?

Along with a lot of spanking, John and I were steadily moving forward in this relationship, whatever it was. He came to dinner with me and my father; they hit it off immediately. Then I met his family, when all of them were gathered for his dad's birthday. Talk about trial by fire: His father, his mother, his two sisters and their husbands, his brother with girlfriend in tow, two nieces and one nephew. A bit overwhelming, but everyone was nice to me.

We argued about B; John said I was still keeping him around because he was "safe." That was absolutely true. B was a sure thing, even though what we had was quite limited and would never be more than it was. John had all kinds of promise and potential, but he scared me to death. And besides, he was still dating someone else too.

Until he wasn't... he ended things with her. And finally, after much deliberation and agonizing, I ended things with B as well. John and I made love for the first time on October 19. And on October 26, he told me he loved me.

My social life had been so neatly compartmentalized. I had friends. I had a lover: B. And I had spanking playmates. Now I found myself with this enigmatic man who was all three and then some. Not what I'd expected, and there were times it felt so overwhelming and unnerving, I wanted to run. When we had fights—and we did, because we're both strong-willed people—I wanted to say, "The hell with this, it's too hard."

But I didn't.

THE JOB FROM HELL

"I don't know why I'm writing now—I'm not ready to write yet. The emotions are still at bay; I feel this eerie sense of calm and numb detachment. I lost my job today; [my boss] fired me. I've never been fired before. I know there's got to be a lot of fear, anger, hurt and resentment welling up behind the numbness, but all I can feel, through the shock, is relief."
—my journal, October 25, 1996

While all these adventures with men were playing out, I had another kind of drama altogether going on with my job.

I had been wooed away from my old job in June 1995 by a woman who got my name from a client for whom I did some freelancing. She owned a graphics company, was looking for a full-time proofreader/office assistant and had heard good things about me. After meeting and having subsequent conversations, she offered me a job.

Her starting salary was more than I was making at my old company, and she promised a dollar raise after three months. Plus fully paid medical benefits, whereas I was now paying 50% of mine. It was a longer drive and I was nervous about leaving my old job. Much as I didn't like it, it was familiar territory and I knew I was good at it. Nevertheless, I took the plunge and accepted the new position.

Practically from the start, I knew I'd made a terrible mistake. My boss, JK, seemed wonderful at first. She was a dynamo, full of energy, very much hands-on with her company, and her chipper, cheery personality was kept from being too sickening sweet by her bawdy sense of humor. Our office was spacious and comfortable, I had my own work area and since I came in at 7:30 in the morning, the traffic wasn't horrible. She ran a very busy outfit and I had much more to do than in my last job.

After three months, she said my probationary period was over and she was giving me a raise—fifty cents. But... she'd promised me a dollar when we were interviewing. I told her this, and she politely but firmly insisted I was mistaken, that the raise was always to be fifty cents.

I knew it wasn't. Thanks to my rigorous journal-keeping, I had a written record that clearly stated I was getting a dollar raise in three months. This was my first sign that JK wasn't quite what she seemed.

As time passed, I realized she wasn't the model of efficiency she purported herself to be, either. She loved to talk with the clients, schmooze with them, joke with them, spend over an hour with them when they came in to drop off work. That was fine, except while she was yapping away, work would back up. Clients' jobs would pile up on her desk; she was the one who scheduled the work, so I'd have to wait until she went over the jobs before I could write them up. I'd have questions for her, things to go over, and she was too busy chatting on the phone or with someone at the front counter.

We had a core group of clients with whom we did work regularly and JK had them all spoiled rotten. Our office was supposed to close at 4:30, but many clients had the habit of showing up at our door at closing time, and JK kept the office open to go over their jobs. Therefore, they had no respect for our hours and came whenever they pleased, often keeping JK or me there until well after 5:00.

They tried to chat me up the way they did JK, but I didn't want any of that; I just wanted to do my work and skip the schmoozing. So a lot of them didn't like me because I refused to play the game and kiss up to them. However, I always did a damn good job on their work, when I'd finally get it. JK would promise them the moon, then let their jobs stack up and back up on her desk. By the time she addressed them, they had become urgent rushes.

She'd leave constantly to meet with clients and I'd have to run the office in her absence. So I'd have to do all the proofreading, faxing and packaging, handle the phones, deal with the front office traffic and more. I was doing the work of roughly two-and-a-half people and there were days I was so busy, I didn't stop to eat lunch until nearly 3:00. I dreaded the days when she went on meetings, because she'd bring back even more work. It didn't matter how swamped we were; she never turned anyone down, made all kinds of promises, and then I was left to deal with angry, bitchy clients when we couldn't possibly keep up with the deadlines she'd assured everyone we'd meet.

I hated customer service anyway, but here, I hated it even more, because these people were so demanding. And doing their work well wasn't enough, either—I had to brown-nose them too, listen to their silly chitchat, and I didn't have the time or patience for it. JK had allowed most of them to become monsters.

Just before Thanksgiving, one guy wanted to give us this huge job that would be due the following Monday, which meant it would have to be worked on over the holiday weekend. I told him I didn't think we could do it because the shop would be closed, and he said, "So have people come in over the holiday—you guys don't have lives anyway, do you?" That pissed me off, but nothing like the anger I felt when JK came back. I told her what he'd said, expecting her to agree with me that he had some king-sized *cajones,* but she simply replied, "Of course we'll do it. We don't turn aside work here." "But... but... it's a holiday," I sputtered, and she repeated that we don't turn aside work. And she had people come in and work that Friday. I refused, of course, and she couldn't force me. But she was none too pleased with me over it.

We fought constantly. I begged her to please stay on top of the work better, to stop with the schmoozing. Sometimes she'd agree she did too much of it, but that didn't mean she made any attempt to cut back on it a bit. When I realized that she wasn't going to change, I tried another tactic; I told her I did not want to do customer service anymore, that I sucked at it, that they didn't like me anyway, and wouldn't she please consider hiring a part-time office assistant so that I could be taken off the front lines and left to do what I did best? A couple of times, she did try hiring someone part-time, but then guess who had to train them? Great, so now along with all my work and the damned phones and the customers tearing me in every direction, I had a "helper" I had to babysit as well. We went through a couple of these and they didn't work out, so then JK gave up on the idea and things resumed as before.

When I was into the job merely six months, JK had to have surgery, a hysterectomy. She was going to be out of the office for four weeks, and then back part-time for the next two or three. I damn near had a nervous breakdown when she told me about this, but there wasn't anything I could do about it and I made up my mind I'd get through this, one day at a time. It was just before the holidays so things were supposed to be a little slower, but of course they weren't. I did the best I could, coming in early and staying late, balancing and juggling and coordinating, busting my ass to run the office properly and make JK glad she'd entrusted me with so much responsibility.

Christmas came around, and I thought what with all this extra work, I was in for a healthy bonus. When our bookkeeper came in to do the payroll, she came over to my desk and said she wanted to tell me about my bonus. *Aha*, I thought, and I smiled up at her, wondering just how much cash I had coming. Then she asked me which one I would prefer: a Honeybaked® ham or turkey.

Huh?

I must have misunderstood. The ham or turkey was extra, along with the cash. Nope... I'd heard correctly. The ham or turkey *was* the bonus, period.

Oh, for God's sake! If I wanted meat for a Christmas bonus, I'd work for a butcher! She asked once again for my preference, and I curtly said, "Neither. I'll pass." I guess I could have taken it and then donated it to a shelter, but I didn't want the bother. I was too damn tired and overwhelmed already.

JK came back sometime in January, and the next several months went by with the two of us struggling to get along. Our relationship became rather formal, minus the laughing and joking we'd done earlier. Meanwhile, she kept coming in late, leaving early and dumping more and more on me, and I felt like I was drowning. The more I pleaded with her to get some additional office help so I could focus more on my work and less on hers, the more she resisted me. Then came a Thursday afternoon in July where everything blew up between us.

I stood stunned while she coldly accused me of being manipulative, saying I didn't want to help out, I just wanted to sit back and let her do all the work. She said I deliberately worked myself up so she'd take on more of the load, and that I exaggerated and overdramatized everything so much that she no longer believed anything I said—I'd lost all credibility with her. I demanded too much attention. On and on it went; even worse than her words was the contempt in her voice. I tried to defend myself, but everything that came out of my mouth sounded lame.

I'd been told before by employers and coworkers that I could be difficult, frustrating, hard to understand. But never had I heard anyone accuse me of deliberate manipulation, tell me I was conniving and that my actions and emotions were contrived. She'd drawn such a malevolent conclusion about me, it made my head spin. And of course, tears came to my eyes, and she said, "Now you're trying to manipulate me with the tears."

Ugh! How could I make her understand? I couldn't help being stressed out and overwhelmed. She didn't know what I went through—the anxiety, the fear, the negative thinking and the fight-or-flight reactions. Why in hell would I *choose* to be this way? I wasn't good with people; I had chosen my profession because it was focused and allowed me to work in a solitary fashion. I didn't multitask well and I panicked when I had too much to do. I could do her job, but what was easy for her was hard for me, and what was hard for her was damn near impossible for me. I laid myself bare, humbled myself, wept copious tears as I stood facing away from her so she wouldn't see them.

She softened slightly toward the end of the conversation, her voice losing some of its harsh edge, but I knew things would never be good between us again. Not only were they not good, but after that day, I believe she launched a campaign to get me to quit.

The next month-and-a-half was tense. JK was cordial to me, but nothing more. She made little digs at me constantly, and made a point of complimenting the others, but not me. When my friend Stephanie and I worked on a complex project together and wrapped it up, JK said to Stephanie as she was leaving, "Thanks for all the great work!" To me, she said, "See you Monday."

Whenever she used to go out on sales calls, she and I would meet and she'd go over the jobs in-house, which typesetter was doing what and which jobs took priority on the schedule. But the next time she was leaving the office for the afternoon, I asked, "So tell me, who's got what?" and she answered, very sweetly, "Why don't you go in the back and see for yourself?" And I just had to suck it up; I didn't dare argue with her.

It was like having two jobs—the office work, plus having to monitor my every word, my every facial expression and my performance, to ensure all I did and said was beyond reproach. Paranoid? Perhaps. But it turned out I was right.

Mid-September, she called me into her office and without preamble, presented me with an 8 ½ × 11 sheet that was completely filled, single spaced, with criticism, documentations of my transgressions, and a threat to terminate if I didn't shape up.

I felt sick and shocked. I'd been trying so hard—I could even see the results with the customers, because they were much more willing to work with me now. My work was excellent—nothing was coming back with typos I'd missed. I tried to defend myself, but I was facing a wall of ice and I could see I'd already been condemned. Either she was trying to make me quit with all this harassment, or she was planning to get rid of me and was covering her ass with all this written crap.

Work was even more hellacious after that day. I was determined to stick this out, not give her any further ammunition. Each day I came to the end knowing I'd done the best I could, but I felt beaten down and discouraged. Still, I persevered.

In the beginning of October, JK took a week off. She didn't say where she was going, left no way we could contact her, and didn't call in to check on things. And we got crazily, madly busy. Jobs poured in—one afternoon, I wrote up 37 jobs from one client alone. I didn't know what to do; there was simply too much work for two typesetters and just one me. I couldn't talk with JK, so I had to make the unpopular decision to bump some work and turn some down altogether.

The clients were furious. However, not at me—they were angry at JK. They couldn't believe she had left her company high and dry and understaffed, with no way to call her and let her know what was happening. They told me that they didn't blame me; that I was doing a good job and they could see I had no choice but to turn aside some jobs. I was relieved and exhausted. When JK finally called in on Friday afternoon, both typesetters refused to speak with her, so I told her they were too busy to come to the phone.

When she came back, she got quite an earful from several people, and I could hear her on the phone, placating and lying, making her usual promises, being as sweet as could be. I did not get any sort of thank-you for the week I'd been in charge, come in early and left late and supervised a massive amount of work successfully.

Two weeks later, she fired me.

I didn't cry this time; I was too numb. It hadn't sunk in. All I felt was relief. It was over. I could stop walking on eggshells, stifling all my feelings and pasting that neutral, pleasant look on my face. I didn't have to knock myself out anymore for someone who would never be happy with me.

She told me that I could stay on their group health insurance plan and pay her month to month until I got another job. But then on October 30, I got a call from her, informing me chirpily that she wasn't going to do so after all, so as of the end of this month, my insurance expired. The end of the month—tomorrow! That was when it really sank in—the degree of viciousness I was up against and how much trouble I was in.

For the first time, I lost it and wept, and I called John. I did not ask him to come over; I would never ask for that, because I don't like to inconvenience people. However, he offered to do so, and was there comforting me 45 minutes later. We'd been together barely two months, and already he was helping me weather a crisis.

I applied for unemployment, and guess what? I got turned down. JK, of course, had painted me to be the worst employee in history. Now I had to decide if I wanted to appeal this and ask for a hearing. At first, I didn't think I was any match for her; my confidence was low, she had all her documentation and it was her cool, ice-princess word against mine.

I talked with Stephanie and she said JK was now harassing and criticizing *her*. I couldn't believe it; when I was there, JK went on and on, praising Stephanie in front of me. So what was *this* about? Was that woman not happy unless she had someone to pick on? I decided to fight, but I knew I couldn't do it alone.

Armed with the Yellow Pages, I first called a legal clinic in the Valley. A very nice woman told me that this was a specialized situation and most lawyers avoided these cases, so I should call the Valley Bar Association for advice. I did that next, and they gave me another phone number to call for referrals.

The forecast was bleak at first. Sure enough, the attorneys and clinics I called didn't want to touch my case, and one lawyer flat-out told me I would lose. But then I heard from a free legal clinic I'd called earlier, and a woman named Dora had me come in for an appointment. After we talked, she thought I might have a chance and she agreed to come with me to the appeal. We discussed all the details and the progression of events that led up to my firing. Thank goodness for my journal and my excellent memory.

Bright and early on a Monday morning, I met with Dora at the court, and the first thing I found out was that JK was sick and wouldn't be there; she was going to give her testimony over speaker phone. That was certainly a relief, not having to face her again.

Dora showed me the final document JK had written up when she denied my unemployment; it made that memo she'd given me earlier look like a hymn of praise. Three pages of character assassination; my throat constricted with nausea. But I moved forward with rubbery legs into the judge's office.

I got the sense right away that the judge was not impressed with JK or her testimony. He kept challenging her statements, interrupting her and cutting her off, and she came off badly. Then it was my turn to present my side of the story, to defend myself. She had written a list of offensive things I'd said to clients and had quoted them all out of context, so I denied the statements.

"Did you or did you not flip off a client?" came her curt voice over the speaker phone. *Oh, so we're going there, are we...* I smiled. I knew exactly what she was talking about and it required a bit of explanation, which I was only too happy to provide.

One afternoon, a couple of months before I was fired, one of our most difficult and demanding clients had come in at 4:30, closing time, with a stack of work. JK was there and she assisted him, so I went to clock out. He saw me and started giving me all kinds of noise about how I was "leaving early" and how lazy I was. I rolled my eyes and said to JK, "I'm off the clock; do I still have to be nice to him?" He laughed, then sneered, "I'm a client. As long as you're on these premises, you *have* to be nice to me, so *there!*" *Oh, up yours, you smug ass.* So, I stepped outside the front door, planted my feet in the parking lot, then leaned back into the door. "Oh, Rich?" I called.

He turned around to look at me. I gave him a sweet smile and said, "I'm not on the premises now!" And I shot him the bird. Both he and JK laughed. So if she thought she was going to throw this one in my face and make it sound like something it wasn't, she had another think coming.

After I told the story, JK tried to argue, but I had more, an ace up my sleeve she knew nothing about. "By the way," I purred, "Rich, that same client you claim I offended so badly, said something very interesting to me the week you were out of the office. He said, 'I like it better when you're in charge. JK screws around too much.' "

This time, she was speechless. The judge raised an eyebrow and made some more notes. And I decided to go in for the kill.

"You know, JK has said a lot of detrimental things about my character and my work performance," I said. "And yet, just two weeks before she fired me, she went out of town and left me in charge of her company, without even giving me a number where she could be reached. Now, if I were really that bad, why on earth would she leave her livelihood in my hands?"

JK had nothing to reply, and the judge had heard enough. He ended the call, then told me I'd get his decision in two weeks.

I got his decision in two *days*. I won. JK had to pay me unemployment, including back pay for the past two months.

The unemployment benefits were merely a pittance, but that's beside the point. I had triumphed. This woman damaged my self-esteem and professional reputation, and the old Erica would have rolled over and slunk away like a beaten dog. But I fought back, efficiently and calmly, and I won.

Oh, and the cherry on the sundae? The same day I got the news about the judge's decision, I heard from Stephanie. She'd found another job, so she'd gleefully given JK notice.

Sometimes, there is poetic justice.

SPANKING VS. BDSM

"I couldn't speak, and I couldn't look at him—I just buried my face in his chest and held on tight. He caressed and soothed me, whispered comforting words to me, telling me it was OK, he loved me, he was here for me. I love this part so much—the soothing and kindness after the chastisement. Pleasure and pain, pain and pleasure, firmness and tenderness, harshness and softness... it's all such a delicious, confusing, exciting dichotomy."
—my journal, November 14, 1996

As with politics and religion, there are scene subjects and controversies that go around and around without ever being universally defined or resolved. One such topic is the comparison of the spanking kink versus the broader realm of BDSM (bondage, discipline, sadism and masochism). Some feel that spanking is part of BDSM. Others think it's a separate entity, while yet others happily combine the two. I have heard spanking referred to as "BDSM's redheaded stepchild" and "S&M lite."

There are definitely some general differences between the two, in ways such as apparel/appearance, protocols and mindsets. Speaking only for myself after much experience, I choose to identify as a spanko, which some say is short for "spankophile."

As John and I got to know each other better, I realized that, kink-wise, we differed significantly. He had come from the BDSM world and had experience in aspects of that scene I'd never heard of, and once I did, I wasn't sure I liked them. He was a switch, and when he bottomed, he did so very heavily, wanting levels of pain and submission to which I couldn't relate.

And his spanking prowess, his naturally toppy demeanor? He had learned that for me. This surprised me greatly—to this day, I wonder why a BDSM (mostly) bottom would answer an ad for a spanking bottom. He said he found my ad irresistible. And he admitted that he'd hoped, since I was so new to the scene, I'd perhaps develop some switch tendencies. But that never happened.

So we slowly learned that while we both could fit into one another's scenes, our preferences were disparate and we'd need to incorporate play with other people. Fortunately, neither one of us objected to this idea nor found it threatening.

John told me all about BDSM/dungeon parties; what they were like, what people did there, what I could expect to see. The Saturday before Halloween 1996, we went to my very first play party, at Threshold in Hollywood. John had bought me a black lace garter belt and some stockings, and I had black pumps, plus a tight-fitting black dress I'd purchased some time ago but never had the occasion (or the nerve) to wear.

Being told what to expect was one thing; actually seeing it for the first time was quite another. I believe my jaw dropped upon entering the club and stayed open for the rest of the evening.

The place was immense and dark. There was a large main room with several scene areas, the bar, food, and a coat check. But there were several hallways with side rooms, an auditorium, more halls, more rooms... it went on and on, and scenes were happening all around us. And the clothes—well, it was a Halloween party, so there were costumes. I wasn't prepared to see so many men in drag, though. One older gentleman was decked out like a Southern belle, complete with a hoop skirt. But lawdy me, Miz Scarlett, he had nothing on underneath it. The rooms were a sea of leather, latex, stilettos, corsets, collars and exposed flesh.

I did my first public scenes that night. First a spanking with John, which I resisted for a while. *Here?* But he insisted, and I realized that once I was in position, I didn't feel as embarrassed about it. My face was buried so I couldn't see, so I was free to simply feel.

Later, John and I befriended a man named Patrick and I ended up doing a lengthy OTK scene with him, while John sat in front of me, stroking my hair and neck, and encouraging Patrick to spank harder. Besides a lot of hand, I felt a

146

strap for the first time and I liked it. And I believe I achieved subspace for the first time too, even though I didn't know what it was at the time. I felt such a high—the room went away and I was submerged in a swirl of pleasure and pain and attention.

There was comic relief, too, with banter and teasing and my bratting. I heard John say, "Hello, Sister!" and Patrick followed up with, "Sister, will you bless this ass?" Immediately, I felt a searing sting that made me jerk. "Aren't you going to thank the Sister?" I looked up and saw a rather large nun smiling down at me, holding a ruler. "Thank you, Sister," I gasped, and the nun replied, "You're welcome, my child." Saints preserve us—the good Sister was male.

When the scene was over, I tried to get up and found I could not. My legs were wobbly and I had a sudden awareness of everyone around me, and I felt overwhelmed. So I knelt down beside Patrick and put my head in his lap; instinctively, it felt like the right thing to do. He caressed my hair, and John crouched down behind me, wrapping his arms around me. I don't know how long I stayed there, but when I was finally able to rise to my feet, John immediately took me into his arms and held me close. I came to recognize that as his way of saying, "OK, you played with her, but the scene is over and she's *mine*." Much as I don't care for the D/s ownership dynamic—I am no one's pet—I find this "reclaiming" of me rather sweet.

After this, we went to several other BDSM parties—another group called Proscenium, plus some private house parties. I collected a few more all-black outfits. One at a time, I gathered scene experiences.

A month after the Threshold party, we went to Patrick's house and played with him and his sub. That night, John used a cane on me. I was terrified of that thing and I'm not sure why. Somehow, he convinced me to let him try it on me, assured me that he would only do six strokes and they wouldn't be hard. I clung to a suspension bar while he did it. He was true to his word and kept the blows on the lighter side and well spaced, but I still freaked out. I was stoic as they were dealt, but after the sixth, I burst into tears. He tried to get me to let go of the bar, but my hands were so tightly clenched around it in panic, he had to slowly peel my fingers off. He had to hold me close and soothe me for a long time before I calmed down.

So bizarre for me to look back and remember that. Just one of the hundreds of memories and reminders of how far I've come. While the cane can certainly elicit trepidation, I haven't been afraid of it since that first time.

In February 1997, we went to the Shadow Lane spanking party for the first time. Back then, they had parties twice a year; February at the Sportsmen's Lodge in Studio City and Labor Day weekend at the Riviera in Palm Springs. Sportsmen's was local to us, so we didn't pay for a hotel room, just party tickets.

The first thing I noticed about this gathering was what I *didn't* notice: I saw no leather or latex, no piercings save for ears. Clothing was light and in a variety of colors, rather than all black. These people all looked like they were at a cocktail party.

A man I'd met through my ad came to the party, and he was wonderful about introducing us around and letting us know about suite parties. One group had three rooms and they opened up the inside doors to conjoin them into one big party room. I didn't have the nerve to play in the main ballroom, but I played in the suites.

One particular scene was very hard; a big man with huge hands, and he whaled on me from the start because I'd been bratty with him. He'd given me safe words to slow down or stop the scene, but I felt this perverse pride kick in and I was damned if I was going to use them.

I buried my face and poured all my focus into absorbing the pain, but I could still hear people in the background as they gathered to watch us. "Oh my God." "Ouch!" "Poor thing!" "John, you didn't tell me she was such a heavy player." I felt hands gripping mine, offering strength. And the scene went on, and on, and on, until I finally capitulated and hollered, "Red!" Because I realized he wasn't going to stop until I did.

Later, a bunch of us were at a nearby deli having a snack and socializing, and this gentleman found me. Grinning, he held out his right palm to me; there was a huge, raised purple bruise on it. Another first! I had never damaged a hand before. It's quite twisted how proud I was of that.

Incidentally, this man had a beautiful young girlfriend, and the four of us hit it off, hanging out together at the parties and playing. Her name was different then, but she eventually became the very popular Niki Flynn.

On Friday night in the vendor fair, I saw some of the people whose pictures had been in the Shadow Lane materials. Butterflies collided with one another when I recognized the handsome Keith Jones. I watched from afar, not having the nerve to approach any of them.

Sometime during the weekend, we were in one of the suites and I was sitting on a bed, taking a break and observing. As I watched everyone around me, something occurred to me: We were all different, and yet, every single person in this room had the same general desire that I did. Everyone here *got* me, knew what made me tick, knew my "secret." I can't describe the surge of joy and freedom I felt after that realization; I wanted to jump up and down on the bed and holler with glee. I belonged here.

* * *

After this party, I was different. We continued to go to the BDSM events and I tried my best to fit in, but found myself growing more dissatisfied. It was not easy to find men there who wanted to do a good old-fashioned spanking scene. To many, spanking seemed like a mere appetizer, whereas for me, it was the main course. I tried different types of scenes—bondage, suspension, various implements, you name it. I even did a "water torture" scene, in which I was strapped down to a table while a suspended bottle slowly dripped on my privates. That didn't turn me on; I was simply wet, cold and irritable. Nothing resonated with me like spanking did. I could not connect with most of the BDSM crowd.

But still, we persevered. We met another couple, A & C, and got to know them well, playing and socializing with them. They were what I came to know as "crossovers":

People who play in both the BDSM and spanking scenes and enjoy each one.

C owned a large, beautiful home and had wonderful gatherings. A topped me and C was a switch, so she could top John. They were a lot of fun and we met many more great people through them, as C was a fetish photographer. She took spanking photos of me that ended up in the amateur sections of *Leg World* and *Taboo* magazines. Anonymously, of course. She referred to me in the caption as "the enigmatic Ms. E." and said I was 29. John got a huge kick out of going into the Hustler Hollywood store, picking up the magazines, pointing at me and saying to everyone within earshot, "She's in this!"

As time passed, my discomfort with the BDSM parties grew. More disconcerting incidents happened. At one party, I walked into a room and saw a man shackled and being bullwhipped into hamburger. I couldn't help myself; I screamed and ran from the room. John had to stay behind and apologize for me, as that action was deemed offensive.

At another party, a guest had a giant leather paddle, and I do mean giant; it was the size of a small child. Perhaps a medium-sized child. He was asking for volunteers to take a swat from it, so I stepped up. The man looked at me and said, straight-faced and completely serious, "Is this all right with your owner?"

I heard gasps and snickers behind me; people knew me. I took a beat and then said, "My *WHAT??????*" I probably could have been heard in the next county.

At yet another party, a man was talking about his wife and referring to her as his "cuttable slave." He ordered her to take off her blouse and she obeyed, smiling in a rapturous manner and keeping her eyes cast down. Her chest and upper back were scarred with several puckered white lines. While others gazed at her in fascination, I turned and left the room.

One more? I once saw a man who had to be in his 60s, if not older, lying on a bench naked save for his briefs, while a woman with sharp stiletto heels stood on his chest and walked up and down his torso. When he moaned in pain, she leaned down, slapped his face and snapped, "Shut up." Again, I had to turn away and leave.

John would get annoyed with me; say I was too intolerant of certain kinks. That their practitioners enjoyed what they did every bit as much as I loved spanking. I knew he was right, but I didn't know what to do about my feelings. Certain things made me deeply uncomfortable; I'm not saying that was right, but I couldn't help it.

At spanking parties, there was great joy and enthusiasm. People laughed, hollered, reveled in the playfulness and naughtiness of it all. At the BDSM parties, the rooms were dark and the atmosphere was solemn. Scenes were watched with reverence. And if you laughed or spoke too loudly, you were shushed. Honestly, it pissed me off and made me want to be disruptive.

And yet, we kept going. I knew John liked being at the BDSM gatherings and we did have some friends there, so I went and did my thing as best I could. But they were becoming less fun and more of a chore. I wanted to be open-minded, I really did. However, the more experienced I became, the more I learned what I *didn't* like.

We met a man who was well-known in the BDSM circles, whom I will call S. He took a liking to me and wanted to scene with me, even though he had women of all ages eager at these parties to play with him. I figured any top that popular had to be great, right? I should play with him, right? That was one of my earliest mistakes.

I did two scenes with him at two separate parties and didn't enjoy either one. The first one, he spanked me so hard with a hairbrush that I was bruised for over a week. The second time, he had me in suspension, making me repeat phrases and doing all this mind-fucky stuff, and hitting me so powerfully, I was howling. I overheard someone say to John, "Is she faking that?" and John answered, "No, she's not—that's pure pain." It was indeed. Not fun at all.

And yet, I said yes to a third scene. Why? Because I was new and foolish. I didn't know how to say no. Plus, since he was so much in demand, he *had* to be good. I figured there was something I was missing, and if I kept playing with him, I'd learn what it was.

We were at a private party in North Hollywood, at a home where the owner had converted his garage to a dungeon. S had told me to bring a spare pair of panties, and make them full-bottom, not a thong. I was mystified by that, but brought them.

Our scene took place in the garage with a crowd of people watching. He was playing too hard, whipping my legs and back, hurting me horribly. He didn't check in with me at all; he was too busy playing to the crowd, putting on a show, and I didn't know what to do. I wanted to use a safe word, but I was intimidated about doing so in front of everyone. John was several feet away and I wanted him so badly, I started whimpering, "John... John..." S overheard me and mimicked me, but didn't stop.

I then found out what he wanted the spare panties for. He'd put them in a bowl and had them soaking in rubbing alcohol. After we'd been scening for what seemed like hours, he put the wet panties on me. The alcohol burned and stung my raw flesh and I screamed. He also had a spray bottle filled with alcohol and was spraying my back with it.

I should have ended it, I know. But I didn't. Part of it, I admit, was my stubborn, stupid pride; I didn't want to be a wimp. I didn't want to cave in and surrender with all those people watching. And John couldn't help me—he kept trying to catch S's eye, tried to signal him without interrupting his scene. But S wouldn't look at him.

He pulled me to my feet and started to shackle me to a St. Andrew's cross, but then someone ran into the garage and yelled, "The cops are here!" I stood there frozen, terrified, as people dispersed and S backed away from me. John lurched forward, snatched up my dress and ran over to me. He yanked the dress over my head—I couldn't move, I couldn't speak. I was wet with the alcohol and it made dark blotches on my dress. Just as John was pulling me into his arms, the police came into the garage.

"What's going on in here?" one of them said. "Nothing," people answered. Then one of them nodded at me. "What's wrong with her?"

John, holding me close, replied, "She's afraid of you." Well, that wasn't untrue.

Somehow, the cops were convinced that nothing untoward or non-consensual was going on, and they told us to keep the noise down and left. John and I said our goodnights, he piled me into the car and started to drive away. But once we were out of there, I broke down. Completely. I sobbed so hysterically, John got worried and pulled the car over to comfort me. I was hurting, wet, cold, stinking of alcohol, and I couldn't stop shaking.

John got us back to his place and opened the car door for me. I tried to get out and nearly fell, and he picked me up and carried me into the apartment. Without any delay, he took me straight to the bathroom, stripped off my clothes and put me in the shower. Once I had all that horrid alcohol rinsed off, I was able to calm down. He then iced my bottom, back and legs and put me to bed.

I learned valuable lessons that night. The first one was a re-learn, one I would unfortunately revisit now and then: Trust my instincts. Just because others enjoyed S's style didn't mean he was a good fit for me. I *did not* have to play with anyone if I didn't want to, no matter what.

Second: If a scene is going horribly wrong, I have the right to end it. That was one I had to revisit as well in the future, but the seed was planted and I knew what the proper thing to do was.

And third: I really, *really* didn't like BDSM parties. I would still go, but I preferred spanking gatherings and the people there. I was tired of trying to shove my ill-fitting puzzle piece into the BDSM picture.

Please don't misunderstand me. I am not saying everyone in the BDSM realm is evil and that all spanking folks are perfect. I have met good and bad people in both scenes, and had both good and bad play sessions in each. But for me, BDSM is a place I can handle visiting, but I wouldn't want to live there. Spanking, however, is home.

LIFE CONTINUES

"After six months of calls, resumes, faxes, networking, more calls, redoing my resume, applying at six temp agencies, resource centers, even more calls, and so on, I can't deny it any longer. I need new job skills."
—my journal, May 1, 1997

As I searched for work after JK fired me, I was in for a rude awakening—nowadays, in my field, I had to have computer literacy. Without at least beginner skills on my resume, it would go straight into the circular file every time.

So I made an effort to learn the basics. I found a small computer training lab near my home and talked with the owner/teacher. He wrote all his own class materials and I noticed they were riddled with typos, so I offered to proof his work in trade for some classes. However, these classes were merely overviews, three to six hours, and without a computer at home to practice on, I forgot what I learned almost immediately. Meanwhile, time went by and I was still jobless, aside from an odd freelance job now and then through former coworkers.

I called my cousin, the one in television, to see if he had any connections with people who might be able to find me work. He threw me quite a curve; no, he couldn't help me in the job market, but he would be willing to buy me a computer and pay for the training I needed.

I certainly didn't expect this, but it gave me something to think about. I mulled it over on the weekend, discussed it with John. I felt embarrassed about relying on my cousin once again, when I was nearly 40 years old. But John said go for it; he wouldn't have made the offer if he didn't want to, and the money was no object to him.

As it happened, we had a dinner date with my father around that time, and when he asked how the job search was going, I told him about my cousin's offer. Not to be outdone, Dad said, "He can buy you the computer; I'll pay for the school."

I don't know what I did, if anything, to merit such generosity. But I am grateful.

So my focus was two-fold: Research computers and buy a good one, and research computer schools. By mid-May, I had a brand-new computer (along with printer, table and desk chair and other odds and ends) in my living room, and I was becoming a student again.

I'd found a 500-hour, self-paced course at a local college that had up-to-date equipment and programs. The tuition covered all materials and students showed up to classes and progressed through the tutorials. I went Monday–Friday from 9:00–1:00, and while at home, I practiced. I enjoyed learning the new programs and testing myself, and I got through the course in record time, achieving a Computerized Office Assistant diploma.

After school ended toward the end of the year, I found a full-time temp position immediately, working for Health Net in their Personal Development department. They had several materials and documents that needed proofreading plus formatting in Word, and several people in the department kept me busy. Best of all? They didn't have a desk for me, so they gave me all the work to do at home.

For the first time in my career, I could work in peace. No phones ringing, no customers, no coworkers, no distractions—I wore what I wanted, took breaks when I needed to, took off in the middle of the day for errands and chores and then worked in the evenings. If I was tired or in a bad mood, I could bury myself in the computer and be left alone.

I would go to Health Net once or twice a week to pick up/deliver projects and have meetings with managers, but I enjoyed those. Unlike my previous jobs, these people were very appreciative and complimentary, and they'd mock-fight over whose projects I would do first ("Hey! Quit hogging Erica!"). The freedom and focus felt like a luxury and I realized this was how I wished I could work permanently.

* * *

Meanwhile, John and I progressed as a couple, in both the vanilla world and the scene. We continued to go to both BDSM and spanking parties, and I amassed new and different experiences, learning along the way what I liked and what I didn't. The world of spanking had much more to it than first met the eye, I discovered—many nuances, variations and styles. At first I was a sponge, soaking up all the experiences and trying things that didn't necessarily appeal to me, just because I thought I should. But as time went on, I became more confident over my preferences.

The parties were a rich source of learning. As I look back on some scenes, whether I participated in them or just observed, I realize they were all part of my journey, even the negative ones.

For example, I discovered that while I love being scolded, I did not like being verbally demeaned or treated harshly. A calm but steely tone turned me on, but a raised or angry voice scared me and made me shut down emotionally. I enjoyed playing hard and I could absorb a lot of pain. But there had to be an underlying awareness that the top was inflicting it with caring behind it, not malice or cruelty, even if that cruelty was part of a role-play.

I also learned that for me, there was a difference between embarrassment and humiliation. While the former added a delicious and squirmy discomfort to a scene, the latter could ruin it for me, make me feel debased. Embarrassment = pulling down my panties. Humiliation = pulling my butt cheeks apart. That's invasive. Don't do it.

Once, at a gathering at our friend C's house, she and a male friend put on a scene show for us; it was one of heavy D/s and degradation. I sat between John and A on the couch, watching it unfold, and found myself struggling. He slapped her face, pulled her hair, tore her clothes and called her ugly names, while she cried and begged.

Logically, I knew this wasn't real, that it had been discussed beforehand and was completely consensual. I knew they were the best of friends and he wouldn't really hurt her. But viscerally, I reacted with horror. Their performance was so convincing and watching my usually strong and capable friend weeping and groveling disturbed me.

When he pushed her to the floor and made her lick his boots, that was the last straw; I got up and left the room. John came after me and found me crying in the kitchen. I felt stupid, but he was very reassuring.

If you spend any amount of time in the spanking scene, you quickly discover that a popular theme is that of the naughty schoolgirl. I saw a fair amount of these outfits at the Shadow Lane parties, particularly the ones they had over Labor Day, because they'd have a "Back to School" theme. I didn't relate to any of this, but I watched with amusement.

One night we went to a costume party in a private home, and John, A and C collaborated and persuaded me to dress up like a schoolgirl. C had a wardrobe of various fetish outfits and she decked me out in a red plaid pleated skirt, white blouse, white knee socks and penny loafers. I drew the line at the little-girl white cotton panties, though—I wore an off-white lacy pair.

They insisted that I looked cute, but I felt like a complete ass. I was 40 years old, for God's sake. I was way too old for this. All that evening at the party, I squirmed, blushed and felt embarrassed, and not in a good way.

All right, now I could say I tried it, and it wasn't my cup of kink. Neither was any sort of ageplay, or anything to do with familial spankings. The Daddy/daughter roles are also very popular in the spanking scene, but that particular dynamic never appealed to me. I may act childish sometimes, but I am not a child. Men may be authority figures in my fantasies, but they are not parental or avuncular.

And yet, hearing the childhood appellation "young lady" gave me butterflies. Go figure! I learned about the power of words; how certain ones could make or break a scene. Some could make me swoon; others made me shudder. I loved the word "bottom"; loved it even more with "bare" in front of it. But "tushy" made my flesh crawl; it sounded too little-girl-ish. And while I had no problem with "ass" in general conversation, within scene I found it somewhat jarring and crude.

Call me naughty? I loved it. But change the word to nasty, and I'd cringe. Brat, bad girl, minx all could evoke a smile. However, call me a bitch or any other harsh name and that would be scene-kill.

And for whatever reason, the word "punish" was a huge turn-on. A top's regretful utterance of "I'm afraid I'm going to have to punish you," or something to that effect, would turn me to instant mush.

Last but not least—I found out that many people into spanking are also anal-erotic. Not this girl. My back door is Exit Only, thank you. Leave it alone.

It was a whole new culture, with its own language, customs and rules, and slowly but surely, I was finding my place in it. But there was so much more ahead.

GOODBYE, DAD

"I am in a fog. I feel a deadly calm, kind of a stupor, a wall of numbness holding back a deluge of pain and fear. I feel like I'm sleepwalking. My father is dying. He has been slowly deteriorating all week, and today I got a call from his doctor. His vitals are dropping, blood pressure and so forth. He definitely has viral encephalitis, an infection of the brain. It is often lethal, and if it isn't, it leaves one pretty much brain dead. Which is how I feel right now."
—my journal, May 15, 1998

My father had been amazingly healthy in his later years, considering how much he'd abused his body with alcohol and chain-smoking for so long. In 1995, he'd had triple-bypass surgery, but he bounced back from that in record time and recovered fully. He kept busy and had many friends, getting involved with volunteer work and senior activities. Life was good. John and I would meet him for dinner periodically and enjoy a few hours with him.

In February 1998, Dad's kidneys abruptly and completely failed. He would need dialysis three times a week, but for the first treatment, there wasn't enough time to surgically insert a shunt into his wrist, so they cut into his neck to access the large veins there. John and I went to visit him the weekend after that and I was shocked at how he looked; very thin and pale, with matted hair and a large bandage on his neck. Still, his spirits seemed good, and he made jokes about how he had a new part-time job, going for dialysis.

After he healed from the shunt surgery, we took him out to eat. I couldn't help noticing how frail he seemed, how his hand shook when he was lifting the fork. He'd always been meticulously neat with his beard, but now he'd be unaware there was food in it.

We had met and befriended a man named Dave at the BDSM parties; he lived near me. He had a wonderful house with a large back yard and a garage that he'd turned into a dungeon, and he had parties and barbecues. Sometimes during the week, he and I would get together to have dinner or coffee, or just hang out.

At the time, the Sportsmen's Lodge held a BDSM mixer on the first Wednesday of the month, and on May 6, Dave was planning to go and he asked us if we'd like to accompany him. John had to pass, because it was a weeknight and he got up extremely early for work, but he told me to go ahead. So Dave picked me up and we had a fun evening, mingling with others in the scene and then heading to the nearby deli for a late snack.

Dave dropped me back home around 1:00 A.M.; I picked up my phone to check for voicemail, and heard the familiar beep-beep-beep, indicating I had messages. Perhaps John had left me one. I dialed in, punched in my password, and the automated voice cheerily told me I had three new messages.

Three? Instantly, I knew something was wrong. I've never been much of a phone person, and I was even less of one after discovering the wonderful world of email and instant messaging. Aside from John, I got very few calls on average, and I could go days without getting even one message. Therefore, receiving three in a few hours was enough to put my senses on red alert.

Sure enough, all three were from my father's friends. Dad was in the hospital. One of his friends, Mike, said I could call him back at any time, no matter how late it was, so I punched in his number, my fingers trembling.

Mike said my father had been falling a lot lately and he'd seemed confused, forgetting their dinner dates and so on. Long story short, Dad was found on the floor of his apartment and taken to Cedars Sinai. Mike had been in to visit him, but Dad was delusional and agitated, and nothing he said made sense. After I hung up, I called the hospital and spoke with a nurse; she gave me Dad's doctor's number and I called to leave a message.

It was 1:30. Normally, I love the quiet and solitude of the night, the feeling like I'm the only one in the world who is up. But that night, I felt panicked and alone, and I couldn't sleep. There wasn't anything I could do except wait for the morning. I managed a catnap from 3:00–5:00, then got up and made coffee. I called John at 5:30, knowing he'd be at work already. He said I could have called him when I first found out, but I said no, he needed his rest and I wouldn't do that to him.

That day was a nightmare. The calls started early— Mike, other friends of Dad's, his doctor. By 9:00, I was dressed and out the door, heading for the hospital. I knew he was in bad shape; the doctor told me Dad was delusional and that they had to put him in restraints, but nothing could prepare me for what I saw when I got to his room. If I'd known he would be the way he was, I never would have gone by myself.

He lay in the bed, twitching and trembling, his eyes rolling around, mumbling incoherently. He had deteriorated tremendously since I last saw him; I couldn't believe how thin and shrunken he was. His body under the blanket looked wasted and small, his legs like sticks. His face and arms were bruised (from various falls, I later found out) and he smelled bad.

But the worst thing was his teeth. I guess the fall had knocked his dentures loose, and his upper teeth were semi-detached, hanging down from his palate and flopping around in his mouth. He grimaced, rattled them in his mouth and tried to speak around them, but I couldn't understand a word. He couldn't eat, so they were feeding him through an IV.

I started to cry and I took his hand, stroking it and telling him I loved him. I think he knew who I was, understood what I was saying, and he tried to talk to me, but it all came out as gibberish. Sometimes he seemed to have a lucid moment; his eyes would focus on me, he'd kind of smile, he'd squeeze my hand. But then the next minute he'd start thrashing around again, his eyes would roll and his face contort, and it was all I could do to keep from running out of the room.

After a half-hour, I couldn't take anymore; I had to leave. I spoke to the nurses and they said he was being moved to another room that afternoon, so they'd be going in soon to give him a bath and so forth. So I left, crying all the way back to my car. I was so scared; I wished I could

161

walk away from it all and not come back. But it was only just beginning.

More phone calls in the evening from my father's friends; they meant well, but frayed my nerves. They were telling me what I needed to be doing, what calls I should make, that I had to get into his apartment and find his address book, get his rent paid and so on.

It dawned on me how difficult this was going to be; I was the only family he had and the responsibility for all his affairs would fall on me. And I was totally unprepared for any of this, especially since he never told me anything. I didn't know who his lawyer was, who his business manager was, how to deal with medical insurance or how to get any of his other bills paid.

The next morning, I started making calls. I spoke again to his doctor, and I called his dentist (who was his friend as well) and arranged for him to visit Dad and take care of his teeth. I spoke to Mike and Dad's other close friend, Sheila. Mike had Dad's landlord's number, so I called her, told her the situation and arranged to meet with her Monday afternoon so she could let me into the apartment.

John and I went to visit him Friday night. He seemed a little better, more coherent, was sitting up in bed and chatting with friends and greeted me with "Hi, babe!" But after a while, he started hallucinating and talking about how people were playing tricks on him and how his being in the hospital was all a terrible practical joke. He grew more agitated until we finally had to call in a nurse, and I left in tears. I knew he wouldn't have wanted me to see him like that anyway.

Over the weekend, his doctor told me they'd put Dad in ICU and his condition was still unknown. They were doing a spinal tap to determine if he had some sort of viral infection in the brain, which would explain the hallucinations and confusion. He said there was no point in visiting, because he was so out of it and they were giving him a lot of medication to keep him calm. John was a rock for me and I did the best I could to put it all on hold until Monday.

Marjorie, the landlord, met me at Dad's condo; he was leasing from her at Shoreham Towers, a West Hollywood high-rise. I hated her almost instantly; she was 60-ish, trying (unsuccessfully) to hide it with stiffly sprayed hair dyed a garish red, fake nails and layers of makeup caked on her face. A cigarette-husky, whiny voice completed the package. She put on a pretense at first of being concerned, but it became obvious that all she cared about was her rent and her furniture. Dad hadn't paid the May rent yet, and it was May 11. At first I thought perhaps I could give it to her just to shut her up, but then she told me it was $1800. Holy cow—for this dump? OK, so they had valet parking, an operator/message service, and he was on the 18th floor so he had a spectacular city view, but the unit itself looked like any other apartment. I didn't have $1800 to spare.

At least she let me in and allowed me some time to look for a few things. I found his address book and a checkbook; the latter did me no good, since he was in no condition to sign checks and I couldn't do it for him. I also found a bulky envelope in his desk that contained his will.

I sat down, opened the envelope and took out a sheaf of papers. As I flipped through them, I realized I had several documents here: His original will and three codicils. I read briefly through the original and the first two codicils, and had to remind myself to breathe.

The first will was drawn up when he was still married to Vampira, and she was the executor. In it, I noticed that he'd left $50,000 to me. She got everything else.

The first codicil was almost identical to the original, save for one detail. I was now to receive $10,000.

Feeling sick, I looked at the second codicil. She was still the executor. All was the same… except now, I got nothing. I was excised completely.

That horrible woman. I could see her influence all over this.

Willing myself to calm down, I then read Codicil #3. This one had been drawn up after the divorce. A new executor had been named; Phil, a friend and former colleague of my father's. Vampira was nowhere to be found.

And I was the sole heir. Everything he had would be left to me.

Tears blurred the papers in front of me. It was too much to process, and yet, I didn't have the luxury of sitting there and absorbing it. Marjorie was hustling me to wrap things up and leave, with her grating voice echoing in my ears. "Aaarica, I'm *sawry* about yer *fahhh*thuh, but I need the rent!" Oh, she was going to be trouble, I could tell.

I took Dad's address book home with me and looked up Phil's number. I had never met him, but I knew my father thought highly of him and when we first spoke, I could see why; he sounded very kind and thoroughly charming. He and his wife had two residences: one in West Hollywood and one in Maine. Unfortunately, he was in the Maine house when I contacted him, but then he assured me that he'd catch the next available flight.

"Are you sure?" I said.

"Of course I'm sure! You think I'm going to let you go through this all by yourself?" he exclaimed. "Are you *crazy*?" (Well, yes, but that's beside the point.) My nerves eased a bit, talking to him. I told him about Marjorie. "Give me her number," he said. "I'll handle her."

More visits to the hospital, endless phone calls. Dad did not improve. His doctor said he had viral encephalitis, which is an infection of the brain. Basically, it was as if his whole body, all his organs, etc. had been short-circuited. They were watching him closely and medicating him, but if there was no change, there was no point in any heroic measures to keep him alive.

In his will he had a Do Not Resuscitate directive. I knew I was probably going to have to make the decision within the week to let him go.

Later that week, I went to visit him, as I was doing each day. The doctor in residence spoke kindly with me, told me that my father was very agitated, clearly struggling against what was ailing him, but he was growing weaker. He gently suggested that I might want to have some private time with him now to say goodbye, and he left us alone.

Dad was in the bed, fretful, muttering, his eyes darting around. He'd kicked the blanket untucked, and his feet stuck out at the bottom. Stupidly, I stared at them. *His toe-nails are too long. Why isn't anyone cutting them?* His hospital gown had slipped off one shoulder, so I pulled it back up and then laid my hand on his chest. At first he flinched and grimaced, but as I kept my hand there, he calmed. And then I spoke to him.

I told him it was OK, he could stop fighting. That I knew he was trying to stay alive for me, because he didn't want to leave me. My voice breaking, I went on to say that he could let go and rest now, that I was going to be fine, and that he wasn't abandoning me. That he'd been a wonderful father, and he wasn't really leaving me, because I would carry him with me in my heart always.

He didn't look at me and he didn't speak. But his hands twitched and clutched at the sheets, his eyes glazed with tears and he let out a sound somewhere between a moan and a cry that I can still hear to this day. Anguish? Grief? Fear? Did he hear me; did he understand? I continued to stroke his chest and shoulder, told him that I loved him. Before I left, I kissed his forehead.

Over the weekend I came down with a cold, so we stayed away from the hospital. On Sunday, his doctor called and told me Dad had gone into cardiac arrest twice and they'd revived him. Did I want them to continue doing so? No, I said. If that happens again, let him go.

Monday morning, May 18, my cold was in full bloom and my voice was a hoarse croak, but I still got up, dressed and drove to Cedars Sinai. Both Sheila and Phil were there when I arrived at around 9:45 A.M., and Sheila ran to me, crying. "Honey, he's gone." He'd passed away at 9:20. Someone—an orderly? A doctor?—brought me a plastic baggie with Dad's watch and a couple of other things, and asked me if I'd like to see him one last time. I said no. I'd already said goodbye.

When my brother died, my world crumpled for a while, because it could. I was young; my only responsibility was to show up for school, and I could take off from that for a while, stay home and weep copiously. My parents didn't have that luxury, of course. Not only did they have to deal with the pain and shock of losing a child, but they had to handle all the details involved with wrapping up a life. Now it was my turn. I didn't cry, I didn't take to my bed, I didn't withdraw into my grief. There was no time; I had too much to do, too many people looking to me for decisions. Mercifully, I went numb.

That day was a blur. I remember bits and pieces: going to lunch at Sheila's husband's tennis club. Talking to my mother, who was vacationing in Vermont. She heard my laryngitis and told me I needed to take care of myself. "I don't have time for that," I said.

Phil took me to Pierce Brothers Memorial, where my father wished to be buried after he was cremated. I sat like a stone, listening while Phil discussed my father's requests with the directors. The only time I had an emotional out-burst, briefly, was when I called home for messages and found that Marjorie had left me yet another message whining about Dad's rent. "He's *dead*, you bitch!" I shrieked into the phone at the voicemail. Phil took the phone from me, hung it up and reassured me that he'd call her back, and that I did not have to speak with her today or ever again.

Phil was such a miracle; I don't know what I would have done without him. Efficiently and smoothly, he took over the legal matters; he got a lawyer and paid him a re-tainer to help with my dad's affairs, he handled Marjorie and her demands, placating her; he took care of the ar-rangements at the memorial park. He found out all the de-tails of my father's bank accounts, insurance and so forth, and got power of attorney so that we could pay Dad's rent and take care of other odds and ends.

I would not be able to transfer Dad's accounts or sell his car for 40 days, so that end of things was on hold. But I had the tremendous task of going through all his things and deciding what to do with them. And very little time in which to do it. As soon as she found out Dad had passed, Marjorie was champing at the bit to get all his stuff out of there so she could clean the place and get it leased to some-one else. She wanted everything done by the end of the week. Phil managed to charm her and got us a little more time, but not much. We had until the middle of the follow-ing week.

The next several days fell into a rhythm. I'd get up early, fortify myself with coffee and a bite to eat, and drive to my father's condo. Sheila, Mike and Phil were constant companions; one, two or all three of them would join me there each day. There was so much to do, so many things to look through. If I'd had the gift of time, I could have spent hours going through it all, reading every scrap of paper in his files, looking at the piles of photos he had, making decisions about things I might want to put in storage for later. But I was rushed; each day was a race against time, trying to get the apartment completely squared away before his landlord had another tantrum.

I heard from many people, including my father's second wife S and my cousin, the one who had helped me so many times, who used to be my father's writing partner. He told me if there was anything he could do, anything, just name it. I didn't have to think about it, I already knew, and I didn't hesitate to ask; I needed all the help I could get. First, would he please arrange for Dad's memorial? He had all the connections and resources to do something Dad would have appreciated, and I knew there was no way any of my efforts could even come close. And second, would it be all right if I stored a few of Dad's things at his home, since he had more room than anyone else I knew? To both things, he said yes.

Sheila and I cleaned out Dad's closets and drawers and gave all his clothing, dishes and linens to the Salvation Army. Always an avid reader, Dad had hundreds of books, and we packed them all (save for a few I kept for myself) and donated them to the Beverly Hills Public Library, where he'd spent countless hours.

I also heard from B, Vampira's son. He and my father had remained close after the divorce, and he asked if there was anything he could do, could he come join us and help out. Absolutely, I said. I knew my dad had been very fond of him.

If I had a bigger apartment, a garage, any place where I could store things, I would have kept so much more. My father had a cabinet of file drawers that were crammed with scripts and correspondences and other things he'd written over many years; a rich history of his career and his life. I wish I'd had the time to read it all, to organize it, catalog it. But again, there was no time and no place to put it all. So I threw a great deal of it away. I regret that deeply, but at the time, I didn't see any other choice.

I did keep many pictures and some articles I found so I could make a scrapbook. But how I wish I could have simply piled all the papers somewhere and come back to them later, with a clear head and several free hours in which I could peruse.

By Wednesday, May 27, it was all over at Shoreham Towers. My cousin's movers had come to pick up Dad's recliner and several paintings and framed pictures. I'd taken the TV and VCR. One of the neighbors took his filing cabinet. We were leaving Dad's car in the garage until the 40 days were up, and then one of his friends was buying it from me, which saved me the hassle of advertising it.

Dad had five Emmy award statuettes. I wish I had kept them all, but I had no room for them. So I kept one Emmy, along with one of the many award plaques he'd received over the years for writing. I gave one apiece to Sheila, Mike and Phil (my "team"), and the fifth Emmy I gave to the Oasis, a senior center where my father had donated a great deal of time volunteering. They adored him there.

I had not cried all this time, nor had I done any work, cleaned my place or exercised. My life had been put on hold and I was an automaton, performing the tasks and making the decisions as they arose. Dad's memorial was scheduled for Tuesday, June 2, and I thought perhaps it would be just the thing I needed to push me into feeling again.

My cousin really came through. The memorial was perfection; my father would have approved. It was held in a large conference room at the Oasis and so many people showed up. Many of my father's colleagues spoke, as well as comedians, including Dick Martin (of Rowan and Martin), Harvey Korman and Louis Nye, who had been Steve Allen's sidekick on the old *Tonight* show. On the buffet table was a tall, beautiful crystal vase with one large, perfect white rose. Carol Burnett, back East at the time, had sent her condolences.

I had been prepared to cry, but instead, I found myself laughing. The speakers were humorous, told funny, ironic and sardonic Dad stories, and the whole affair was free of the usual schmaltz and melodrama of the typical funeral/memorial, for which I was grateful, as I hate that. And I know Dad would have hated it as well.

I learned things about my father I'd never known. For example, one writer, Frank Tarloff, spoke of how Dad fronted for him, ghost-writing his scripts after Tarloff had been blacklisted during the McCarthy era. Why had I never heard about this?

Later, I also learned that when Dean Martin started a solo lounge act in the 1960s after his professional breakup with Jerry Lewis, my father helped him create the character he embodied for the rest of his career: the lovable lush. I wish I'd known more of these things when Dad was alive; I was so proud of him and I couldn't tell him so.

John took off work to come, and my mother and stepfather attended as well. S came too, so two out of three of my father's ex-wives were there. The night before, B had called me. Sounding sheepish, he said he was sorry to put this on me, but he had to—his mother had heard about the memorial and she wanted to come. She had pushed B to ask me if I'd extend an invitation to her.

I suppose I could have taken the high road and said yes, go ahead, tell her to come and pay her final respects if she wants to. Then I thought about all the years of pain she caused, how much damage she did to my family, her many vile, vicious words...

Screw the high road. I told him no. He understood.

* * *

In the coming weeks, life slowly returned to normal. My temp assignment continued at Health Net, I went back to the gym, the phone stopped ringing every five minutes. All my father's odds and ends of paperwork had been handled, his car was sold, his bank accounts were now in my

169

name. Phil had gone back to Maine. It should have been a relief, but emotionally, I crashed. The feelings I'd held at bay finally broke through, and I cried a great deal, felt overwhelming fatigue and sadness. But everyone assured me this was normal.

My temp job concluded toward the end of 1998, and my first instinct was to seek another full-time job. Because of my new computer skills and the fact that I'd been able to put them to good use for the past year or so, I was able to get another position fairly quickly, this time doing data entry/proofreading in a research company. However, from the first day, I knew I didn't want to stay.

They offered no vacation/holiday pay. The work was unbearably tedious, and they did all the data entry in MS-DOS. Who the hell used DOS anymore? They gave me a big fat employee manual with all sorts of rules and regulations, some of which were rather insulting. Don't say this or that, don't do this or that. Don't use the copier. Don't use the phone. Don't spill on the carpet. Sleeping in meetings was prohibited (yes, really). And the company timesheet was ridiculous; I had to account for every minute I was there, literally. I had to log each job I worked on, how many minutes/hours I spent on each one, plus account for breaks (food and restroom), no matter how small. It could take up to 20 minutes each day just filling out that stupid thing.

I thought back to the past year of taking work home and doing it on my own time, and how much better suited I was for that. It might take a while to establish myself, but why didn't I go freelance permanently? Contact old clients and companies, redo my resume, put the word out that I was now a free agent and I could handle people's outsourced overload work. And here was the key: while I was building my business, I could supplement my earnings with the money Dad left for me. Without that, I never would have had the financial flexibility to venture forth into this new aspect of my career.

So I quit the new job after six days and never looked back. No more soul-crushing office jobs for me. No more Bosses from Hell. Ever. What freedom!

A couple of years into my freelancing, I got a gig at a small advertising agency that put out the bulk of its ads on Friday, so they needed an extra proofreader to work on that day. It paid fairly well and I worked 10–12 hours each Friday, so you'd think it was a nice regular mini-job to have.

It wasn't. My co-workers were nice, but the place was run by a Holy Terror named Byron, who bullied and blustered and created a very unpleasant work environment. People were scared to death of him and hated him at the same time, so there was a lot of skulking around, whispering, note-passing and fearful looks cast about. But I figured it was just once a week; I could put up with it. Until they told me one Friday that they wanted me to start working Thursdays, too.

One full day of this negative atmosphere was enough, thank you. I declined. Next thing I knew, one of the other proofers pulled me aside that afternoon and whispered, "I'm not supposed to tell you this, but they're firing you. They're putting an ad out this afternoon to replace you."

Nice. Easy come, easy go. I didn't want to leave my colleagues in a lurch, since it was crazily busy, so I decided to finish the rest of the day. Byron, however, was openly contemptuous and rude to me. In his eyes, I guess I was already gone and he didn't have to bother prevailing upon his precious few social skills.

Around 6:00, the other three proofreaders and I were struggling through piles of ads. Byron stormed into our room, came over to me and snatched up the stack on my desk, loudly announcing, "I'm going to give these to my secretary. They'll get done *much* quicker."

That did it. No boss was going to treat me this way again. I slammed my hands down on the desk, stood up and slung my purse over my shoulder. "Byron," I said, "kiss my ass." As he sputtered, I went and hugged each of my fellow proofers in turn, and then walked out.

How many people fantasize about saying that to an obnoxious employer? I actually got to do it. Yet another gift from my father, one that keeps on giving.

Thank you, Dad. Again and again, and always.

INTRODUCING ERICA SCOTT

"The Shadow Lane video is a GO! We're shooting on January 9, and Keith Jones is going to be my partner. Yes!! And I don't have to carry the whole female part of the film, since there will be another woman in it as well, so that's a relief. Eve made an announcement of it on the [soc.sexuality.spanking] newsgroup, and I've been getting all kinds of congratulations and good wishes—I'm so excited! And nervous!"
—my journal, December 14, 1999

John and I had befriended Ralph Marvell, one of the Shadow Lane video actors; we'd gotten together a few times, gone to jazz clubs, had dinners out. At the Shadow Lane Labor Day party in September 1999, I did a public scene in the ballroom with Ralph, one that drew a crowd of onlookers, including Tony Elka and Butch Simms (the third Shadow Lane owner).

The spanking was long and intense and when it was over, I wasn't ready to get up, so I crouched down next to Ralph and put my head on his leg. As he stroked my hair, I heard applause and I peeked up. We were surrounded by people watching us, and getting a standing ovation. Along with the rush from spanking-induced endorphins, I felt an altogether different kind of high. I liked this attention. I wanted more of it.

What would it be like to get spanked on camera?

I thought about it for the rest of the weekend, going back and forth, working up my nerve. On Sunday morning at brunch, I found Tony and Butch sitting at a table and I approached them before I could talk myself out of it. Smiling, I said hello, introduced myself and asked them if they remembered watching my scene with Ralph from Friday night. Oh yes, they most certainly did. Taking a deep breath, I plunged. "So, are you guys still looking for new people to do videos?" Tony replied by enthusiastically pushing a napkin at me, fishing a pen out of his pocket and saying, "Always. Here, give us your name and email address, and Eve will contact you."

And sure enough, she did, the following week. She asked me to please send a photo along with my height, weight, clothing and shoe sizes. Along with that, she wanted a brief description of my preferences and limits. She was quite thorough, even asking what types of colors I thought I looked best in. I answered her immediately, attaching the only picture I had of myself scanned in, a headshot. After that, I did my best to put the idea in the back of my head, waiting to see if I'd hear from her.

In December, Eve wrote me again and said she'd written a script for me and another new video actress named Alexandria Panos. We'd be playing secretary and receptionist, and our boss would be Keith Jones.

Say *what?*

Oh, my God. Keith Jones? *The* Keith Jones? I was doing my first spanking video and *he* was my co-star? He'd be spanking me on camera? We'd met briefly at the last party, maybe exchanged a dozen words, and even *that* had damn near given me a stroke. My nerves exploded. She gave me the shoot date (January 9) and told me that I was going to take care of all the outfits, but I should bring a few things as backup just in case her choices didn't fit.

I asked Eve if I could please have Keith's email address, so I could introduce myself and have a bit of dialogue between us before the shoot. That was one of the best things I could have done; Keith was wonderfully responsive to my tentative note. He wrote back a fairly long message, saying the most important thing I needed to remember for the video was relax, focus on what I was doing and on him, and block out the cameras. Pretend we were doing a scene together at a party. He asked a lot of questions about how he could help me: Did I like scolding? Did I want him to hold me down firmly? How hard a spanking after the warm-up? Did I like fast swats or slower, more deliberate ones? Which implements did I prefer? I could tell I was going to be in the best of hands.

I had to consider a video name; what would I use? One of the men I'd met from my ad had said that I had "Victorian white" skin, so I toyed with the idea of Victoria White for a while. But then I decided I didn't want the confusion of two first names, so I would keep Erica.

So which last name? I wanted something simple, easy to remember and spell; I'd seen how some scene names got butchered every which way online. One particular Shadow Lane actress came to mind: Kiri Kelly. Seemed like a simple enough name, right? But I saw Kirri, Kyrie, Kerri, Kelley; never underestimate the public's ability to misspell. My real surname begins with an S, so I wanted an S name. There were several choices, but I was partial to either Scott or Stevens. Scott won. I'd also considered Steele, but then had visions of it being misspelled Steel, Steal, and Steale, so that choice was quickly discarded.

The holidays dragged on and on; I am not one who enjoys them, and I find all the socializing and parties tedious. I certainly didn't need all the extra calories, wanting to keep my weight down for the shoot, and I worked out like a fiend whenever I could. John was working for two companies at that time, so there were two office parties along with an endless string of familial obligations, and I was already a nervous wreck, trying to memorize my lines and prepare myself mentally. All that Y2K nonsense was going on too, with people predicting that the worldwide computer systems were going to crash *en masse* when 1999 rolled over into the year 2000.

But finally, it was all over, we were into January, and I was ready. I had gone over my script so many times that I not only knew my own lines, but Alexandria's and Keith's as well.

That Sunday, I showed up at 11:00 A.M. at the office building where we were shooting and met everyone. Keith, Alexandria and I had an immediate rapport and we worked well off each other; I felt comfortable with them right away. Eve showed us all the outfits she'd bought for us, and I was pleased at how everything fit perfectly and looked great. Particularly a skintight gold halter-top dress that was the sexiest thing I'd ever worn.

The day is a blur—our shoot started at noon and went until nearly 9:30. The script was quite ambitious, with sev-

174

eral scenes and four costume changes, and one hell of a lot of spanking for Alexandria and me.

Shadow Lane videos are scripted, but somewhat loosely. The scripted dialogue (usually written by Eve) is often used to introduce the characters and set up the scenes and their transitions, but a great deal of the dialogue during the spankings themselves is left to ad-libbing. For this reason, SL prefers to shoot people who are truly into spanking, because they tend to naturally deliver more authentic spanking patter.

I had some interesting realizations: One, I found it was remarkably easy for me to shut out not only the camera, but the crew—I was completely focused on my co-stars and our action.

Two, I had an aptitude for ad-libbing, and Eve liked it and told me to keep it up.

Three, I seemed to instinctively know what to do, as far as the nuances of posing were concerned. I kept my head up, even though my natural inclination when playing privately was to bury my face. When they posed me leaning over the desk for some pictures, I knew to deeply arch my back and thrust my bottom upward. Behind me, I heard Eve say, "Can you believe this is her first spanking video?" and heard Tony reply, "Nahhh… she's a natural."

And four, and most important—I learned about the power of endorphins. I was on such a high all day, my tolerance was off the charts. If I felt any pain, I don't remember it. All I remember is that I wanted more and more, and I didn't want the shoot to end. Both Alexandria and I turned out to be insatiable, and Keith was impressed.

What can I say about Keith? Everyone was wonderful, but he really made that first shoot exceptional. He was funny, sexy, skilled, and, once he got into that toppy character, very believable. Which made his off-camera personality even more fun; such a strange juxtaposition of his natural goofiness with his strictness once the cameras rolled. He encouraged and complimented us, made us laugh constantly. When we were both leaning over the desk, he was behind us, singing, "Heaven, I'm in heaven…" During a break in the action, I looked around for my panties but couldn't find them. "Has anyone seen my—" I started to ask, then looked across the room and saw Keith sitting at the desk with my panties on his head.

When we finally wrapped up, Eve said they were all going to Jerry's Deli; would Alexandria and I like to join them? All I'd eaten all day was a banana, a few baby carrots and half a bagel, and I was suddenly and ravenously hungry. Besides, I didn't want the day to be over yet. So we caravanned over to Jerry's and to my delight, I ended up sitting next to Keith. The bantering continued all through dinner and when it was time to leave, I felt like a little kid who doesn't want Christmas to end. We were exchanging hugs outside of the restaurant, then Keith took me aside and said, "Hey, how about I ask Tony if I can borrow his place for about an hour, so we can play some more?"

Well, you know, that sounded like fun, but it had been a long day, I was exhausted, and after all, I'd just been spanked, paddled, strapped and caned for hours, so I was played out. But thanks anyway...

NOT! Of course I said yes. At the time, Tony, Eve and Butch had an unusual setup: They lived in three separate apartments, all next to one another (they used to call it the Shadow Lane Compound). So when Keith asked Tony if it was OK, Tony said sure, he'd just hang out at Eve's for a while. Keith got into my car with me so he could direct me to the apartments. As I turned the key in the ignition, "Hurts So Good" blared out of the speakers. What are the odds that *that* particular song would be playing?

And so we played for another hour, this time incorporating a lot of caning. No one can believe that I wanted to continue with more spanking after a nine-hour shoot, but I could not get enough. Finally, I had to concede to the late hour and go home. Keith walked me to my car, hugged me goodbye and said that I owed him a three-hour scene at the next party.

It was midnight when I walked into my apartment, still completely wired. John had told me to call him when I got home no matter how late it was, so I did, bubbling and blathering about the day and all that we'd done. I didn't go to sleep until 3:00 A.M., but I guess that was to be expected.

176

What a rush the following week was! Among other things, I found a post Eve had made on an AOL spanking newsgroup:

> *Had a great shoot with Erica S. and Alexandria Panos over the weekend. They co-starred with Keith Jones in Naughty Secretaries Week Volume 2. Both women gave outstanding performances as the mischievous office help who give their new boss all kinds of headaches. It was a very complex script, covering three days of action, with numerous scenes, costume changes and lots of fun dialog. Erica S., witty and real, was also slender to a fault with showgirl legs and a flawless small-sized bottom that could take an amazing amount of discipline. Alexandria P., with her exquisite hour glass figure and stimulating irreverence was ready and able to endure just as much hard, sustained spanking as Erica, plus spanking with a number of wooden and leather implements. Both women brought the kind of energy, enthusiasm and integrity to the shoot that only comes with real scene people. We couldn't be happier about our charming new discoveries.*

Showgirl legs, *me*? Witty and real? I read that post over and over, and then copied it into a Word document to keep. It was my first "review."

I had not joined the Shadow Lane member site yet, and I put in my credit card information to buy a membership so that I could see the pictures they put up from our shoot. Shortly thereafter, I got email from Tony, cancelling the charges and telling me that girls who get their bottoms smacked in gold dresses don't have to pay. I think that was my first inkling that my status in the spanking scene was going to change, and change it did.

The first time I saw my pictures on the Internet was a mixed bag of emotions for me. I was thrilled to pieces and at the same time, horrified—I hated my face! Silly of me, I know. (Who was looking at my face anyway, right?) Unfortunately, I had either inherited my mother's harshly critical eye, or I had absorbed it via osmosis after a lifetime of hearing her pick at other people's bodies and features, my own included.

Writing about this, I had a flashback to a classic example. When I was in my 20s, my mother wanted some new pictures of me, so I went to a photography studio and had some taken. I wasn't thrilled with any of them, but I chose the one I thought was best, bought a nice frame for it and gave it to her. She hung it up on the wall in her bedroom.

The next time I came to visit, I went into her bedroom and noticed that there was a small painting on the wall where my photo used to be. When I asked her about it, she had the grace to look a bit guilty, and she opened a dresser drawer, where I saw the picture lying face down. And her explanation was:

"It's a horrible picture of you. I didn't want anyone to see it and think that's actually how you look."

Yes, that hurt as much as you're imagining it did. Multiply that comment by several hundred of its kind and there's little wonder why I viewed myself with such a relentlessly disparaging eye. I can't really blame my mother; she was riddled with her own insecurities, and sadly, those who are hard on themselves are often the same with others, because it's all they know.

Anyway, negative reaction notwithstanding, it was a very exciting time for me. On the whole, the year 2000 was tough one. My freelance work was very slow and I had a lot of financial challenges, including multiple car problems and a broken crown that needed replacing. John had an ongoing issue with work that was stressing him dreadfully, and he and I argued on a regular basis, everything from irritating spats to full-blown fights that went on for hours and left me drained. And I had been diagnosed with uterine fibroid tumors—benign, but their symptoms were painful and distressing. Yet running parallel with all these aggravations was the video and all my new experiences around it.

Before the video came out, I received the new issue of *Stand Corrected* in the mail. As it turned out, this would be their final issue in print. I tore open the envelope and saw the back cover, and the magazine slipped out of my fingers and fell on the carpet. There we were—me over Keith's knee, with Alexandria standing beside him and smirking. And there was a write-up about us inside.

And then, of course, the video came out. I watched it by myself the first time, because I didn't know what I'd feel and I thought it was best to be alone so I could process the various reactions. Delight ("Damn! I'm funny!"), horror ("Is my nose *really* that big?"), surprise ("Well, I'll be—all those hours in the gym *do* pay off!"), embarrassment ("Ack! Why does everything show even when my legs are closed?")—on and on it went, all 90 minutes of it. But overall? I loved it. I loved that I had done this, and I couldn't wait to do it again.

* * *

Because of the lack of work and the stress I had over finances, John, health issues and so on, I found that the Internet offered a distraction and a refuge. I made more friends and spent time emailing, instant messaging and talking in chat rooms, the Shadow Lane room in particular. I knew exactly what I was doing, but I couldn't seem to make myself log off until hours had disappeared.

In July, Eve told me that Keith was coming out from New York for a visit and that he'd love to play with me again. I had heard a great deal about discipline scenes from others, but never experienced one for myself. I emailed Keith, telling him of my online "addiction" and asking if he could help me out with that when he came to L.A. He assured me that he could and I wouldn't like it, but I had to trust him and know that everything he did was out of caring. Damn, he was good. Just reading that message made my knees liquefy.

We met at Tony's apartment on a Wednesday at 4:00. He was in character immediately; he sat me down with a pad of paper and a pen and told me to write down every single one of my "crimes" and not to leave anything out. I had to stipulate to needing very strict discipline, and then I had to sign it and date it! I was giggling and asked if we

179

should have it notarized as well—I could tell he was trying not to laugh at my irreverence.

That was definitely the hardest scene I'd had to date. I started out as a smartass, but dropped that quickly, as he was clearly not going to accept it. After a long OTK hand spanking, he bent me over the couch arm and was alternating paddle and cane, and every time I sassed or disobeyed, didn't call him "Sir" or answer his questions properly, I got penalty strokes. He left the room briefly to get some water and I could have sworn he said "Stand up," so I did.

"Did I tell you that you could stand up?"

"You told me to!"

"I said 'stay there,' not 'stand up.' You weren't listening." I apologized and looked pleadingly at him, but he was implacable. "Three hard ones for not paying attention."

How many friends on my Buddy List, he asked. Thirty, I replied. So I got 30 very hard whacks with the paddle, 15 on each cheek. He kept me engaged, lecturing me and asking questions, not allowing me to zone out. This went on for nearly two hours, with the riding crop thrown in for good measure. I was burying my face in the couch cushion so I could holler into it.

He kept mentioning the "final caning," but every time he'd do a round of caning and I'd gasp out, "Is that it?" he'd answer "Nooooo." He began to seriously cane me; he stopped speaking, and the only sound in the room was the whir of the air conditioner. He'd take long pauses, whip the cane in the air (which always made me shudder), and then lay a hard one on me. I didn't want the scene to end, and yet I did. I didn't know how much more I could take.

When a really intense round stopped and he started to rub me, I said, "Was *that* the final caning?"

"No, but you know what?"

"What?"

"It would have been—I was all prepared to have it be the end, but…"

"But WHAT??"

"You didn't count any of them."

Oh, God… "You didn't tell me to count them!" I cried.

180

"I told you in the beginning to count every cane stroke, didn't I? Did I not say that?"

He had. I'd forgotten. Tears finally came to my eyes.

"OK, *now* it's going to be the final caning, and it's going to be the hardest one yet." He bent down and pushed my hair aside. "Look at me." I did. "I'm doing this because you need some strict discipline and I'm trying to teach you a lesson, not break you. Do you understand?" "Yes, Sir," I said, resigning myself to more. "Be sure to count these," and he started.

Again, long, long pauses between each stroke, and God, were they hard. My tears ran into the cushion, but I never lost count, and it went on until he hit 24 and stopped. It was over. I lay there and didn't raise my head, panting, trying to catch my breath. I felt like I was on fire.

I stayed in position, and he got some ice and rubbed it all over my bottom and thighs. I felt the melting rivulets trickling down my legs, cooling the burn. After my hot flesh dissolved the ice, he toweled me off, then massaged in some sweet-smelling lotion. Keith the Disciplinarian was gone—he was back to his bantering and easy-going self.

Several minutes into the massage, I heard him mutter, "Jesus."

"What?" I asked.

"Well, pardon my French," he replied, "but your bottom is fucking bionic. It's healing right before my eyes."

And there it was—my scene nickname was born. Although I wasn't fully bionic yet, it seemed; I had bruises and cane stripes for eight days. I loved them, of course, and was sad to see them fade.

Eve and Tony took Keith and me to dinner later. We ate outdoors on hard metal chairs with crisscross mesh patterns…what are people thinking when they design things like this? Keith grinned evilly at me as I squirmed on mine. A little boy walked by wearing a T-shirt with "Satan, Jr." on the front. Tony asked, "Keith, would you like to have a shirt like that?" I couldn't resist piping up, "No—he's Satan, Sr.!"

* * *

Before I knew it, the Labor Day Shadow Lane party was upon us. I wondered how different it would be this time, now that I'd done my first video. The answer was: VERY. It had been great fun before, but now, it was especially magical.

First of all, John and I were comped in (the economy was much better then; that generous perk became an unaffordable luxury and had to be discontinued, unfortunately). Second, Eve asked Alexandria and me if we would work their vendor table Friday night and Saturday afternoon. And third, we were both asked to model pajamas and baby-doll outfits for Bobbi Tawse for two hours on Friday evening—and yes, we'd be paid for that.

Friday night was surreal. Being on the other side of the Shadow Lane table was an indescribable high for me; Alexandria and I had so much fun, and all the copies of our video were sold out. We put on Bobbi's various outfits and circulated the ballroom, showing them to all the guests. People recognized us and complimented us; every time I turned around, it seemed someone wanted to greet me.

We were supposed to have some photos taken in these clothes, so I was striding across the ballroom heading for the vendor area where we'd be meeting the photographer. Keith suddenly materialized, grabbed my hand and stopped me in my tracks.

"Where do you think *you're* going, young lady?"

"Uhhhh... to get pictures taken?" I stammered.

"That can wait," he said, and he led me over to a chair near the middle of the room, where we did our first public scene.

Amazing. A year ago, I was gawking at this man from across the room, too shy and self-conscious to say a word. And now look at me!

The weekend was nonstop activity. We met a lot of new people, got invited to room parties we'd never known about before, and I played more than I ever had. I know it shouldn't be this way, but I have to be honest—people treated us differently.

I recall one woman whom I won't name; the year before, she was quite standoffish with me when I saw her at room parties. She'd been wearing this beautiful long flowing gown, and I'd said, "I love your dress; it's gorgeous." Without a smile or a thank-you, she'd merely looked at me and said, "It's a robe." However... cut to the present, post-video, and this same person greeted me effusively, gave me a hug, complimented the video. Very strange indeed. But as it is in life overall, the scene can oftentimes be a popularity contest. I was to see a lot more of this over the years.

John was amused to discover his own change in stature. He could walk into a room by himself and, due to being an unfamiliar and unaccompanied male, have his attempts at striking up conversation greeted with wariness. But then, should I join him, the same people who were previously cool suddenly regarded him with warm interest. He'd joke and say I gave him credibility. I had a hard time wrapping my head around that one!

On Sunday night, our perfect time was capped off by being invited to a private dinner out with Eve, Tony, Butch, Keith and a few others, including Dolores Cortez. I felt like Cinderella at the ball all weekend, and kept wondering when I'd wake up from this fun dream, but it was real.

All my life I'd wanted attention, to be noticed, to feel like I was, well, *somebody*. I never thought I'd end up taking this avenue to accomplish that, however. But I sure as hell loved it. Reality still existed, but I was inside a bubble of fantasy-come-true. And there was so much more to come.

It didn't occur to me at the time that all bubbles have to pop eventually. But for the time being, I soared on the high, eager to experience everything the spanking scene had to offer.

* * *

John was raised Catholic and received his primary education at small Catholic private schools. That summer, we were invited to his grammar-school reunion. Yes, grammar school, not high school. It was being held outdoors at some club, and I thought, what the heck. John remembered all of his classmates and his stories about them were rather entertaining (not to mention his horror stories about the strict nuns). He was curious to see how all of them had fared (read: aged) and I figured it could be somewhat interesting.

Once there, John kept me amused by pointing out the various alumni and telling me their background tales (the budding babes and jocks, the brains, the geeks, the troublemakers). Overall, it seemed to be a very clean-cut and vanilla crowd.

And then there was Susie Bright.

In case you aren't familiar with her (I wasn't, at the time), Susie Bright is a renowned writer, editor and speaker. Her topics? Sexuality and erotica.

How delicious—a sex expert at the Reunion of the Repressed! I could not make that up; it was too perfect.

Later in the evening, I was in the ladies' lounge, fixing my hair and refreshing my makeup. As I primped, I heard a sing-song voice call out, "I know who you a-a-are!"

My head snapped around, and there across the room, grinning at me, was Susie. No one else was in the room, so she had to be talking to me.

I was completely flabbergasted and sputtered, "Uh… um… you do?"

She laughed. "John told me. Congratulations on your first video!"

We talked for a minute; she wrote down the URL of the Shadow Lane website and the video name. And then we exited the restroom and that was that.

If anyone had told me that I'd be discussing my new spanking video "career" with one of the alumni at a Catholic school reunion, I would have asked them to share their drugs, whatever they were.

* * *

Also that summer, there was a grand opening of a new dungeon in Los Angeles, and Eve and Tony were invited. They asked John and me to join them. I'd never been to a pay-for-play dungeon before and the place intrigued me—a

184

huge space with several themed rooms and areas, and an immense collection of implements and equipment, all types. Everything was new and immaculate. Long story short, my curiosity overwhelmed me and I accepted the general manager's offer to come work there a couple of days a week, doing sessions as a sub. Getting paid to be spanked sounded ideal and exciting.

So every Tuesday and Thursday, I worked there from noon to 7:00. The rule was that the doms wore black and the subs wore white, with a silver collar. I've never liked wearing white, so I had to shop and find some inexpensive white clothing—a couple of dresses, a white bra, white thong panties, stockings and garters. A pair of white sandals. As for the collar, that was the only time I've ever worn one and I never will again.

The rule at this club was that the women had to keep a thong on at all times. Otherwise, everything else could come off. Of course, there were always clients who tried to talk us into slipping the thong off; who would know? There was to be no penetration, no exchange of bodily fluids, etc. Just the various forms of BDSM.

I lasted just a few months, and only that long because I enjoyed the other women who worked there so much. The femdoms in particular had fascinating tales to tell (some of the things that sub males want done to them are beyond comprehension). And as for the gifts and "tributes"—one woman had a client who took care of her rent, her car payments and her laser eye surgery. Another told of having an old car that kept dying on her and how one day, a client got fed up with her cancellations due to car trouble, handed her a blank check and said, "Go buy a new car." *Damn*, I thought. *I'm on the wrong team here.*

We had a very comfortable room where we could sit and hang out, read or watch TV when we weren't in sessions, and we'd often munch on microwave popcorn and share stories, laughing ourselves silly.

But I was not cut out to be a pay-for-play bottom; most of the things asked of me were not to my liking, and I ended up turning down a fair amount of sessions (we always had a pre-scene interview and the girls had the right to say no to any scene if they felt a bad vibe). I wanted to be spanked, of course, and I would accept all the different implements. I didn't mind bondage and I could tolerate tickling (although a half-hour to 45 minutes of it was pretty tedious).

But acting submissive, kneeling, crawling? Talking dirty on command? Watching clients jack off into a towel? Didn't appeal to me in the least. Elaborate role-plays where I had to spout contrived dialogue and wear ridiculous outfits? Nope, that didn't flip my switch either. One client came in with a huge suitcase filled with clothes. He wanted me to play a wanton secretary and I had to put on panties, a girdle, a slip and a thick skirt. I wouldn't have felt a spanking from King Kong through all those layers.

As much as I disliked the trash talk, the cheesy-spanking-story talk was even worse. One gentleman had me role-playing as his wife, and I had to greet him coming home from work by jumping into his lap and cooing, "Hi, honey! How would you like to spank the world's sexiest bottom?" Who talks like that? It was cringe-worthy.

My first session ever was someone who claimed he wanted to tie me up and "play with me" a bit, which sounded harmless enough. Once I was tied to a chair, though, he started wrapping scarves around my throat and pulling them tight, until I had to tell him to stop. He kept trying different things, all centered on cutting off my breath in some manner, and I kept safe-wording because it scared me; this definitely hadn't been part of the pre-scene agreement. He cooperated and I knew I wasn't in danger, but it was very uncomfortable and I wondered what I'd gotten myself into. I also figured that because I kept stopping him, I could kiss any tip goodbye.

But when the session was over and he untied me, he pulled out his wallet and fished around through the bills. "You were good," he said, tossing a $50 on the chair. Then he hesitated for a moment, fished out another bill and tossed it on top of the $50, adding, "You were *very* good." It was $100. Very bizarre indeed. Of course, tips like that were not the norm. Many clients didn't tip at all.

One quickly learns that nothing is too weird. One client, in between bouts of spanking, sang to me. Swear to God. It was sweet, but awkward. Another, who booked me twice, was pleasant enough; he enjoyed tying me up and then masturbating, and he didn't expect me to watch. Unfortunately, he had a pronounced lisp. When he whispered, "You're driving me *nut-th*," I had to grit my teeth to keep from laughing.

I grew more uncomfortable and dissatisfied as time went on, but hung in there, thinking it would get better. Then came the day where the first client wanted me to say filthy things to him as he got himself off (and this time, I had to watch), and the second client had no idea how to handle implements and he wrapped my hip badly with a flogger. After those two, I knew I was done; I was hurting and felt rather unclean. I quit that night.

I don't regret my time there, because I learned another valuable lesson. Spanking was a joy and a pleasure for me, and in order for it to stay that way, I had to choose my play partners—not have them choose me. Without chemistry and attraction, the same activity that thrilled me to no end became a chore and a business, and there was no way I was going to let that happen. I made a little bit of money, but I was much older than the other subs there and between that and my limited range of fetishes, my appointments were few. At best, I came out of my sessions feeling neutral. But more often, I felt uncomfortable and sleazy, as if I'd somehow compromised myself.

There is a certain emotional detachment necessary if one is going to do pay-for-play, I think. I was not able to achieve it, but I wouldn't have known that without trying it. I'd had this idea in my head that working in a dungeon was glamorous somehow, and saw for myself that there is absolutely nothing glamorous about it.

Still, it was yet another item I was able to check off on the spanking experience list. Next!

DEVELOPING ONLINE PRESENCE

"I just checked the member count—we have 997 members, and 10 pending. That means our club now has over 1000 members! You guys are the greatest! Thanks to every one of you for joining and helping us make this the best, kick-ass (er...spank-bottom) club on the Web."
—from *Southern California Spanked Wives and Girlfriends*, November 21, 2000

Around the time my first video was released, spanking forums were the hot ticket online. The term "blog" wasn't ubiquitous and Twitter was in the future, as were MySpace and Facebook. Nearly everyone was on AOL and people had things called "homepages."

One day, a friend emailed me, "Erica, your picture is on someone's homepage," and he included a link. I clicked on it, and lo and behold, there I was in that infamous gold dress and stretched across Keith's lap. The page belonged to a woman named Becca, and I noticed that, underneath the photo, she clearly credited it to Shadow Lane and added, "No, this is not me, but I wish it was!" All right, so she was honest, and this was pure flattery, not a rip-off. I continued reading the rest of her page and she talked about her love of spanking and what she enjoyed about it, and how the picture above perfectly captured the essence.

Pleased, I located her contact address and wrote to her. "Hi—you don't know me, but my picture is on your homepage!" She wrote back, effusive and excited, and we struck up an online friendship immediately. She lived in Southern California as well and was eagerly exploring the spanking scene.

It turned out she was quite web savvy as well, because she started one of those spanking forums, building it from scratch with several pages, photos and more. Then she asked me if I'd like to co-manage it with her.

Why not? It sounded like fun. We didn't think it would be that big a deal anyway, since there were so many clubs and forums at the time. After discussing it, we chose to keep it strictly Male Spanks Female. Switches could join, but we requested that the discussions and photos be kept to M/F. It was our club, it would be small and local anyway, so we could have it any way we chose, and M/F was our personal orientation.

Both of us had been disgruntled by the flaming and disrespect we saw on the unmoderated AOL newsgroups, and so we made another rule: NO flaming or insulting allowed. Discussions with all opinions were encouraged, but they had to remain civil. We wanted this little corner of the Internet to feel safe to its members. We had an off-topic board as well, but we asked people to refrain from discussing politics and religion. That was just asking for trouble and there were plenty of other boards for those subjects.

We called it *Southern California Spanking Wives and Girlfriends*; it eventually came to be referred to as SCSW. It was on MSN, which had several "adult" groups at the time. Ours was unique because of the M/F-only orientation, and we figured it would remain small. Little did we know.

Becca was a very active, hands-on manager. She posted and advertised us all over the spanking sites and recruited members, built new pages, posted lots of photos and constantly started new discussions. I did not have her website ability, but I posted often, making sure to be an equal presence. I was comfortable following her lead. We were a good team; both of us with strong opinions, a love of writing and the Internet addiction necessary to keep a site like this one running. We agreed on many things, and when we didn't, we provided complementing views and agreed to disagree.

For example, Becca had a strong view of the spanking-and-sex controversy. At the time, she saw the two as completely separate entities, not to be combined. She used the metaphor of "chocolate cake and pecan pie," her two favorite desserts, which she adored separately, but would definitely not like if they were mashed together on the same plate. I did not agree; personally, I like to keep them separate as well, but I also know that many enjoy them combined and I understand the appeal. So I developed my own metaphor of "cake and ice cream." Many people love both, and ice-cream cake is delicious, but some prefer the two separately rather than commingled.

Between Becca's advertising and the word-of-mouth that increased steadily, we began to grow. In a short time, we hit 1,000 members, and before we knew it, the member count had grown to 5,000. New people joined every day and the board flourished with dozens, then hundreds of threads.

Our club title rapidly became a misnomer, because our membership was quite literally worldwide. When the club grew too big for Becca and me to manage by ourselves, we took on two assistant managers. One of them lived in the Netherlands! She chose the name "Helen."

Many assistant managers came and went during our heyday, but Helen holds a special place in my heart. She was married with two small boys, and when she became pregnant with her third child, she announced it to us and the entire club went through that pregnancy with her. When the baby was born, she posted a picture of herself with the little one in her hospital bed. Our SCSW family gathered around, *ooh*-ing and *aah*-ing and bestowing congratulations.

SCSW became my home away from home and a haven for many of our friends as well. At first only spanking was discussed, but as the club grew and friendships were forged, people began sharing personal thoughts and experiences, and we had many deep discussions. We watched lives change: Becca met a man through a Shadow Lane ad and ended up marrying him, posting her wedding pictures on our board. Helen had her baby. Relationships began and relationships ended. People kept up with each other's life situations.

For example, in June 2001, I had surgery for my fibroid tumors. They had become problematic, causing pain and bleeding, and there were hard lumps I could see and feel protruding from my abdomen. Ignoring them was not an option; I'd had one friend who'd done so, and hers grew to the point where they occluded her bladder and she had to be catheterized, and then had to have emergency surgery that left her with a large abdominal scar.

So I had three choices: 1) hysterectomy (the most drastic, but definitely cures the problem); 2) myomectomy, which was surgical cutting out of the tumors (often not effective, because if even a tiny bit is left behind, they grow back), and 3) a fairly new procedure, uterine artery embolization (UAE). In this, they cut a small hole in the groin and inserted a tube into the main artery that fed blood to the tumors, and then blocked that artery. The optimal result would be that, without the blood flow, the tumors would shrink and die. I chose UAE.

I talked about my surgery on our board and the support was gratifying. There were good-luck and get-well threads for me, many well wishes and notes asking how I was, how it went, how my recovery was going.

Our board had a wonderful reputation among the forums because of the no-flame rules; people felt extremely safe revealing their private feelings and that was exactly what we'd wanted. We enforced our rules firmly; if a member posted something nasty to another, we deleted the comment and gave them a warning. We did not allow X-rated photos (gratuitous gynecological shots or "dick pics"), so if they were posted, we zapped them. If warnings were not heeded, then the offenders were banned. A few naysayers said we practiced censorship, but most agreed that how we ran the board was the best way to keep it clean and safe.

Topics ran the gamut from the lightest to the most serious. We had our share of cheerful baiting and bratting, but there were many threads with long, thoughtful and heartfelt posts on personal subjects. There could be a deep discussion regarding how to tell vanilla mates about your desires, and directly below it, a post where Becca had taken a picture of Keith and me from *Naughty Secretaries Week Part Two* and Photoshopped PeeWee Herman's head onto Keith's.

Of course, all spanking events were fodder for much discussion. We had lively threads after all the Shadow Lane parties with detailed reports. Once, Becca even had a SCSW party in her hotel suite, where several of us gathered and got to meet in person. I wrote about my video shoots, not omitting a single facet. Members who gave/received their first spankings told us about them. I even talked about a couple of bad scenes I'd had, because I wanted the less-experienced women to know that these things could happen to anyone, that it wasn't their fault, and even those of us who had several years into the scene could make errors in judgment.

I did not name names, of course, even though people asked me to. Becca, in her classic blunt style, made one of the best comments I can recall, regarding a player at Shadow Lane with whom I'd had a negative experience. "Tell us who he is! By the time we all get through spreading the word about him, he won't even be able to make a spanking date with his monkey!"

I also kept an ongoing log of my fantasies concerning my handsome and sexy personal trainer, whom I was convinced was a spanko because of comments he made and how he was so obviously a butt man. After a great deal of banter and teasing, I outed myself to him, and it turned out he wasn't one of us after all. However, he was extremely fascinated with the idea of spanking and thought it sounded fun and exciting.

So he asked questions, teased me about it endlessly, and borrowed one of my videos. During our sessions, he did pitch-perfect "top speak" and even swatted me on occasion. And each encounter got recorded on SCSW as the members read eagerly and commented, waiting for the next installment. Ultimately, I got to triumphantly post the story of how I convinced him to give me a spanking, on my 45th birthday. Thousands cyber-cheered.

As a side note, he turned out to be a natural, but confessed that, aside from enjoying seeing how much I got into it, he didn't really care for spanking a woman—it felt like "hitting" and it did nothing for him to inflict pain. Go figure. But at least he tried. And I milked the hell out of that story for a long time; the thread stayed alive on the board for two years.

* * *

I met so many wonderful people over the years, several of whom became my friends (and sometimes play partners) outside the board. I could tell stories that would extend this chapter to dozens of pages, but I won't. However, I'd like to mention one exceptional young woman.

From the early days on, we had a member who at first called herself Sassipants, but then revealed her name was Jesse. She was in her 20s, lived in New Orleans and was a smart, witty little spitfire. She didn't mince words; if you pissed her off, she let you know it, but she was equally outspoken with her support and praise. If she loved you, she was fiercely protective. She wrote all her posts with a red font and signed them with a rose emoticon. You could count on her writing to be articulate, incisive, warm, funny, and always essentially Jesse.

Eventually, she and a couple of other women branched off and formed their own MSN group, *The Brat's Place for Spanking*. We were kind of like sister groups, sharing many of the same members and supporting each other. Once there was a flap on our board over a huge misunderstanding and one of our few flame wars erupted. I was criticized harshly along with another member; he was on vacation and hadn't had a chance to come on and tell his side of things, so I left the discussion in place instead of deleting it as I normally would have. Jesse came on several times and defended me like a mama lioness.

She and I would Instant Message now and then, and during one of our discussions, she was expressing admiration for the way I'd handled the situation on the board. I can't recall the quote word for word, but the essence was: "Erica, you have such class and I admire you so much... I want to be you when I grow up!" I daresay that of all the compliments I've ever received in my lifetime, those words ranked in the top ten, if not number one.

Jesse didn't get to "grow up." She was very private and didn't reveal details of her personal life on the boards, but she confided in me: she had leukemia. She requested I keep that between us, because she couldn't bear the thought of people feeling sorry for her or treating her differently if they knew, so I never said a word.

Hurricane Katrina happened in fall 2005 and devastated Jesse's beloved New Orleans. Her family home was spared, but not so the homes of so many people she knew. Normally, Jesse was a very upbeat and positive person, a fighter, but seeing all the destruction and misery around her was too much, and she stopped fighting. In December 2005, she succumbed to the leukemia and passed away, just two months short of her 29th birthday.

I'd never met her in person, but I still cried and cried at her death. Both SCSW and Brat's Place reeled over it, and endless tributes were posted to her. Such was the nature of these boards back then—we got close. People touched us in ways we never could have imagined.

Regarding the aforementioned occasional bad scenes, I once posted about a particularly wretched episode I had with someone whom I'd considered a friend. We were at a private house birthday party and he and I played, but things went south and he got very harsh and non-consensual with me. I was in shock and I went along with it because I didn't know what else to do; I didn't want to make a scene and spoil it for the birthday girl. So I shut down and went within, and didn't melt down until after the scene was over and I could disappear into the bathroom, where John found me sobbing. The worst and most confusing part? After this abusive scene (which culminated in his slapping my face), he said, "You know I love you. But I needed to push the envelope; you've grown too complacent. And I will do it again, every time we play."

Since when was that his decision to make? Of course, he never got another opportunity to "push the envelope" again; that was the last time we played together. But I was at a loss for how to handle seeing him at parties in the future, since we were in the same general group of friends and encountering him often was inevitable.

When I spoke of this on SCSW, the thread fairly exploded with supportive, enraged and thoughtful comments. But one in particular stands out for me—the following from Jesse. It completely encapsulates her character: outspoken, witty, fiercely loyal, loving and a bit hot-tempered.

Erica, my darlin'... how can you POSSIBLY call this man your "friend"? He's a sadistic, arrogant son of a bitch who humiliated you...PURPOSEFULLY ... and has promised to DO IT AGAIN. He's everything negative I've always thought BDSM was. You were feeling a little too superior, so he cut you down to size... sorry in advance to all you BDSMers, but that's your rap. How did he cut you down to size? Let's see,

he violated you sexually,
he pulled your hair to the point of curving your spine severely,
he slapped your legs,
he BIT YOU FOR GOD'S SAKE....
and then he slapped you in the face.

Then... "it's ok, you know I love you."
Honey, if that's love, he can take it, fold it, and stick it where the sun don't shine. Love, my ass. That's an extreme hatred and anger towards women... he's dangerous, Erica.
This man isn't your friend, Erica. I AM. And I'm telling you to tell him to go to hell!!!!
Dammit, for years now I've been hearing about BDSM and how we are giving it a bad rap... that's it's just as safe, sane and consensual as what we do.... but what you've described is rape, pure and simple - the trust of a long standing friendship destroyed by an aggressive angry dom. (One who enjoyed the hell out of it soooo much, he's PROMISED TO DO IT AGAIN!)

Jesse, FURIOUS!

A few posts later, she softened her stance after cooling down.

I'm not being fair, lumping all BDSMers into that category. I was so furious I wasn't editing myself... but what I really meant to say was, that was the impression I'd always had of that whole scene... humiliation, degradation, etc. It's taken me a long time to accept that what people consent to do is none of my business, and that I should keep an open mind about it. And along comes this so-called friend of Erica's, and plays into every prejudice I have battled against.

God, I loved that girl. Rest in peace, sweet Jesse.

* * *

As SCSW continued to blossom, so did Erica Scott. I now had a presence of sorts, online and at parties. People knew who I was. Of course, some of it was due to "flavor of the month" syndrome: I was a new face and bottom, and was getting the requisite press and attention. But after a while, I noticed that people weren't just commenting on my butt or my video sass. They were calling me funny, smart, open and real.

Real? Please! The *real* Erica was the insecure depressive, the curmudgeon and loner, the shy, awkward being floating on the outskirts of life with her nose pressed against several windows, looking in hungrily. Erica Scott was merely a persona, a fantasy fabrication, an alter ego. Right?

That's what I thought, at first. Then I came to realize that Erica Scott and the "real" Erica were one and the same. The former was simply a facet of my whole package; a part of myself that I hadn't allowed to come out before. Yes, the real Erica still had a laundry list of neuroses. But when she felt comfortable, accepted and loved, she could indeed be engaging, articulate and quick-witted.

Who would have thought that the key to unlocking some of my best components would be a spanking fetish?

Noisy Neighbor...

"Ralph and I played wonderfully off each other, Eve and Tony were very pleased, and I was on a huge high afterward, just as I was after my first shoot. We finished the shoot around 5:30, and then spent some time taking still shots. By 6:00, we were done and packing everything up. I went to pick John up and we all went out for dinner, Shadow Lane's treat, of course. They are so incredibly generous. They even reimbursed me for the manicure/pedicure!"
—from *Southern California Spanked Wives and Girlfriends*, April 2, 2001

After the positive experience of my first shoot, I was dying to do another video, so I was thrilled when Eve suggested that I do my second one with Ralph Marvell. She asked me if I had any plot ideas. I'd always thought that my first spanking scenario ever—the one where I acted like an inconsiderate apartment neighbor—could be made into a fun video script, so I suggested that. Much to my surprise, Eve said, "Sounds good—why don't you write something up?" *Me*, write a Shadow Lane script?

I took the idea and expanded on it, creating a script with two separate scenes and spankings, adding a twist for the second one (I'd make noise on purpose, to provoke my irate but attractive neighbor into visiting me again). I decided to call it *Spank Thy Neighbor*.

When I sent it to Eve for review, I thought perhaps she'd edit it a fair amount, but she made just a couple of tweaks and left it mostly as I'd written it. Then I got another email from her, asking if maybe I'd like to do a little something "naughty" in this one, because videos with that element tended to sell better.

Ummm... naughty? "Well, I don't know—what'd you have in mind?" I wrote back. She replied that perhaps he could finger me to orgasm while I was OTK, at the end of the second scene. Well, now.

I admit, the idea intrigued me and it fit in well with the scenario. But did I really want to go there on camera? And

197

how would John feel about it? I asked him about it, but he just made jokes about it, which was his way of saying, "Sure, it's fine, go for it." Next, I wrote to Ralph and told him of Eve's suggestion. What did he think? He replied, "Well, if you don't mind doing it, I sure don't!" And he punctuated it with a smiley face.

Oh, what the hell. I rewrote the second scene, adding in the little extra activity. I gave it a romantic ending, with the two of us exchanging a kiss and then him lifting me up and carrying me off camera, with the intention of sharing a neighborly shower.

Eve gave me the final OK on the script and I brought it over to John's so that I could run lines with him. He read through the script and toward the end, he said, "Hey, wait a minute!" Uh oh. Maybe he wasn't so hot on this idea after all.

"Honey, I told you about that scene, remember?"

"Never mind that," he blurted. "You didn't say you were gonna *kiss* him!"

I was dumbfounded. "So, let me get this straight— you're OK with the fingering business, but you don't want me to *kiss* him?"

"No!"

OK, so I deleted the mingling of tongues. Too funny!

We were shooting on a Saturday this time, and using Kristine Imboch's home. Before I headed there, I stopped for a manicure/pedicure, toting along a gorgeous pair of brick-red platform sandals from Eve's shoe collection so I could match the shade.

As with the first shoot, Eve had new outfits and lingerie for me. For the first scene, she put me in a slim navy blue skirt with a sleeveless top in the same red as the shoes. For the second, I had a beautiful halter-top wrap dress in a print of brick red, pink and cream, and then for the part where I was stripped to lingerie, a matching bustier/panty set in a rich lavender-blue color.

It was a fun, energetic shoot. Ralph and I had natural on-camera chemistry and the sparks flew during the first scene as I fought and kicked and screamed at him, all to no avail. Our ad-libs flowed naturally, and I was handed a perfect opportunity when Ralph scolded, "Do you know how many times I've had to lay there trying to sleep, with your music blasting?" And I snapped right back, "*Lie* there, stupid." Oh, I paid for that, but it was well worth it.

One of the pleasures of writing the script is the ability to insert inside jokes. When Ralph was complaining about my horrible choices in music, I wrote myself replying, "It's better than that Springsteen crap *you* play." Ralph Marvell is a die-hard Bruce Springsteen fan; he's been to countless concerts, probably numbering around 30 by now. I also wrote in a line about how he left SCUBA tanks strewn about outside his apartment; Ralph is a deep-sea diver.

Bizarre dichotomy about these shoots: When the cameras are rolling, I am oblivious to my exposure, but as soon as the director calls "cut" and I return to reality, then I'm overcome with modesty. Every time we had to break for whatever reason, I grabbed my panties and put them back on; I did that so many times, Tony took them away from me and stuffed them in his pocket!

After we finished the first scene, Eve called Ralph and me over, and then she knelt down behind me, indicating that he do the same. She then proceeded to point out the red areas on my bottom, indicating where I could use more spanking. I kid you not. "See, she's nice and red *here*, but over *here*, you need to even her out." I'm sure I was blushing purple, because one of the cameramen caught my eye and snickered.

We had a snack, I changed my clothes and they turned the A/C back on (it has to be shut off when we're shooting, because of the background noise). The second portion was a lot more intense, with hairbrush and belt added in. Once again, my adrenaline was soaring and I don't remember feeling pain, but I know I must have. In fact, after one very hard hairbrush stroke, I gasped and sucked in some air— and promptly began to cough and choke. "Cut," I spluttered, and as I hacked away, Ralph scrambled to get me some water. I could hear Tony in the background, plaintively crying, "Don't die! Please don't die!"

And then it was time for that "little extra naughty something." Amazingly, even though I had five pairs of eyes on me, I was able to shut them all out and disappear into the scene. I couldn't bury my face in the pillow, as that had to remain visible to the camera, so I turned my head to the side and closed my eyes; I was surprised at how easy it was.

Perhaps this is a rationale on my part, but I think we handled that portion as tastefully as possible. I didn't go over the top with my reactions, and it was only a few minutes at the end, not the primary focus of the video. For spanking enthusiasts, there was plenty of that, and for those who like the sexy stuff, they got to have their little treat too. Overall, it seemed like a well-balanced video with something for everyone.

We finished in about six hours and we all went for dinner at an Italian restaurant in Studio City. This time, John was able to join us and he got a kick out of seeing me post-shoot, all spacey and giggly and bubbling with lingering endorphins. I couldn't believe how much fun this was; I'd thought perhaps the first time was a fluke, but the second time proved to be as much of a joy.

And then there was the post-shoot anticipation and buzz, pictures being posted on the SL site, waiting eagerly for the release. When it finally came out, Tony invited Ralph, John and me to his apartment to watch it.

Yes, if you think that was a bit strange for me, you are correct. There I was, sitting on Tony's couch, with Ralph on my left and John on my right, and *that scene* comes up. I didn't know which way to look as I sat and squirmed, heard Ralph chuckle and John say, "Well!" Watching oneself on video is a bizarre thing to begin with, and I've heard of some spanking video actresses who never watch their own films. I don't mind that, but when I'm watching with friends and the graphic shots appear on the screen, part of me wants to disappear.

The feedback was gratifying and the video sold well, according to Eve and Tony. Funny side note, in case anyone wonders if I got a big fat head over all the extra attention. Not to worry; I had John to keep me in check.

A few months after we had that viewing at Tony's place, John asked me to bring the video over because he wanted to see it again. I obliged and we put it on. He was fairly quiet as the scenes progressed, and then, about half-way through, I heard a soft sound and turned to look at him.

It was a snore. My boyfriend had *fallen asleep* during my spanking video. I guess he could afford to be blasé about it; after all, he could see my bare bottom any time he wanted!

"They didn't start shooting my portion until 4:30. By then it was an inferno in there. But the show must go on, yes? ...Honestly, I don't know how we did it. We were both pouring sweat. I had to stop once, because sweat ran into my eyes and I looked like I was crying. We both forgot our lines, and had to keep re-taking to get them right. At one point, I guess it really showed that we were struggling, because Arthur's girlfriend suddenly called out, "CUT! These people need water, now." We stopped, put the fans on, drank a ton of water, mopped off the sweat, and picked up again. And just kept on persevering."
—from *Southern California Spanked Wives and Girlfriends*, August 16, 2003

One of the most fun things about SCSW was the pre-Shadow Lane party networking, where members would post if they were going and we'd make sure to look for one another once there. A regular poster who called himself Brushman was coming to his first party over Labor Day 2002, so he uploaded a photo in order to be recognized and encouraged others to say hello. I always found his posts clever and he was quite easy on the eyes to boot, so I was eager to meet him.

We met him and his girlfriend on that Friday evening and hit it off immediately. I did a scene with him in one of the suites and was very much impressed with his technique as well as his play personality. By then I'd gotten into the habit, whenever I played with a man who had unusually good presence and proficiency, of tossing out, "Hey! Ever think about doing a video?" The answer was always no, but I figured it was worth a try. So I casually said to Brushman, "Hey! Would you ever want to do a video?" Much to my shock, he answered, "Sure!"

So I introduced him posthaste to Eve, giving his play style great praise and planting the seed. He came to the next party and Eve got more glowing reports about him. Finally, a year later, she decided to cast us together in his first and my third video.

We opened the forum for video name suggestions. As I had done, Brushman also wanted to keep his real first name and change the second. Several ideas were thrown in: Steve Payne? Nope; there was already a femdom named Alexis Payne. Steve Wood? Nah, that sounded like a porn star. I came up with Steve Hertz and people seemed to like that. But then Becca chimed in with: "He's Brushman—how about Steve Fuller, like the Fuller Brush Man?"

Ladies and gentlemen, we had a winner. Becca just named a video star.

* * *

The plot of our video was changed three times, but the final choice sounded brilliant. Called *The Spanking Professor*, it would actually be two videos. The first would be subtitled "Incorrigible Coed," and in that, Steve's college professor Ronald Woodward would be stalked by Charlotte, a relentless student in love with him, played by a newcomer named Raven. It would be revealed during this portion that the professor's wife was an incurable flirt who was rumored to be rather "free and easy" and fooling around on him all over the place. Therefore, Charlotte's argument: "She won't care; go ahead and have an affair with me." Of course, Professor Woodward would have none of this and spanking would ensue.

In the second video, to be subtitled "Faculty Wife," the professor would then go home and take his errant wife to task for all her flirting, her various personal trainers and coaches, and the fact that she refuses to look for a job. Promising premises, right? It didn't quite work out that way. I will preface all the following with this disclaimer: The video turned out fine, SL was thrilled with Steve and we were able to laugh everything off after the fact. But this particular video became the Shoot from Hell, from start to finish.

Because the plot had been revised several times, we didn't get our final scripts until less than a week from the shoot. Poor Steve had *two* scripts to memorize with a fair amount of dialogue, and he was stressing over this. I did my best to reassure him. "Just do the best you can," I encouraged. "The dialogue isn't carved in stone, and a lot of the videos end up being ad-libbed anyway. Just pretend you're doing a scene with [his girlfriend] and be yourself. And you'll be fine once you get there; the shoots are so much fun. They treat us like stars, put out a ton of snacks, you'll see. It will be great."

We were shooting this time at the home of SL star Arthur Syre and his then-girlfriend, Anna Valentina. Arthur often did background work for them as well, both camera and lighting. It was a typical mid-August day—triple digits. I arrived at Arthur's place on Saturday morning; the first thing I noticed was that it was the top floor of a triplex. And once I entered, I quickly realized there was no central air, just a small wall unit bravely whirring away in the corner of the living room. It was already quite warm in there, and I knew that even that meager A/C would be turned off due to the noise. Oh, boy. Add the hot lights and the heat produced by three cameras, and we were looking at a long, scorching afternoon.

Steve was on the couch going over his lines with Raven, who was cute and friendly. Eve had hired her on the recommendation of a trusted friend, and she looked good and seemed to know her lines. I settled in, trying on the outfits Eve had purchased for me. She'd gotten me a cute skirt and sleeveless blouse for the first scene, but the blouse didn't fit. Fortunately, I'd worn a white tank top that day and it looked great with the skirt, so we went with that.

As with the first two shoots, I hadn't eaten anything that morning. Since the last two sets had had good healthy snacks like fruit, veggies, peanut butter and bagels, I figured I'd munch a little something once there, just to keep my blood sugar up but not fill my stomach. But much to my consternation, all there was available to snack on this time was potato chips and cookies. Fortunately, they did have copious quantities of bottled water. We'd need it.

Setup took longer than usual and they started shooting Steve and Raven's portion first around 1:30. While everyone else went into the den area, I sat in the living room, went over my lines and kept an ear on the progress in the next room. Raven and Steve both nailed their opening lines and were ready to begin the spanking. Then things went horribly wrong.

Raven couldn't take a spanking. Not at all. From the first light swats over a thick denim skirt, she was howling OW OW OW, and it wasn't an affectation for the video, either. She called "cut" several times in the first few minutes, imploring Steve to go even lighter. He was barely patting her as it was. They managed to get in a brief spanking, doing the usual skirt-panties-bare progression, but it was clear that there was no way they were going to get an entire video out of this girl.

Eve, who could see where this was going, thought quickly and made a snap decision. She cut the action and came into the living room to speak to me. "This is a disaster," she whispered. "She can't take anything. I'm getting rid of part one. We'll salvage a few minutes of this footage and use it as an introduction to your scene. You're going to be carrying the rest of this video."

Oh, my. Let's review: we now had a thoroughly stressed-out new male star, an aggravated crew, a scrapped video and a set that was about 150 degrees. And I had to come in and help salvage this? Pressure, much?

Eve cut Raven a check for a full day's work even though she'd only put in an hour and sent her home. The crew took a break and Steve came in to join me on the couch. He was upset, not only because Raven had so thoroughly spooked him, but he had spent so much time memorizing that first script for nothing, and he didn't have the second script down as well. I told him once again not to worry, we'd make it work, and we sat and went over our lines. Neither one of us had eaten and we were hot, hungry and lightheaded, but didn't want chips or sweets. Fortunately, Steve had two protein bars with him and he gave me one of them.

I don't remember why we didn't start shooting our portion until 4:30, but by then, the den was in full broil mode. Steve and I bravely tackled our first scene, but as soon as the OTK action began, we were both dripping sweat. Steve kept soaking through his shirt, so we'd have to stop action so he could take it off and Anna would run her blow-dryer over it. My bangs were matted to my forehead and perspiration ran into my eyes. We forgot our lines and had to be cued repeatedly.

And yet, we kept going. Somehow, I went into autopilot and was still able to kick and scream and thrash around, even though I felt like I was going to pass out. Poor Steve was light on me at first because of all of Raven's complaining, but I assured him it was OK, he could (and should) ramp it up, which he eventually did. He never did go the full force I know he can do (and has done in subsequent videos), but I have to cut the guy a break, considering what he'd been through in that earlier scene and the fact that it was so freaking hot.

Finally, the first scene was done and in the can. Immediately the A/C unit and the portable fans were turned back on, water was gulped and we cleaned up as best we could for the next scene. There would be a spanking bench in the second part, so Steve and I rested while they set it up and adjusted the lighting.

Can I just say here what a trouper Steve was? He never lost his good nature, never grumbled. I felt terribly guilty, since I'd waxed rhapsodic to him about how much fun shoots were and this one was anything but. Despite it all, he insisted he *was* having fun and I was helping him get past the Raven incident.

I stripped off the skirt and top and put on the light blue boy-shorts and bra set Eve had gotten for me. As for Steve, he didn't have to worry about his soggy shirt any longer; Eve decreed that he'd do the second portion shirtless. I'm not sure he was all that crazy about the idea, but I knew the female viewers wouldn't object.

The second scene flowed better. By now, Steve and I had relaxed a bit, he'd regained his confidence, and we ad-libbed and bantered a great deal. I discovered how very quick-witted he is; that no matter what I threw his way, he'd have a response. It was still hot as hell, but since I wasn't lying over his lap this time, we didn't have to absorb each other's body heat, and we were both wearing less clothing. So it was bearable.

My strict professor husband did everything in his power to convince me that I didn't need all these other men in my life and that I needed to spend my time a bit more constructively, perhaps with job-seeking. Naturally, I argued and fussed and hurled insults at him, but he was quite unflappable. Damn, but that man's comebacks were impressive. Toward the end, he'd accused me of saying something or another and I protested, "I didn't *say* that!" "No, but you inferred it," he said. *Inferred?* I quipped, "Actually, I implied it. What kind of professor *are* you?" Steve didn't miss a beat; he calmly came back with, "History, dear. And your *butt* is going to be history in about five minutes." Nicely done, my friend.

Our bad luck wasn't quite over yet, however. About two-thirds into the second portion, one of the cameras died. Much cussing and fuming and further delays as they tried to revive it, to no avail. There was no choice but to do the remainder with two cameras. Not a tragedy, but certainly annoying and the last straw. By now, the overall consensus was "let's get this effing thing done already."

The finale had a wind-down chunk of scripted dialogue, but it got thrown out. I wish they hadn't done that, because it was cute—Steve's character finally compromised and told me that if I gave up my trainers, I wouldn't have to get a job after all, and then admonished me that I needed to "practice economy." But that's the way it goes. I sat in his lap at the end, and as I recall, I kept sliding off because I was so sweaty.

But we did it! We had a video despite it all. I knew Tony had one hell of an editing job ahead of him, but he assured me that when he was done, the cuts and retakes would be undetectable.

That night, Tony and Eve, Arthur and Anna, and John and I went out for dinner. Unfortunately, Steve couldn't join us because he had another commitment. All I'd eaten the entire day, with all that activity, was a protein bar, so I was half out of my mind with hunger and could have eaten sawdust. Actually, we went out for Indian food, so for me, sawdust would have been preferable. But I didn't care; I did my best, ordered a salad with chicken in it, which seemed fairly innocuous. When the spices on the chicken peeled off the roof of my mouth, I drank my water and most of John's. It didn't matter—the day was done.

I emailed Tony and Eve, thanking them as always for everything. When Eve wrote back, she said this had been one of the most brutal shoots they had ever endured, but we were great, Steve was amazing and she'd love to work with him again. It was all worth it.

Sure enough, when the finished product came out, I watched it and it was quite seamless. I thought our rivers of perspiration would show on the footage, but for whatever reason, it wasn't that obvious. In the first scene, there's a close-up of Steve's arm and my bottom, and you can see beads of sweat glistening on both. But other than that, we look fine.

We ended up with excellent on-screen chemistry and *The Spanking Professor* remains one of my favorites. Even though Raven's mini-scene with the pitty-pats wasn't the greatest, it was brief, so it had little impact (no pun intended). It served as a good little intro to Steve and me, and we took it from there.

I watched Steve grow into a star over the years, working with several companies and with many of the most beautiful and popular young models. Recently I read that he has retired from videos, and I know he will be missed. I still get a huge kick out of the fact that I got to be his first!

SPANKING EPICS PREMIERES AND ERICA TOPS (RELUCTANTLY)

"Yup, it's true. I'm going to top another girl for the first time ever (and the last, folks!). When Bethany first contacted me and told me about the mother-spanking-daughter scene, my first instinct was no, I can't do that. But then I weighed that one short scene against everything else—working with Keith again, getting to be in Bethany's premier video (which looks like it's going to be awesome!), the whole experience of it—and I realized there was no way I could pass this up. ...So OK, open season, guys—you can tease me all you want! And you men with your F/F fixations, have at it!"

—from *Southern California Spanked Wives and Girlfriends*, February 16, 2004

Early in 2004, Tony, Eve and Butch of Shadow Lane moved away from Southern California to Las Vegas. For a long time, they had been synonymous with the Southern California scene and I couldn't imagine it without them. But I was going to have to anyway.

At the end of January, several of us pooled our resources and put on a big going-away party for the three of them. It was so much fun; we had 22 people, loads of food and drink, a "memory book" for everyone to sign, and we'd written "The Top 10 Reasons Shadow Lane is Moving to Las Vegas." (The #1 reason? The slot machines drown out the sounds of spanking.)

That night, I played my heart out and my butt off, feeling like this was the end of an era. The Shadow Lane parties would continue, but in Vegas now—no more Palm Springs. And all the small local parties that were centered around Tony and Eve would be no more. I had loved having them as neighbors and I felt quite bereft, but it didn't fully hit me until the day after the party. John and I went to brunch; I was tired, sore and feeling low. All John had to say was, "Is someone depressed?" and I starting crying into my pancakes.

209

My spirits were in need of a lift around that time, and they got one, quite unexpectedly.

* * *

I was familiar with the name Bethany Burke; she ran a popular site called "Bethany's Woodshed," which featured spanking stories by various writers. In February 2004, I received email from her, telling of a new endeavor. She was partnering with another production company and was going to start filming her own spanking videos. However, they would be different from the usual; these would be full-length shoots with complex plots, several characters, indoor/outdoor scenes and the production values of mainstream films.

The new company was called Spanking Epics and she had the first video scripted and ready to shoot; she just needed the performers, five total. Would it be all right if she posted about this on SCSW and put out a call for people who might be interested in any of the parts? The shoot would be in Virginia and they would pay for all travel expenses, hotels and meals, along with the standard payment for a spanking video. Of course, I told her yes.

So with Becca's and my blessing, Bethany wrote a detailed post about the upcoming shoot. The plot centered around two 18-year-old schoolgirls, circa 1912, who had been caught cheating on their final exam. The schoolmaster gave them a choice: They'd either fail the exam and have to take the year over, or they could take a spanking from him, then go home and tell their families what they'd done; after that, they could repeat the exam. Naturally, they'd choose the spanking. Further punishment would ensue when both girls went home; a woodshed strapping from a brother-in-law for one and a spanking from an angry widowed mother for the other. However, Mom would also be quite pissed off that this teacher had the nerve to strike her daughter; seems there was a bit of history between them, and she'd go to the school to confront him.

Our members loved the sound of this and the thread was lively with responses and questions. Then Bethany wrote to me privately once again…and asked me if I'd like to play the mother. She realized I was purely a bottom and I wouldn't be too thrilled about doing a topping scene. However, that scene would be very brief, and then I'd get to do a much longer bottoming scene with the schoolmaster. Oh, and she'd gotten Keith Jones to take on that role.

Oh, my. What an incredible adventure—being flown back east, working with Keith again, starring in this new company's premier effort, wearing period costumes. It sounded exciting and I wanted to say yes. But… me, spanking another girl? Ugh.

I had now been in this scene for eight years and had discovered that many women who start out as bottoms eventually tap into their inner tops and experiment with switching. Many of the video bottom females had become tops, especially when they got past a certain age and their opportunities to bottom on camera grew more infrequent.

But for me, this wasn't an option. I didn't have a toppy bone in my body and the idea of spanking anyone gave me the creeps. I certainly didn't want to spank a male. And while I love my female friends, I have no desire to get physically intimate with them in any way. And let's be honest; spanking is an intimate activity, even when sex isn't involved.

So despite my personal skeeve factor over topping, I'd still have to do it on camera *and* make it look real. I didn't see how I could. And yet, how could I turn this opportunity down?

Bethany understood my trepidation and she assured me that I could do this. It would be a home-style discipline scene between mother and daughter in a kitchen, and I would not be taking her OTK; I'd be paddling her with a wooden spoon while she was bent over a table. So I wouldn't actually be in physical contact with her. It would not have to be very long or hard, since she would have already been well worked over by Keith's character. With this new information, I thought about it some more and then told her yes; I knew I'd kick myself repeatedly if I walked away from this.

So we announced on the board that I was playing the mother and Keith was playing the schoolmaster. Bethany kept us updated regularly, letting us know when all the roles were filled and about the sets, including the house they were using that had once been a real schoolhouse in 1910. I took the expected amount of razzing, both for playing a mother and for doing a topping scene. Some of it I could have done without, but for the most part, it was all in good fun and very supportive.

The shoot was scheduled for the weekend of March 13–14, and on March 12, I took a shuttle to LAX and arrived there at 6:30 A.M... for a 9:00 A.M. flight! As I recall, I actually had a meal served to me on that flight; those days are long gone! There was one stopover at Dulles and I caught a commuter plane to Charlottesville, where Bethany picked me up. I liked her immediately.

She took me back to her home, where I greeted Keith and met her husband Jim, her business partners Colin and Angie, her daughter and a couple of her assistants. I also met Lamia DeLion, the stunning 19-year-old who would be playing my daughter. She was a beautiful girl, but a complete Goth; she had purple hair and was wearing a leather dress, studded boots and a long black coat with a silver boa collar. Eslynne Weaver, who would be playing the other schoolgirl, had not arrived yet; she was coming with her husband (who would be playing her brother-in-law) and their baby.

We ate dinner and talked, then Bethany drove Keith and me to the Red Roof Inn, where we each had a room. I was so jazzed that I had a king-sized bed all to myself; you can see I don't get out much! Keith and I hung out together for a while in my room, running our lines. During our confrontation, it was scripted for me to try to slap his face, but he'd block me. "Nahh," Keith said, "there's no way to do that and have it look real. Just hit me."

Huh? I'd never slapped a man's face in my life. "Don't think about it too much," he instructed. "Just aim for the center of my cheek. Don't hit me in the nose, and don't club me in the ear." Easy for him to say.

The next morning we all convened once more at Bethany's and I met Eslynne, her husband Miklos and their 11-month-old daughter, who was a little beauty with red hair and startlingly blue eyes. Mom was lovely too, with long auburn hair and a classically beautiful face like a Renaissance portrait.

She, Lamia and I went upstairs to change and put on makeup. Bethany had vintage dresses for both the girls, and for me, a long black skirt and two blouses (one red, one white). And of course, real drawstring, split-back bloomers. Eslynne put her hair into a demure bun and Lamia's purple tresses disappeared under a wig. They were shooting the scene with Keith and the girls first, so I had time to have a bit of breakfast, look over my lines yet again and have Bethany's daughter attempt to do something with my own hair.

I was supposed to be a 1912 widowed mother, but I definitely did not have Mom hair. What could we do with it? Putting it up would be the usual option, but for me, that was out. Why? Because I hate my ears. They're huge and I never show them. I don't wear my hair up and I don't pull it up into a ponytail, ever. And I sure wasn't about to on camera. So Bethany's daughter fussed with it a bit, pinning up pieces of the sides but leaving most of it down, so I had a much tamer, Mom-ish look. What with the hair, the long skirt and black flats, I thought I looked frumpy, but I guess I was supposed to.

I sat and watched Keith, Lamia and Eslynne tape their scene; they were amazing. Lamia had never been spanked before; she'd done some BDSM photo shoots with simulated action, but this was her first real spanking, so she was quite the trouper. Eslynne was in a domestic discipline marriage and therefore used to spanking, and it worked out well because her character was supposed to be the instigator anyway. Keith didn't hold back with Lamia, but he definitely gave Eslynne more.

He was so good with them, so patient and kind, just as he'd been with Alexandria and me four years ago. It was quite a joy to see him working his magic and how these young women responded to him. The set looked amazing with all the authentic touches, including old-fashioned wooden desks and other items from that era.

Next, they shot a brief outdoor scene with the two girls and then it was time for Keith and me to have our confrontation scene in the schoolroom, where his character decides that's what's good for the daughter is also good for the mother. It wasn't very long, but it was quite vigorous, starting with heated words, then a brisk OTK spanking capped off by a caning and paddling.

I was particularly nervous about the slap to Keith, but I was determined to get it right the first time. When he let me up from his lap so he could go get the implements, I was supposed to slap him. One little problem, though—Keith forgot about the slap and after I got on my feet, he gripped my left wrist hard, scolding me and saying, "Don't you move!" Oh dear—I'm left-handed!

It ended up playing out well, though; I wasn't acting when I forcefully shook his hand off, hissing, "Let go of me—let *go*!" Finally he dropped my hand and I clocked him. The camera got a great close-up of his shocked, angry face. The caning/paddling that followed was intense, with more heated arguing and my furious resistance. And as usual, I don't remember feeling a thing, because I was so fueled with endorphins.

After lunch, we went back to Bethany and Jim's house and they prepped the dining room/kitchen area for my scene with Lamia. As with everything else, Bethany went all out with the details—I had a full-length apron and the table was set up with pie-crust dough, flour, peach filling and a rolling pin, and they'd rented an old stove from that time period. Everything was ready... I just had to do this and get it over with.

We exchanged our pre-spanking scripted dialogue, and then it was time for me to drag her over to the table, bend her over and paddle her with the kitchen spoon. When I lifted her skirt and undid her bloomers, I cringed; that poor girl was already marked like crazy from Keith. I shut off my mind and went on autopilot, ad-libbing scolding. That part was easy; I'd certainly heard enough "Top Speak" over the years, so I could call it up and parrot it myself. "Aren't you ashamed?" "I work my fingers to the bone so you could go to that school and you do *this*?" "Keep still!"

However, that had to be the one of the wimpiest paddlings in spanking video history. I rapped her smartly with the spoon several times, but I didn't put any force into it. Nevertheless, she got plenty red and hollered in protest, so it looked reasonably real. And when it was done, I knew for certain there was no inner top within me. I didn't like doing that segment of the scene and I hate watching it to this day. But it was worth it.

I then had to do one more quick scene with Lamia, and then we shot a fun alternate ending that was used as a DVD bonus. In that, Keith and I were now a married couple and he was disciplining me, and my daughter would come in when he had me facing the wall with my skirt up post-strapping. What the crew didn't tell me was that when Lamia entered the scene, she wouldn't be in costume. So when she walked in and yelled, "Ma, what are you doing?" I turned around, saw her in all her purple-haired, black-leather glory, and I completely lost it, doubling over with laughter.

The next morning we all caravanned to the house with the woodshed, so Eslynne and Miklos could shoot their scene. Their little girl had been a perfect angel the day before—didn't cry, didn't squawk or fuss, seemed very content. Eslynne was so serene and patient with her and she was fine—as long as she was with her mom or, if her mom was shooting, her dad. But Sunday morning, it was almost as if she could sense that both Mom and Dad were going to be busy and she'd be apart from them, because she was clingy and fussy and Eslynne couldn't get her makeup on, so she asked me to hold E, who didn't like that in the least. And as soon as Eslynne and Miklos left the house to head for the woodshed, E burst into tears.

She cried and cried and cried... not just baby fussing, but big fat tears spurting, and she was inconsolable. I was alone with her and I did everything I could think of to calm her down. I held her, jiggled and rocked her, hummed to her, tried to distract her with her toys, her Cheerios, the dog. She wouldn't have any of it. She fought hard to get

215

down, but whenever I'd put her on the carpet, she'd crawl to the front door where she saw her mother exit, sit in front of it and sob piteously. It broke my heart; I wanted to cry myself! After about 45 minutes (which felt like three hours), Eslynne came back in and E was immediately fine; she stopped crying and went right to sleep, exhausted. So much for my worrying that she was scarred for life.

Just for fun, Keith and I shot another bonus scene in the woodshed, pretending we were on a tour and we'd snuck away from our group to check out the barn…and Keith discovered the razor strap on the wall. After that, we were done! I flew home that night and came straggling into my door at 1:45 A.M., completely wiped out. I took the next day to sleep and catch up with email and phone calls and such, and then wrote a full report for SCSW.

The thread about the shoot bloomed to 143 replies, with Bethany and Jim both chiming in and waxing enthusiastic about how well the weekend went and how good the film was looking so far. The Spanking Epics website was built and pictures, synopsis and trailer were put up. The trailer featured all of us, including me right after my daughter tells me that the schoolmaster spanked her—slamming my fist down onto the dining room table and making flour fly, and yelling, "That *bastard!*"

The photo close-up of Keith gripping the paddle looked fabulous and ominous—until someone noticed his wrist-watch and pointed out those didn't exist in 1912. Oops! Thank goodness for Photoshop. When the DVD came out, it was well reviewed; the consensus seemed to be that the Spanking Epics premier was a success and they had many more creative projects ahead. I thought my participation was a one-shot deal, but I was to be very pleasantly surprised in the future.

FURTHER ADVENTURES IN KINKDOM

"Have you ever gone to a wedding, a nice prim and proper occasion, having to behave sweetly and demurely (well, as much as your personality will allow), after engaging in a LOT of spanking play (including cracking a @#$%ing hairbrush with your butt) and still stinging from it all under your dressy outfit? If not, I highly recommend it, it's quite delicious."
—from *Southern California Spanked Wives and Girlfriends*, July 19, 2004

As the first decade of 2000 progressed, I continued to have miscellaneous spanking/BDSM adventures apart from video shoots, many of which I detailed on SCSW or on my blog. Rather than deal with them chronologically, I thought I'd devote a chapter to some of the random highlights.

John and I were once comped into a downtown L.A. club on a Friday evening, in exchange for doing a BDSM mini-show. Not with each other; he would be playing with a female friend of ours and I would be participating in a demonstration of whips with famous bullwhip artist Robert Dante.

Whips?? Yes, you read that correctly. My first answer was a most emphatic *no*; I'd seen what whips could do and I wanted nothing to do with them. John suggested I go to Robert's website, read more about him and think about it. If we went there and I decided I couldn't go through with it, I could back out and he'd still do his part, so it would be fine. *Come on, Erica,* I thought. *Stretch a little. Get out of your comfort zone.* And after all, the night would be free.

Robert Dante turned out to be a gentle and soft-spoken man in perhaps his late 40s or early 50s with a full head of silver hair, and I liked him right away. He sat me down and talked with me for a while, explained what he would be doing with me and about the illusion he'd create. The whip would crack *near* me, but not *on* me, and then it would drape around my arm or waist or whatever, giving the appearance that he'd struck me. The whip looked scary, but

217

somehow I trusted him instantly and knew he wouldn't hurt me.

I changed into black lingerie with stockings and high heels, and we played on a stage with a pole to which I was tied. He cracked the whip all around me—my legs, arms, waist, chest—and true to his word, he made sure I felt light impact but no pain. I heard the loud snap and felt the whoosh, but nothing more. I knew I was in the presence of skill, competence and complete focus, and ended up having fun with it. After the demo, he untied me and flogged me while I clung to the pole and writhed.

Did I mention that the club we were comped into was a swing club? John and I had friends who dabbled in swinging, but we'd never tried it ourselves. So that evening, we experimented with (read: fucked) the host couple who had taken a liking to us. Interesting indeed, quite the different and surreal experience, and something we don't regret doing, but we had no desire to do it again. As much as I love sport spanking with many partners, that love doesn't extend to sport screwing.

The host couple enjoyed us both and invited us to return; we politely declined.

* * *

And speaking of s-e-x...

John and I are not poly-players—we don't seek out sex from our other play partners. When I play with other men, spanking is my main course and dessert, not an appetizer that segues in sexual entrees. However, I won't lie—every now and then over my years in this scene, there have been times when the chemistry between my partner and me is so explosive, I do want a bit more than spanking.

The same goes for John. Some femdoms like to order their male subs to sexually service them. I can't really blame them, in John's case. John is... well, let's just say that his naked body is magnificent. If he says, "But honey, what if she wants me to...?" my standard reply is, "Whatever, sweetie. Have fun. Use protection." Honestly, I don't care. They're already doing things to him that I don't want to think about, so what's one more?

John has a name for this play-and-sex blurring: Scene Sex. If the sex is an offshoot of a spanking/BDSM scene, a natural progression, not just a sex act unto itself, then it's acceptable between us. It may sound like a rationale to some, but it works for us. His one rule: "Do whatever you want, but don't fall in love with another guy and leave me for him." As if that could happen. No man I've played with has ever tried to come between us; they have all been completely respectful of John.

I wish I could say the same for some of the femdoms John has known. A couple of them, in the past, made it clear that they do not approve of his having a girlfriend and they did their best to sabotage our relationship. I've never been in a catfight, but I wanted to slap these individuals into next week. Sorry, ladies. You can play with my love, you can do unspeakable things to him, you can use and abuse him however you see fit and to his heart's desire. But you don't get to own him; you need to give him back when the scene is over. And (give or take a few marks) please return him the way he came to you, thank you very much.

Back to the subject. In February 2001 at the Shadow Lane party, I met a man who had come from back East to attend. The attraction was instant and mutual and we had a wonderful first scene in one of the suite parties. We did not exchange emails and all I had was a first name, so I had no way of following up with him.

However, he showed up again at the next SL party in Palm Springs, September 2001. This time, we played privately in his room a couple of times, and things were rather steamy, but we cut them short before they went too far. He teased a lot, though, telling me he had a crush on me and he'd love to be able to "have his way with me" just once.

Cut to February 2002, time for another SL party at the Sportsmen's Lodge. Once again, M was flying out for it. He didn't want to carry all his spanking implements on the plane, so he asked if he could UPS them to me and I could bring them to him at the Lodge after he arrived. I said yes, that would be fine. And then I thought about it...

The opportunity was there; it was undeniable. I had to at least try.

So I asked John, "Sweetie? M is coming to Shadow Lane and he'll be at Sportsmen's Lodge Thursday night. I have his toys; would it be OK if I brought them to him on Friday morning before the party, and then we'll play, and then, uh…?"

John just shook his head and said, "Oh, you slut." Which I knew meant, "Sure, go for it—you have my blessing." Have I mentioned that I love that man?

So that Friday morning, I went to M's hotel room with the UPS package. He opened it and started shuffling through all the straps and paddles, looking for his cane. I mischievously started grabbing fistfuls of the packing peanuts and flinging them all over the room, saying, "Perhaps it will be easier to find if you get rid of some of these!" He then made me get on my hands and knees and crawl around, picking them all back up while he struck me with a crop. The morning was off to a fun start.

Later that evening at the party's vendor fair, I was working the Shadow Lane table and I watched as John and M greeted one another. "Hey, M!" John said heartily, pumping his hand. "Good to see you again! How are you doing?"

"Great, thanks," M replied.

"So you got in last night? What'd you do today?"

M grinned, and I blushed mightily. Well, at least John didn't ask *who* he did today. "Nothing much, really."

"Yeah," John smiled, "that's pretty much what Erica did today too, she just kinda screwed around." I had to turn away and focus on someone who was looking through the stacks of videos, because I knew by now I was probably a charming shade of purple.

Late Sunday night, John and I went to M's room to retrieve the box of implements, so I could UPS them back to him after he got home. He gave me some money and we hugged goodbye. Then I watched as my boyfriend and playmate exchanged a man-hug; M clapped John on the back and said, "Thanks, man, you're a trouper!"

Surreal? You bet. But also pretty damned hot. I loved the forbiddenness of it.

* * *

I may have preferred spanking parties, but I don't want my readers to think I didn't have any fun at the BDSM gatherings John and I attended. I have some fond memories of specific party incidents, including the following.

It was at a private house party; the host had play parties about once a month. This one in particular had a special theme: It was a "Slave Auction." The tops/doms would put up their subs for "sale," and the highest bidders got to do a scene with them.

I can imagine what everyone is thinking: Erica, in a slave auction? Has the world as we know it come to an end? But it was all in good fun, quite tongue in cheek—the currency was Monopoly money, and each participant got a set amount. The "slaves" didn't have to do a scene with the individuals who won them if they really didn't want to, but of course, the sense of obligation was there anyway. So we all hoped for desirable bidders.

When it was my turn, I stood up on the platform and John introduced me as Slave Erica, a bratty bottom whose specialty was taking a good spanking. The bidding began; I was flattered when several men offered higher and higher monetary amounts in hopes of winning me.

But as the stakes increased, they dropped out one by one, and the lone persistent bidder was a creeper. Come on, we all know them. He'd come to the party by himself and spent most of the evening standing off to the side, staring at various women, not speaking. He was older, unkempt and very unappealing. *Oh, crap,* I thought. *No way am I going to play with this guy. Please, please, someone else bid!*

I knew I could refuse the scene, but I wanted to be a good sport. If my winner were even halfway decent, I'd go along. But this guy was utterly gross; I cringed as he leered at me. Looks like I was going to have to be a bitch and say thanks but no thanks.

Just then, another man bid for me. I looked over in the direction of his voice and... woo*HOO!* Jackpot! He was all in black, with dark hair and eyes and a mustache, trim and quite attractive.

Creepo bid again; so did Handsome. It was down to the two of them. I kept casting beseeching looks toward Handsome as if to say "Pleeeeeeaaase, keep bidding! Save me!" But then he ran out of money.

My heart sank, until I saw what the enterprising gentleman did next. He turned to the men around him, including John, and said, "Gimme some money, would you?" He was so charming about it, and I guess they all wanted to see him win—I watched gleefully as several men pressed fake bills into his waiting hands. He then had more money than anyone else and he won me.

Creepo glared at all of us, but said nothing and skulked away. I went into another room and happily did a fun spanking/paddling scene with Handsome (whose name was Robert). He was more into D/s than spanking, but we enjoyed each other anyway. I saw him one more time at another gathering, and then he moved out of state. But I'll never forget the image of him standing there, his hands open, wheedling Monopoly money out of his competitors!

* * *

On one of our anniversaries, John and I went to a nearby park. It was a hot August night around 11 P.M. and no one else was around, so John made me walk on the bike path by myself, with him several feet ahead watching me. What's the big deal about that, you might ask. Just one itty-bitty detail—he'd removed all my clothes, save for my stockings and heels.

I'd known for a while by now that I had a strong exhibitionistic streak, but this was taking it to a new level. It was one thing to bare my bottom or my body in places where it was sanctioned, such as a party or a video shoot. To get naked in a park, which was quite illegal and therefore risky, was another.

222

So I did my model-runway walk down the path, backlit by the moon, trembling all over with a cocktail of nerves and arousal thrumming in my blood. All we needed was for a police car to cruise by and we'd be screwed, but thank goodness, they must have all been enjoying their evening doughnuts at the time. John then retrieved a blanket from the emergency bag in my trunk and we found a semi-private area on the grass behind a large tree.

That was my first foray into outdoor sex—oh, wait. I forgot about that one time with John on a side street off of Melrose Avenue in West Hollywood—up against a transformer. Good times. Mind you, I'm not advocating risky public sex. But for someone like me, so closeted and cautious all my life, it was freeing to be a bit wild.

When we were done, John gathered my clothes, wrapped me in the blanket and helped me back to the car; I could barely walk, I was so out of my head with excitement. Something about the forbiddenness and the fear of getting caught enhanced this adventure greatly. But it was time to take our little show home and continue it in private.

* * *

Speaking of the police—we've had them called on us three times. The first time was early in our relationship when John lived in an apartment in North Hollywood. It was July 4 and all the neighbors were home, and we'd accidentally left a window open. Four cops showed up on his doorstep; two of them (one female) came in to talk with me and the other two took John outside. Fortunately, we both told the same story and they believed us when we said it was consensual and there was no abuse happening.

They wanted to see my driver's license, which was in my wallet in the bedroom. I started to go in there and the female followed me. Nosy! Then I remembered that the bed was strewn with spanking toys, so I dashed ahead of her, snatched the bedspread from the floor and flung it over the strap, paddle and hairbrush just as she entered behind me.

The next two times occurred at his house. The second time was pretty much a carbon copy of the first—four cops, two with me (one of them female) and two with him. Lots of questions; John said one of the cops with him was clearly trying to keep from snickering. Once again, we managed to convince them that we were just having a special sort of fun and I was unharmed.

The third cop visit was different and a great deal more unnerving. This time, we hadn't even been playing! It was a Sunday morning and for whatever reason, the dogs on John's block were in full cry, barking incessantly for a half-hour or more. John and I were lazing around in bed and he pinned me and started tickling me, and I yelped at him to stop it. That was it. Certainly not anywhere near the racket we'd make when we were playing.

We got up and while John went into the shower, I put on his bathrobe and started to brush my teeth. Suddenly there was a loud BAM BAM BAM on his front door, so forceful it rattled the shower door. "Police! Come out now!" John opened the window by the shower and peeked outside; there were two cops with guns drawn, and one of them whirled around, pointed his weapon and yelled, "Come out, NOW!"

John scrambled out of the shower and, dripping wet, pulled on shorts. I was so startled that I walked out onto his front deck with the toothbrush still in my mouth. One of them had evidently seen way too many cop shows; he was Mr. Alpha Tough Guy, demanding that I put my hands behind my head and feeling inside the robe pockets. I was mortified, as the robe was huge on me and the sash was slipping, threatening to fall open and completely expose me. "Can she at least tie her robe?" John asked. "In a minute," Alpha Cop said.

"We got a call about a disturbance with barking dogs and someone thought there was domestic violence going on." Meanwhile, all the dogs were still in cacophonous chorus. John said, "You hear the dogs now? Do you see any violence going on? This is what we live with—the dogs bark." The cop said, "Well, we were told that someone was heard crying 'No, stop it.'"

Oh, for Christ's sake. Enough was enough. Obviously, one of John's neighbors doesn't like us.

Some women have spanking policeman fantasies. I'm not one of them. Cops don't turn me on in the least; I don't feel like messing with someone who could blow my head off. And I knew that if they didn't believe us, they could haul John away and then we'd have a huge mess.

So I pulled the robe tight around me, sat on the bench on John's deck and tried not to tremble. John, on the other hand, kept his cool. When they asked if they could search his house, he asked if they had probable cause. No, they didn't. He then offered to walk through the house with one of them, and he and the non-Alpha Cop went inside. "Can I go in and spit out my toothpaste?" I blurted around the toothbrush still sticking out of my mouth. Alpha Cop let me go into the bathroom, but then I had to go back outside.

When John and the other cop came back, they asked us if we'd gotten these types of calls before. Uh oh. No point in lying; they surely must have a record of the last visit, at least. So John took a beat, shrugged, dropped his voice and said, "Well, here's the story…" And he told them everything; about our kink, about how I love being spanked, how it's all part of the game for me to scream and holler "no" and "stop," but I really like it.

The cops stood there speechless and I turned six shades of crimson. John wrapped it up with, "If you don't believe me, I'll show you on the computer; she's all over the Internet." By now, they'd let us stand together, and I buried my face in John's chest.

"Uh… that won't be necessary," Alpha Cop muttered. "I can see that she's all right and that she's not afraid." "Only of *you!*" I couldn't resist retorting. They asked us a few more questions, said "Your secrets are safe with us," (gee, thanks a lot), wished us a good day and left.

Side note: two of John's neighbors ended up getting citations for their dogs disturbing the peace. It's been much quieter since then.

* * *

Late in 2002, my aforementioned friend Jesse wrote to the Dr. Phil show, just for the hell of it. She explained who

225

she was and what she was into, and posed the question to him, "Why? What's your take on why we like spanking so much?" She didn't expect to get an answer, but suddenly, she was bombarded with emails from various contacts at the show, asking her to come on the program. Since this was out of the question, she told the producers that if they wanted, she'd pass this along to a couple of other people who might be interested. Then she told them about Eve Howard and about me.

When this was first presented to me, my reaction was, *what the hell, why not.* I wrote to one of the producers, sent her a picture and told her my own story. Within 24 hours, *I* was getting bombarded with emails and then phone calls. It seemed that the Dr. Phil show was highly interested in us. My primary contact, R, said they loved the question and thought it would make for a fun segment.

At first, caught up in the excitement, I said I'd appear in person. My exhibitionist side had taken over and I thought, *so people will see me, so what? I have nothing to hide or to be ashamed of.* Then I talked to John, who in essence said, "What the hell are you thinking?"

I wrote back to R and said I was sorry, I hadn't thought things through. I'd not only be outing myself, but my boy-friend by association, and there could be a lot of repercus-sions that I didn't want. I figured that would be that, but she called me the next day and begged me to do it anyway, but over the phone. She said I could use a fake name and be completely anonymous; they loved how articulate I sounded and that even though they might be able to get someone else in the scene to do it, they wanted me. When she put it that way, how could I say no?

On the show, they make these phone-ins look rather spontaneous, but they are anything but. I had to sign release forms and do a phone interview with R so she could have a background of how I got into spanking and why I like it so much.

R then took my extensive interview and boiled it down to a question I could pose on the air. On the scheduled day, they called me on the phone to hook me into their system and so I could listen to the segments before mine. So, while

I sat there listening to two sisters bitching about their hypochondriac mother and a wife whose husband gave her a weekly household allowance of $10, I read and reread my question, because I was supposed to sound upbeat and not have any "ums" or other pauses.

The segment right before mine was another phone question, and it was intimidating. The woman was friends with a married couple and she knew that the wife was cheating—since she's as fond of the husband as much as she is of the wife, should she tell the husband what she knows? Dr. Phil basically told her that it's not her job to fix the world and to mind her own business, and she was left looking rather foolish. I was not about to let him do that to me.

Then it was my turn... I heard him say, "OK, we have Louise on the phone (yes, I used my middle name; it was R's idea), and she says sometimes she likes it a little kinky—Louise, what's your question?" I read my question, which went like this:

"Dr. Phil, ever since I was about five, I've been fascinated by spanking. I was not spanked as a child, but I made my Ken doll spank my Barbie doll, and whenever my friends got it, I wanted to know all the details. [Had to pause for a big audience laugh here] Cut to seven years ago, I found an ad in the back of a magazine for a spanking organization; I joined and have been hooked ever since. I discovered there are thousands of people like me and I love it. I get weak in the knees just hearing 'You're in BIG trouble, young lady.' [again, pause for laughing] So, my question is, WHY do I like spanking so much? What's your take on this?"

He didn't answer at first, so I said, teasingly, "Are you still there?" More laughs. He said, "Yeah, I'm still here," and then he completely bailed, asking the audience what *they* thought. One woman said she thought I sounded like a freak—nice! He asked me if *I* thought I was a freak. I firmly said no, I do not, I am very confident in my sexuality, I feel good about what I do, and all I can say is, "Don't knock it till you've tried it!" Big laughs.

The next woman he asked, who sounded a little more on the ball, said, "It sounds like she's found her niche, and she doesn't really need you!"

After a few more audience reactions, he gave a little canned spiel about how he could go into all kinds of psycho-babble about the origins of fetishes, but basically, he thought that whatever happens between consenting adults is fine, as long as no one is hurt and it doesn't interfere with one's job, children, etc.

He then asked me what I thought of that, and I replied that I figured he'd say something like that. In fact, I added, I was calling on behalf of a group of friends who were fans of his, and we all suspected he'd be cool about this; truth be told, we thought maybe he might like it himself!

The audience exploded with laughter, and for a brief moment, the good doctor looked rather nonplussed. Then he sputtered, "I consider myself rather avant-garde—but I think I'll leave the spanking to you!" And that was the end of that.

After a commercial break, Dr. Phil asked the audience what they thought of my question—was it worth the show's time? Did they find it entertaining? Over the phone, I heard a lot of clapping, then he said, "Well, there's your morbid curiosity happening!" Cheap shot, but I guess he had to have the last laugh.

I wrote to R and asked her how she thought it went. I wondered if it would air or if it would be considered too edgy. She wrote back:

"You were great and I thought the segment worked. I do know that Dr. Phil was a little uncomfortable but I don't think the segment will be cut. We all loved it!"

Well, how about that. And the segment did air. They saved it and aired it in February 2003—during sweeps! (For those unfamiliar with the term, *sweeps* are television rating periods. Shows often save their best episodes for sweeps months.) Not only that, but in the promos for that particular show, the clip they showed as a teaser featured the voice of yours truly, saying I was fascinated with spanking.

I think if I'd allowed it, Dr. Phil and his audience could have made me look like a fool and yes, a freak. But I didn't let them; I held my ground and came on strong and confident. I was proud of that.

* * *

Over the years, I've met a lot of interesting people in both scenes. When John and were first getting to know one another, he introduced me to a good friend of his I'll call M. She was about five-foot-ten with long hair, an athletic body and beautiful eyes. We went out a couple of times, and she joined us when we went to a spanking workshop at Threshold. I liked her.

One Sunday after we'd seen her the night before, John and I were having brunch and chatting about her. I knew she preferred women, so I asked, conversationally, "Has M ever been with a man, do you know?"

John hesitated, cleared his throat and replied, "Well, no... there's something I need to tell you about M."

"What?"

"Well... you saw *The Crying Game*, right?"

Huh? What did that have to do with anything? "Yeah, why?"

"You remember that one particular scene?"

Who could see *The Crying Game* and not remember that scene? Stephen Rea's character takes that stunningly beautiful woman home, they start to get busy and then Rea realizes his date has a...

"NO!" I yelped, nearly choking on my pancakes.
"Yes," John said.

He then went on to explain to me that M was a pre-op transgender. She had had several cosmetic surgeries to feminize her body and face—breast job, cheek implants, her hairline lowered. She'd even had her Adam's apple shaved down, and her vocal cords were altered so that her voice was husky but no longer masculine. She'd been taking female hormones for years, she'd legally changed her name and essentially lived as a woman. But she was still considered pre-op because she hadn't had the surgery to alter her genitalia.

I was amazed. I hadn't even guessed; was it my naïveté, or was she especially convincing? Probably a combination of the two.

You know, there have been times in my life that I've cursed being female; there are a lot of inconveniences, mostly physical. Periods. Hormone hell. Worries about breast and ovarian cancer, and all the other things that can go wrong with a woman's parts. Society's dictate to remain young and fresh-faced. But overall, I love being a woman. I love my body and how it works, how it interacts and connects with a man's body. I enjoy feeling sexy and flirty and feminine. And I can't imagine for the life of me hating my own gender; feeling as if I'm one sex in my mind, then looking in the mirror and seeing the opposite sex. It was bad enough all those years, feeling out of step with the rest of the world, but at least I was comfortable with the sex I was born to.

Therefore, I gained a powerful respect for transsexuals/transgenders (Ts, for short) for what they have to go through and how they have the courage to go forward and make such deeply personal and fundamental changes.

Several years later, M had a birthday and she invited us to join her celebration. John and I met with her and a group of her girlfriends at a restaurant; they'd reserved a banquet table and we had balloons and streamers and a wonderful dinner. At one point, I looked around the table at John, M and her gal pals, and was struck with a thought that made me stifle a giggle. *Holy crap. I'm the only one at this table with ovaries.* All the women were Ts.

Dinner was followed by a show at the *Queen Mary*, a club that was known for its drag shows (it has since closed). I'd heard of it but never been; the show was hilarious and I remember that evening with great fondness. You don't find nights like that one in the vanilla world!

* * *

I've never been much for BDSM fetishwear. When we went to those parties, I made do with various black outfits; I had no interest in leather or latex. John wanted to buy me a corset, but I told him no. For one thing, they are obscenely expensive and I didn't want him spending all that money on something so frivolous, and for another, I happen to like breathing.

Our friends A and C were going to a BDSM costume ball at a place called *Club Stiletto*, because C was doing a photo shoot there. They invited John and me and another couple and got us comped in (I certainly got a lot of comps in my day, didn't I), and John said, "Oh, you have to let me buy you an authentic fetish outfit." I really didn't want it, especially since it wasn't even a play party, just a posing party. But he insisted, so we went shopping.

I ended up with a black latex skirt and sleeveless latex tank top. When I say these things fit like second skin, I am not exaggerating. The top was easier to put on, since it had a zipper down the front. But the skirt was simply a very small, narrow column, and getting that thing on required a lot of powder first and then a great deal of pulling and tugging and inching it on. I had to go commando, since there was no way I could wear underwear; even the skimpiest thong would have made lines.

Can I say I don't understand what people like about these clubs? It was quite the fancy venue and I watched the parade of very attractive people with very expensive fetish clothing sashaying in after the valets took their cars. Industrial music pounded throughout the place and some people were dancing, but most of them were standing around talking. Although I don't see how they could hear one another, since the music was so loud. I found the place tedious and my outfit dreadfully hot and uncomfortable, but I thought what the hell, it's another experience to chalk up. Stick it out and it will be over soon.

Eventually, nature called and I went to the ladies' room. Once in the stall, I tried to lift the skirt, but it clung to my legs like shrink-wrap. Plucking at the bottom, I attempted to peel it upward; with a SNAP, the skirt rolled up all at once like an old-fashioned window shade and ended in a tight little roll at my waist.

I did my business, stood and pushed at the bundle to unroll it back down. It wouldn't budge. It was stuck to itself and that bunched-up latex at my waist *would not move.* If I'd been wearing panties, I would have walked out of the stall and asked for help; that's how bad it was. But I wasn't about to do so buck-ass naked.

So I stood in the stall for several minutes, fuming and cursing to myself, wrestling with that freaking skirt— finally, I was able to get it rolled back down into place. I can't even begin to imagine how ridiculous that would have looked, had it been filmed. When I came out, John and the others said they'd been concerned because I'd taken so long. They had a damn good laugh when I told them what happened.

I wore that latex tank top once or twice more. The skirt? Never again.

* * *

When I first joined the Shadow Lane member site and was spending time in their chat room, I befriended a lovely woman whose screen name was EllieO. She was bright, funny and a late bloomer in the scene like me, so it was great fun to watch her own journey unfolding.

A favorite party memory is one in which I surprised her by setting her up to play with Keith Jones at a Shadow Lane weekend. After pre-arranging things with him, I found her in the Riviera ballroom, grabbed her hand and said, "Come with me; someone wants to talk to you." I then delivered her to Keith, who fixed her with *that look* and said, "Are you Ellie? I have a bone to pick with you."

Oh, her face—part absolutely thrilled and part deer in headlights! They went off to play and when she came back to the ballroom, she was soaring six feet above the floor. I'll never forget her coming over to where I was sitting, leaning down and whispering, "You're in my will—you want the Porsche or the pearls?"

EllieO met G through the SL personals and in July 2004, they got married. John and I were invited to the wedding in Northern California; it was on a Sunday afternoon. John was having a very busy time with work and he'd been sick, so he suggested I make a weekend out of it and go on my own.

My feverish little mind went to work on how I could fully capitalize on this, and I remembered that one of my favorite play partners at the time also lived in Northern California. Long story short, I contacted him and asked if we could coordinate something that Saturday, and he was all for it.

So, with John's full blessing, I flew to No. CA on Saturday and took a shuttle to a nearby Best Western. I had to switch rooms; they'd put me in a room right at the top of the stairs above the lobby and I knew that would be problematic. Fortunately, the room at the far end of the hall was available.

Late that afternoon, Joe showed up and we played long and vigorously; he broke a hairbrush on me. After dinner, more play. I went to bed a sore and happy girl.

The next morning, he came by the room again and gave me one more spanking before I showered/washed my hair/dressed up/made up. It was a hot day, so I was wearing a sleeveless turquoise shift dress and white sandals. The dress had been given to me by my buddy Dolores Cortez, who'd worn it in one of her videos.

Joe drove me to the wedding, I thanked him profusely and he took off. Now I had to switch gears from kinky to vanilla; Ellie might have been a fellow spanko, but this was a vanilla gathering and I had to mind my Ps and Qs. Easier said than done.

After a beautiful ceremony, there was a reception and buffet luncheon. Along with family, colleagues and other friends, Ellie and G had invited a small group of spankos, and the plan had been to seat us all at the same table so we could chat among ourselves without worrying about non-spanking tablemates. However, it didn't quite work out—because of unforeseen circumstances, our table ended up with one vanilla couple.

We tried to be subtle and discreet, but as the champagne flowed, it got more difficult. One woman knocked over her drink and her husband loudly said, "I think she should be spanked, don't you?" And the matron of honor, who was quite adorable but very outspoken, kept saying every few minutes to anyone within earshot while pointing at me: "She's a movie star! Did you know she's a movie star? Oooh, I'm sitting with the movie star! Hey, take a picture of me and the movie star!" I was getting a few strange looks and I'm sure some people were wondering, "Just who the hell *is* she?"

Later, a few of us were in the ladies' room and someone complimented my dress. I told of its origin, and the aforementioned matron of honor shrieked, "Oooh! Get it off of her; we can sell it on Ebay!" So three women descended on me and we playfully tangled as they pretended they were going to strip off my dress. We thought we were alone in the bathroom… and then a toilet flushed. The stall at the far end opened and a woman who looked a bit like Ellie came out, smiled at us, washed her hands and left without a word.

Oooops.

We told Ellie about the incident, describing the woman, and she laughed, "Ah, that was my cousin." Double oooops. However, Ellie didn't bat an eyelash; she wasn't in the least bit concerned and her cousin hadn't said anything about it. She was such a good sport about what came to be known as "the rowdy table." As for that one vanilla couple at our table, they seemed quite unfazed by the naughty kids. I would have loved to eavesdrop on their conversation after they left!

STAND CORRECTED

"Once we started, it was magic. We just came alive, ill-nesses forgotten, the energy ran high, the lines flowed, the chemistry crackled. Devlin is every bit as verbal as I am, so we had incredible dialogue. I can't say anything about the spanking, because truth be told, I was so high on endorphins and Sudafed, I don't remember feeling a thing."

—from *Southern California Spanked Wives and Girlfriends*, February 22, 2005

I was dying to do another shoot for Shadow Lane, but Eve was running out of choices of tops. I'd already worked with three of their regulars (Keith, Ralph and Steve) and she preferred not to pair the same people twice. Then Eve asked me if I'd like to work with Devlin O'Neill, writer of the *A Maid For All Seasons* book series.

We'd never officially met, but I knew who he was and I'd seen him at Shadow Lane. Friends spoke highly of him and Eve said he was a pleasure to work with. He'd recently joined our SCSW board as well. I told her yes. She then suggested that since we were both writers, we should collaborate on our script.

How fun! Devlin and I decided to play exaggerated versions of ourselves: He'd be a writer about to publish a book about a girls' school with corporal punishment and, as his editor, I'd take exception to his subject matter, saying it's just masturbation fodder and schools like this could never really exist. Then I'd edit the book to the point where it becomes a farce—and hand it in to the publisher without Devlin's approval.

We emailed the script back and forth, adding notes and edits in various text colors, and when we had what we thought was pretty close to final, we sent it to Eve, who approved most of it with a few minor tweaks. With the script finalized, we ran lines over the phone.

The shoot was scheduled for February 20 and Devlin was going to drive us to Vegas. He'd stay at a friend's house and I'd occupy a spare bedroom in Butch's house.

In a case of spectacularly rotten timing, we both came down with colds right before the shoot. We were quite the pair on the drive, popping Sudafed and lozenges. The drive took seven hours due to rain and a couple of accidents, but we finally made it.

After a nice dinner out, Eve showed me the dresses and lingerie she'd bought for me; everything was lovely. My throat was very sore, so she made me a hot toddy with tea, lemon, sugar and a shot of whiskey. That knocked me out and I was happy to settle into my room. I felt like a queen in a four-star hotel—I had my own bathroom, an A/C and heat register inside my room, a huge closet, and Eve had stocked the bathroom with lots of little luxuries.

Despite being tired and sick, I was too excited to sleep much. The next morning, I woke up with no voice. I'd open my mouth to speak and all that would come out was a hoarse croak. We were supposed to shoot that afternoon— what the hell was I going to do now? How could I deliver all that dialogue, not to mention the screaming and yelling, without a voice?

Tony and Eve took it in stride; Eve directed me to rest my voice, and to drink hot tea with honey when we went to lunch. Devlin wasn't feeling well either, but his discomfort was all in his ears and sinuses, so no laryngitis for him. I kept quiet, drank my tea and tried to relax—miraculously, my voice came back. It wasn't perfect, but it was there.

That afternoon they set the cameras and lights up in Butch's living room while Devlin and I ran our lines and then got into our first-scene clothes. The A/C was turned off as usual, because of the noise; in fact, they even un- plugged the refrigerator. Fortunately it was February, so heat wasn't an issue this time. And once we got started, the energy and adrenaline kicked in for both of us.

I so wish Shadow Lane would put out a blooper DVD. Every shoot has them and some of them are hilarious. Tony sent me one of ours; at the end of the first scene, there was a close-up on me after I said my final line, looking very diabolical. But as I stood there smirking, Eve suddenly said, "Oh wait, I'm going to sneeze!" and she did. I cracked up, and you heard Tony off-camera saying, "Say bless you,

Erica," which I did. Then they set up to shoot the last line again and called "action," but before I could speak, there was another loud "AHHHHH-CHOOO!" from Eve. Then you heard Tony say, "Oh, for fuck's sake."

After a break for a snack, water and costume change, we shot the second scene, which included hairbrush, belt and other implements along with a lot of hand. Throughout, Devlin and I had lively repartee, with me snarking and sniping so relentlessly, Tony finally said, "Erica... you *do* realize that he eventually has to win, right?" (sigh) All right, if he must. I slowly came around and admitted that I was secretly fascinated with the subject of his book, I'd been curious about spanking and I wanted to see what it was all about—and I liked it. We agreed that I would help him edit the book's second edition at no cost, there was one final strapping and we wound it up.

The power of the mind over the body is amazing. After we finished and my endorphins receded, exhaustion set in and I lost my voice once again. We went to dinner and I had to repeat my order three times, because the restaurant was loud and the server couldn't hear my whisper.

No matter; we did it. Both of us were ill, but we pushed through. If you watch the DVD and listen carefully, you can hear my voice cracking here and there, but it held up. Then, once we were done, my body sent a clear message: "OK, we're done, so screw it, I can be sick as hell now."

The next morning after I got up and packed, I went over to Tony and Eve's to have some coffee and wait for Devlin to pick me up. Tony and I chatted and I confessed how stressed out I'd been that this cold was going to ruin the shoot. Tony the Unflappable just shrugged and said, "Wouldn't have mattered—we'd just keep you here until you were better!"

On the ride to Vegas, Devlin and I had been very chatty, but now both of us were wiped out. So the ride home was fairly quiet, but it was a companionable silence. I was so grateful that he had driven and all I had to do was sit back, relax and be a passenger.

After we came back, I posted a full report on SCSW, with Devlin chiming in with his own notes. When Steve

Fuller came on to comment, Devlin asked him if his arm had been sore after shooting with me. Steve came back with, "I don't recall my arm hurting, but my ears were ringing for days." Humph.

Another wonderful shoot experience with Shadow Lane. Sadly, it was to be my last with them.

THE KEITH JONES TRILOGY, PART I

"I am a wreck—I'm so nervous! Would you believe I still have one more script coming? I've been reading and reading the other two, and running my lines with John, and have them down pretty well. The third scenario is a culmination of the first two, so there will be a lot of action and not as much dialogue and buildup, so Bethany has assured me it will be a lot easier than the others. But still... agggghhhh! My perfectionist little self wants to have it in my hot little hands so I can start familiarizing myself with it. And of course, because I'm such a rotten traveler and a nervous Nellie overall, I've got a million 'what ifs' going through my head. All this aside, I'm still excited, and know it's going to be great fun. And I get to work with the two best men in the business!"

—from *Southern California Spanked Wives and Girlfriends*, June 2, 2005

In spring 2005, I heard from Bethany once again. Flush with the success of *Schoolmaster's Revenge* and her subsequent shoot, *The Vacation*, she was preparing to tackle a new project true to the name of Spanking Epics. When she told me the details, I couldn't believe how ambitious it was, and how completely original.

It was to be a trilogy called *Being Keith Jones*. Keith would play himself, visiting a therapist to uncover the root of his spanking fixation. This therapist, who specializes in past life regression, uses hypnosis to send Keith back into his past lives.

In the first installment (*The Puritan*), Keith is taken back to Puritan times, where he is a widower struggling with his recalcitrant daughter and the spiteful town widow. In the second installment (*Trouble in Carson's Gap*), he is a sheriff of a small Western town in the 1800s, dealing with a feisty saloonkeeper who shows up in his town with two young girls in tow. All three pretend to be nuns there to build a convent, but their intentions couldn't be more dissimilar. Finally, in the third (*The Reckoning*), Keith confronts his therapist in the present day, realizing that her own past selves were those who tormented him long ago.

I was to play three parts: the therapist, the Puritan widow and the Western saloon proprietress. Keith and I would co-star with several others and Bethany was having us all come out to Virginia and shoot throughout June 4–9. Much of the shoot would take place at Camp Albemarle, a large campsite in Charlottesville, and we would have our own makeup artist and chef on hand. Bethany would provide all the period costumes and once again, all flights, hotels and meals were on Spanking Epics/Wasteland.

What an undertaking! My head was spinning just trying to deal with three scripts and my own travel details, so I can't begin to imagine what Bethany was experiencing, coordinating this whole endeavor and so many people (there ended up being 12 performers in the trilogy, plus several extras and bit players). There were many trips to arrange (we were coming from all over the States), elaborate costumes to rent and myriad preparations. She was always accessible to us for questions and her demeanor was calm, organized and efficient. I don't know how she did it.

As June 4 approached, more people were added to the cast; I found out Sierra Salem and Steve Fuller were included, as well as Eslynne Weaver from *Schoolmaster*. I had met Sierra a few times at local parties and she was an active member of SCSW—beautiful girl of 19, with a dancer's body and eyes you could get lost in. Bethany arranged for us to be travel companions, sitting together on the flight to Virginia.

The scripts were daunting—lengthy and dialogue-intensive—but I had to remember that I wasn't in every scene. I went through and highlighted all my lines, three-hole-punched the pages and put them into separate binders, and studied them day and night. My head was bursting with lines and scenarios and I could swear I was rehearsing in my sleep.

On Saturday, June 4, I woke up at the ungodly hour of 4:00 A.M. My bedroom looked like a war zone with clothes and toiletries piled up all over the carpet, but I was packed up and ready to go by 5:30, when I went downstairs for my shuttle pickup. I ended up getting to the airport and squared away with an hour-and-a-half to spare, so I sat with a very expensive coffee and bagel and read my scripts.

When it was time to board, I found Sierra in line and we went to our seats. We were in a row of three but the third passenger didn't show up, so we had plenty of room. The flight went fairly quickly, as we were both excited and chatted away the time, forging a sort of big sister–little sister bond. There was one stop in North Carolina to pick up a connector flight, but we finally arrived at Charlottesville Albemarle Airport at 7:00 P.M. Virginia time.

Jim picked us up and took us to the Red Carpet Inn, where several of us would be staying, so we could check in and drop off our things. Then we went to Bethany and Jim's for the evening. Steve and Keith had arrived as well and we all had dinner. Around 10:30, they took the four of us back to our motel. Most of the others would start arriving the next day, and we would convene at lunchtime, have something to eat and then get to work on shooting the first scenes on the itinerary.

Because all three scripts had office scenes (for the hypnotherapist and her patient) and we could only have access to this particular office on Sunday, we had to shoot all the office scenes that day. Plus, the office was being used for three short "boarding house" scenes in the Western scenario as well, so we had quite a bit to shoot that first day. Thank goodness, I was able to sleep Saturday night.

The next day after lunch, we got to the office around 2:00 and met up with Colin, Angie and the camera/lighting crew. Since we were shooting three separate sessions, I'd brought three complete outfits with two pairs of shoes, all the requisite underwear and stockings, etc. But I hadn't brought a scrap of makeup, because I'd been told we'd have a makeup artist on the sets—and then I found out she wasn't coming until later. Oh, dear. Bethany's daughter had to drive me back to the motel, where I picked up my cosmetics bag and blow-dryer and we headed back. I didn't have a lot with me, but several of the women on the set had some makeup with them also, so between all of us, I had enough stuff to get my face on for the camera.

We set up for the first scene and about 30 seconds into it, the power went out. Can you say "heart attack"? Fortunately, Jim was able to find the circuit breakers and got things back on shortly. Keith and I were the only people in these scenes, except for a couple of lines from Bethany's daughter who was playing my receptionist. We filmed one spanking scene and that was a blast, since the two of us could adlib and be creative. I took a long OTK hand spanking and then was bent over the couch for the razor strap, then back over Keith's lap.

It was fun, but of course, things got warm with the lights and all. Plus we had the usual flubs and subsequent retakes, so the three therapist/patient scenes took a long time. Paris Kennedy had arrived, as well our makeup person, so once Keith and I were done, the three of us (Sierra, Paris and I) started getting into the nun costumes for our brief scenes in the Western boarding house. Bethany had gotten the real thing with all the various pieces—habit, wimple, veil, etc., plus crosses and rosary beads. The room where all of us had changed was now being used to shoot in, so we had to clear out all the piles of stuff and set up in there.

Someday, I'd like someone to figure out the ratio of time spent setting up vs. the time actually shooting.

We got those three mini-scenes shot, and that was it for that venue—everything else would be shot at the camp, starting the next morning. By now it was around 10:00 P.M. and everyone was heading to a barbecue place for a late dinner, but I begged off; I just wanted to go to bed, since I had to get up around 6:00 A.M. But of course, once I got there, I was wired and couldn't sleep! This happened every night—I'd come back tired, but with my mind whirring with activity from the day, running lines in my head, thinking about what I could have done better and so on.

* * *

Since everything was being shot out of order, they grouped scenes according to the sets, the video theme and whether they were inside or outside. Monday and half of

Tuesday would be all the Western scenes, and then the latter half of Tuesday and all of Wednesday would be the Puritan scenes.

So, at 7:00 on Monday morning, we all met outside in the motel parking lot and made the trek with three vehicles to Camp Albemarle. Bethany and Jim and crew would meet us there; it was about a 20-minute drive from the motel.

For this city girl, the camp was quite a sight—nothing but green. One of the cabins would be used for us to dress in, get made up, lay out all the costumes, etc. Each cabin had several bunks in it, but they had vinyl mattresses and no linens; apparently you had to bring your own. The lighting was a bare bulb hanging from the ceiling at either end of the cabin. Outside and around the back of that cabin was the community bathroom, with a row of toilets (hidden by shower curtains), a row of sinks and a row of open showers with no doors or curtains. Past the cabins, there was a main lodge with a full kitchen, and we'd make good use of that lodge for several scenes, as well as a place to hang out, eat and talk. Outside, there were several paths, hillsides and a river, which is where Sierra, Steve and Paris would shoot one of the Western scenes. There was also a pavilion area in the field with picnic tables and benches and a barbecue pit, and we ate dinner out there on two nights.

And tons of bugs! Camp Albemarle was lush and beautiful, but extremely rustic, and I've never seen so many flying and crawling critters in all my life. Mosquitoes, huge bumblebees, wasps, dragonflies, gnats, spiders, ants, you name it. I am amazed that I didn't get a single bite, but John had warned me in advance and I made sure I had plenty of Cutter's spray.

C, Bethany's assistant and our cook, took such good care of us, keeping us supplied with lots of wonderful food, copious quantities of bottled water and sodas and of course, the life's blood of many of the crew—coffee. But he took care of all the individual needs too.

He knew I like to eat lighter, more healthful food and he made sure there were always plenty of fruits and vegetables, Diet Coke, turkey and fish for me. He stocked up on sugar-free Red Bull for Sierra and Paris. When he grilled steaks on Monday night and sausages on Tuesday night, he also grilled fish for me, since he knew I don't eat red meat. I always feel so weird about my fussy eating habits, so I was deeply grateful for his efforts to cater to us. We truly were treated like celebrities.

Sierra, Paris and I went into the bunks to change into our nun costumes, and we had Lori and another assistant Patricia to help us. That morning, we first shot all the scenes that required the nun garb, and then I had a break while Steve, Keith, Sierra and Paris did their scenes. After lunch, I had a wild spanking scene with Keith in the sheriff's office—we were both keyed up for it and I was supposed to be a real hellcat, so I kicked and screamed and yelled insults at him and fought like crazy. We were both running sweat when it was over, but triumphant, knowing we'd nailed a really hot scene.

Next was a bar scene with Keith, Steve and the two girls, with me coming in at the end. I was scripted to clobber Keith with a liquor bottle—he would be advancing on me threateningly and Bethany had purchased a prop bottle for me to grab and break over his head. However, I had no idea of how very fragile and thin these bottles are. When Keith dropped his hat and bent to pick it up, I grabbed the bottle by the handle and swung it down at his head. The handle completely crumbled in my hand, and the rest of the bottle, instead of breaking on his head, flew across the room and nearly hit Bethany. I gasped, clapped my hands to my mouth and yelled, "Oh SHIT!" (That ended up in the Bloopers section of the DVD, by the way.)

We had one more bottle for a second try... but once again, the handle disintegrated in the palm of my hand and the bottle separated. This time, it did break on Keith's head—and I actually cut his forehead, along with my hand! I can laugh now, but I felt awful at the time. For one thing, I certainly hadn't meant to hurt him (although it was just a tiny nick) and for another, I'd wrecked two takes with two very expensive prop bottles and that's all they had. However, Colin assured me that he did have a very good shot of me swinging downward, and the camera didn't catch the bottle flying across the room—it just looked like I'd totally clocked Keith.

Everyone in the cast and crew was great fun, but Ben, one of the cameramen, was particularly entertaining. He was tall and as thin as a 14-year-old boy, with the baby face of roughly a 20-year-old, but he was 38. He was clearly into Goth—bleached blond hair with black roots, black-rimmed glasses, black clothes, spiked collar and wristlets—and he was the most hyper person I've ever met in my life. This guy was a force of energy, always moving, always talking, always running—whenever anyone needed anything, Ben was the one who would go running for it. And I do mean *run*. We'd be sitting on the lodge steps and he'd come tearing across the field, yelling, "Look out, coming through!" and he'd run by us so fast, we'd get a huge breeze, which felt quite good in that thick humid air.

Full of funny stories, he had me laughing so hard in the cabin once, I was doubled over in one of the bunks with tears coming out of my eyes. When he wasn't telling outrageous tales, he was proudly mentioning his two daughters, showing pictures of them. He was sweet, nutty and a lot of fun to have around.

That was about it for Monday—we had a barbecue that night, and I got to use my Cutter's insect repellent; once the sun went down, the bugs came out in full force all around us. The air was filled with them! We all left shortly after dinner—two days down, two to go.

* * *

Tuesday morning, we were shooting a McLintock-esque scene for the Western. After I bashed Keith with the bottle, I would go running out of the saloon with him after me. He'd chase me up and down the roads and through the field, and we would end up at the sheriff's office. It was early morning, but it was already hot and extremely humid, and here's what I was wearing: a long-sleeved blouse, buttoned all the way up to my neck; a heavy dark green jumper-style dress that weighed more than I do; bloomers;

petticoats, and thigh-high stockings. And I had to run like a maniac in all this?

We shot three separate chase portions and they took three takes of each one. And in each one, I had to be turning around and yelling insults at Keith while I ran. Particularly challenging was the run through the field. Halfway through that, I heard Colin yell, "Trip and fall!!" So I went *splat* into the grass, stumbled back up and went on running… and had to do that two more times. The grass was soft so I didn't hurt myself, but I did rip one of my stockings. On top of everything else, we had to keep pausing because of ambient noise—there were jets, plus some piece of machinery that was mowing the grass or cutting hay or whatever the hell, going back and forth around the camp, and it kept coming within earshot of the shoot.

When Keith finally caught me in front of the office, he took me OTK for a hand spanking on the bench by the office steps. By then, I was dripping sweat and very grateful this scene was almost over, but then we hit a bunch more delays. Colin wanted to do a bit where Ben hands Keith a switch and suggests he use it on me, and we couldn't quite get that right. Then we had to stop again for jets.

Lying there with my head down, I felt like I was going to pass out. My face was so wet I couldn't stand it—Paris was off to the side as part of the crowd scene, and I panted at her to please come over. When she did, I wiped my face on her apron. It was a dark color, so I knew it wouldn't show—everyone laughed, but I just couldn't handle the sweat anymore; it was running into my eyes!

For the crowning finale of that outdoor scene, Keith would decide this wasn't cutting it, so he'd throw me over his shoulder and carry me—kicking, screaming and caterwauling—into his office so he can take my bloomers down in private. When we finally got in the doors and off camera and he let me down, he was laughing, and he blurted, "Do you know what you were doing?" I said no, what? He told me that during the trip up the stairs when I was kicking, I was kneeing him repeatedly in the chest! Oh, my…I had absolutely no awareness of that. Poor Keith—between flailing knees and prop bottles, he took (almost) as much abuse as I did!

After that, I needed to rest—the heat and exertion and profuse sweating really wiped me out. Fortunately, I had no more scenes for the Western portion and I could break until we started the Puritan scenes later. I showered and had a late lunch; it was 2:00 and I hadn't eaten since 7:30 that morning. Lunch had already been served earlier, but C had reserved a turkey sandwich and some grapes for me. Once again, I felt like a celebrity.

Now it was time to switch gears and start shooting the Puritan scenes. We said goodbye to Steve, who was flying back to California. Enter Eslynne (with her five-week-old baby girl), Isobel Wren and Hans Stromfield—they'd be playing Keith's daughter Purity, her friend Sarah, and Sarah's brother, respectively. Everyone on the set fell in love with the baby, R (her older sister E had stayed home this time with her dad). She was beautiful, and such a mellow infant—never cried and rarely fussed, no matter who held her (and pretty much everyone did).

We all got into Puritan outfits, even the extras, because we had to shoot a couple of group scenes. The outfits, once again, were very authentic and the women had to wear assorted hoods, bonnets and caps because our hair wasn't supposed to show. Lori gave me more of a subtle look with makeup this time. In the Western, I had bright reddish-pink lipstick, lots of blush and black eyeliner. For this, she just used some foundation, a little blush, mascara and pale pink lipstick—after, I was a Puritan. And underneath the long conservative dress and the petticoat—no panties or bloomers. They didn't have underwear in the 1600s, apparently.

One scene was shot inside the lodge, which was made up to look like a church with benches and a podium for the preacher. We actually had to sing a hymn; of course, none of us knew the words, so one of the crew took the big white board used for light check and a black marker and wrote out the words, so we could use it as a cheat sheet. It was funny for me to be sitting behind Paris, who was one of the extras in this video. There she sat, looking very prim and proper in her shapeless dress and her hair up in a bonnet, but from where I was, I could very clearly see the bold black tattoo of "PIMP II" across the back of her neck.

Then there was a scene outside the "church," pre-service, with all the cast and extras. I was standing to the side in a small group with Ben, Sierra and Patricia (who stood behind Ben to hide the fact that she was wearing sandals under her Puritan gown). Colin directed us all to have some normal, soft-voiced conversation and look natural. Easier said than done; when you know cameras are on you and you're supposed to be background and look perfectly natural, what do you talk about? Well, we were hanging around Ben, so it was bound to be something unexpected. So while Keith and others were shooting their scene, we were off to the side chatting about condoms. I have no idea how that subject came up, no pun intended, but here we were shooting a Puritan scenario in a spanking video, standing in front of a fake church and discussing male contraceptives. It was laughably absurd.

The rest of the afternoon was spent filming indoor Puritan scenes. There were three separate scenes in my character's "house" (the lodge, once again). I had one argument scene with Keith that was fun—I got to smash a cup in the fireplace. I was such a horrid woman in this video; the town widow, embittered and mean, and living to gossip and get others in trouble. Next, we shot a scene where Keith, his daughter and sister come to visit me, after I've had a fall (caused by the daughter and her friend, because they greased my porch). Of course, I'm not really injured, I'm just faking it, and Keith discovers that later.

Then it was time for my spanking scene with Keith. Bethany wanted me to play this one out a little differently—still defiant, but whereas my Western character was feisty and spirited, my Puritan character was to be a little darker and more poignant. But there was still plenty of action—I almost killed Keith again. I had to grab the lid of a very heavy cast-iron pot and swing it at his head (he blocked it, though). Then he put me over the table.

For an implement, Bethany had this old wooden paddle that had been used to churn butter in those times; it had holes in it. Keith started using the paddle, but then he stopped and I heard everyone in the room laughing. When you're bent over a table with your bare butt facing a roomful of people, hearing laughter is a bit unnerving. I asked what was so funny, and Keith held the paddle in front of my face—he'd broken it! Or my butt broke it, as the case may be.

They actually kept that in the film—they had Keith say, "Oh well, looks like you need a new butter paddle," and then he picked up a wooden spoon and continued. We ended the scene by going into the bedroom area for a final OTK hand spanking. I wish I could cry on cue, because the scene really did call for it, but my acting skills aren't that extensive. Nonetheless, I think I got the right mood.

That was my last scene of the day, so I was able to change and clean up. One more scene was shot and then it was time for dinner. C grilled sausages with peppers and onions (swordfish for me) and Colin made a little speech to thank and congratulate all of us, even though we still had one more shooting day, since a lot of people were leaving the next afternoon.

After dinner, Ben and I started chatting. As the days had progressed, he grown increasingly wired, and when I asked him if he'd had any sleep, he said no. He confessed to me that he was bipolar and he had stopped taking his medication, because he didn't like the side effects. That certainly explained a lot—all this energy had been due to his being in a manic phase.

He asked me a strange question: What was my impression of him? I certainly thought he was intriguing, but I didn't say that. I thought about it, then answered, "I think you're smart, creative, very funny, and I have a feeling when you care about someone, you're very giving and fiercely loyal." I paused, then added, "And I think you're an accident waiting to happen." Why I said that, I don't know. But he wasn't offended; just gave me a sad little smile and said, "Yes, I am—always have been."

One more day of shooting to go!

* * *

249

On Wednesday we finished the Puritan video, doing a lot of the outside scenes. I didn't have much to do, just a few short scenes, including one where I had no dialogue—I was spying on the two girls (who were plotting to sneak out of church early) and smirking, since I planned to rat them out. There was also a quick scene of me striding out my front door, even though I'm supposed to be horribly injured, and am surprised by Keith waiting to ambush me.

Then there was my final scene for the entire shoot: the fall on the porch. After I got the girls in trouble, they would retaliate by greasing my porch steps with tallow. Then I'd come walking around the building with a bucket of water, slip and do a pratfall on the steps, landing with the bucket on my head.

It was one thing to take a fall in some tall soft grass, but I'm no stuntwoman and I wasn't about to risk breaking my back on those stone steps. So we faked the fall—they took a shot of me walking up the steps, then another with my foot sliding out and my arms flailing, and with the bucket flying up in the air (my bonnet flew off too, which was a nice touch). Cut the action; Colin held the microphone in front of my face and instructed me to let out a loud scream, which I did and he recorded. Then they cut away to the girls hiding in the trees and running away after they hear me scream. Final cut back to me lying sprawled on the porch, with the bucket on my head and water splashed all over my dress.

After that, I was done; all my scenes were shot. I felt extreme euphoria for about five minutes…and then I crashed. Once I got out of my Puritan garb and back into my own clothes, the adrenaline that had been gushing for days abruptly ceased and I felt the most overwhelming wave of fatigue I can remember. I went back into the lodge and ate some lunch, feeling like my limbs were filled with lead pellets. There were still a few more scenes being shot outside, but in the lodge, people were starting to clean up and pack things up. I said to Jim, "I know I should be doing something, but I just can't move." He assured me that my job was done and I didn't have to do another thing.

Eslynne was in the last few scenes being shot, so she'd left the baby in the lodge for all of us to watch over her. She began to fuss a little bit, so Patricia picked her up and R immediately mashed her face into Patricia's chest. Clearly, motherhood was calling; we had to interrupt Eslynne's scene so she could feed the baby. (I wonder if, in the history of shooting spanking videos, there has ever been another case of a break in the action called so a mother could breastfeed. I doubt it. But again, such is the absurdity of these things sometimes.)

After R was fed and changed, she settled down, happily looking at everything going on around her. I lay on the bunk, bent my knees up and placed her on my legs, bouncing her a bit, and she eventually fell asleep. And there we stayed until it was time to leave.

Several of us went back to the motel to shower and rest a little, while others left to go home, including Patricia and Ben. Later that night, those of us who were left met at Bethany's house for Chinese food. I enjoyed being there, but I was so very tired, I could barely talk, and around 10:30, we caravanned back to the motel. Sierra's and my plane wasn't leaving until 3:30 the next day, but Keith was leaving in the morning, so we said our goodbyes, exchanging hugs and thank-yous and marveling at how we pulled it all off. I went to bed and slept for 12 hours straight.

After all that, the trip home was anti-climactic. We took the quickie connector flight and were delayed in North Carolina, so we had time to get some food and make phone calls. On the main flight home, Sierra got headphones and listened to music, and I dozed on and off all the way.

How do people handle frequent travel? I suppose they get used to it, but I can't imagine how. I felt grubby, jet-lagged and disoriented, and I was beyond eager to walk into my front door. But I was happy. We *did* it. Now all I had to do was rest, settle in back home and then write up shoot reports. And of course, impatiently wait for the finished product.

THE KEITH JONES TRILOGY, PART II

"As I was relaxing in the den, I overheard Sierra say-
ing something in the kitchen about a spank-off. She had
mentioned that earlier, that she and I should do a spank-
off, with Keith and Steve as our spankers, and see who
could hold out longer. Then she came into the den and said,
'Erica, I challenge you to a spank-off!' Huh? Was she kid-
ding? It was already late, we were done shooting, it was
time to wind down. But the more she talked about it, the
more I thought, hey, this could be fun."
—from *Southern California Spanked Wives and*
Girlfriends, September 5, 2005

As summer 2005 passed, we eagerly waited for notices
of the first installment of the trilogy being edited and released, but there were none. Then in August, Bethany contacted all of us with some bad news.

Something had gone wrong with the audio portion of
the footage shot outdoors. I don't know the technicalities,
but in a nutshell, most of the outdoor scenes had inaudible
dialogue. The indoor scenes were all right, but before the
videos could be completed, we would all have to come
back and dub our outdoor lines.

And so, the first weekend in September, most of the
cast and crew reconvened in New Hampshire (at Colin and
Angie's house, this time) to recreate the outdoor dialogue.
Bethany, in an attempt to make the most of the weekend,
said that while we took turns in the sound booth, the others
would shoot what they called "spanklets"—mini-scenes,
about 10–15 minutes in length, for streaming.

On Friday, September 2, I got up at 2:45 A.M., since my
shuttle was picking me up at 4:00 (for a 7:15 flight). Once
again, Sierra and I were seatmates, so we found each other
before boarding. The flight was uneventful, except it
seemed we were talking about the purpose for our trip a bit
too loudly, because the man behind us told us to be quiet!

C, the same gentleman who had been our chef during the week of shooting in June, picked us up at the airport and delivered us to Colin and Angie's home.

What a great house they had! Downstairs was an entryway, a room off to the side of the entry that they used as a music room, a formal dining room, large kitchen and dining area, living room, a huge office area and a half-bath. Then upstairs, four bedrooms and two more baths. Plus a big back yard, a pool and a Jacuzzi, and a large basement, where they shot some of the spanklets. Many of the cast and crew were camping out here and there were air mattresses set up all over the house.

It was great fun seeing everyone again. I couldn't help noticing that Ben, the goofy cameraman from the first shoot, was not present. I asked about him and was told, "No, Ben will not be joining us." Nothing else was added and I got the distinct feeling that I shouldn't ask why not, so I didn't.

Our first night was dinner, then watching some rough cuts of the three videos. Later, C drove Sierra and me to the Residence Inn, where we'd be staying with Eslynne, her sister and the two babies.

The Residence Inn was so cool! Well, at least it was to me, as I'm not much of a traveler and I'd never stayed in a place quite like this. It was a townhouse, and the bottom floor had a living room (with fireplace), full kitchen, a bedroom with king-sized bed and a bathroom. Upstairs was another bedroom/bathroom, and the bed was queen-sized. Sierra and I took the upstairs suite and went to sleep around 1:00 A.M.

The next morning we were up at 7:30, and after taking our showers and dressing, we went downstairs to see Eslynne and the kids. E was now a beautiful toddler with long red curls, and R was five months old, and just as mellow and happy as she'd been as an infant, beaming at all of us and never fussing. E was shy at first, but then she warmed up to us and was absolutely adorable.

The children were *never* exposed to any of the film action; I want to make sure that is very clear. They were with Eslynne any time she wasn't shooting or dubbing, and if she was, her sister watched over them. The baby went into any pair of arms willing to hold her (and there were many, including my own) and E was a sunny, sweet child, engaging with whomever was around her at the time.

Saturday was a blur of activity. Colin had set up a sound booth in the attic for our line dubbing. We would take turns reading our lines, a couple at a time, while watching the film snippets, wearing headphones so we could hear ourselves talking and try to match what we heard. Colin would have us repeat the lines until we got a good match, then we'd go on to the next couple of lines. Some were harder than others, and it was more challenging than one might think—all the inflections, plus every sigh, pause and stutter had to be duplicated. They did the Puritan scenes that day and I didn't have all that many, so I had time to shoot two spanklets: one with Steve and one with Keith and Sierra.

The spanklet scenarios were very simple and unscripted. In the first one I did with Steve, we played husband and wife, and he discovered I was buying lottery tickets and gambling when he told me not to. He had to go into my purse to answer my cell phone and found the tickets, so I got a spanking in the basement over his leg and over the tool table. The dialogue was completely improvised and Steve was his usual talented self at matching my comebacks with his own, so we had some fun banter. They wanted lots of kicking and yelling, and I was only too happy to comply.

In the late afternoon, Sierra and I got dressed up in a couple of the Western period dresses and did a spanklet with Keith. He played my husband and my character was gossiping too much with our next-door neighbor (Sierra). Her husband was always away on business, so she came over every day and we had a hen party and tore all the townspeople to shreds. Keith took us both to task and it became quite the funny scene. The two of us never shut up the whole time we were being spanked and Keith did his patented, exasperated slow burn. I believe he said more than once, "For the love of God, will you please, *please* just shut your mouths?" Of course, we didn't.

After dinner that evening, they screened *The Puritan* for us, and Bethany and Colin set up microphones in the kitchen so we could record a "director commentary" as a DVD extra. Keith had gone to bed and Eslynne was with the children, but Isobel, Hans and I participated a bit, talking about our parts. Around 12:30 A.M., it was time to go back to our townhouse to sleep.

Sunday morning we were up at 7:00 and I wandered down to the lobby to check out the free breakfast buffet. I got myself some coffee, but it was weak as dishwater so I dumped it and decided I'd wait until we got to Colin and Angie's, where I knew the giant urn would be on all day for our coffee-and-cigarettes crew. Eslynne, her sister and the girls were leaving that morning, so we had to say our good-byes. So hard to let those babies go!

The house was buzzing with activity with many sleepy, disheveled people milling about, strong coffee perking and breakfast being cooked. After we ate, it was time to do the Western voice-overs, which took up the morning and some of the afternoon. More spanklets were shot as well, including one with Steve and me in our Western garb, doing a "behind the scenes" bit for *Trouble in Carson's Gap*. Of course we were no longer at the camp, but the back yard had trees and a lot of greenery, so we were able to fake it.

In this spanklet, I was teasing Steve about how Keith had all the hard work in this trilogy and he (Steve) was merely a sidekick, an amateur, Tonto to Keith's Lone Ranger, so Steve decided to show me he was no amateur when it came to spanking. The scene was vigorous and funny, with Keith doing two walk-ons.

After that, one more lengthy spanklet was shot, in which I played a stunt butt. Yes, really—one of the women in it, who had been an extra in the trilogy, wanted to be in the spanklet but didn't wish to show her bare bottom on camera. So they shot with her up until the part she was put over the stair railing for a strapping, then the action was stopped so I could put on her dress and take over. The camera stayed on my bottom and didn't show my face, and I tried to pitch my voice up to sound more like hers. Then three other girls were to be strapped, so I stepped off camera. I ended up being credited in that spanklet, which was no doubt a bit confusing for the viewers, because they'd watch it and say, "Hey, where's Erica?"

By now it was Sunday evening and those of us who were still there were relaxing in the den; all the camera equipment had been put away and the plan was to watch the Western, do a commentary on that and call it a weekend. However, Sierra had other plans. She thought it would be fun to have a spanking contest, with Keith and Steve as our tops, to see which one of us could take the most. When she challenged me directly, my first thought was *No way, it's too late, I'm too tired, I'm spanked out.* But of course, there's always a part of me that wants more, that doesn't want the shoot(s) to come to an end. We took our idea to Bethany and Colin, who liked it and talked with the crew about setting the cameras up once again. Everyone was on board for it, so we decided to go for it after dinner.

As I ate a very light dinner, I saw Sierra drinking a beer. "Oh, no you don't," I said. "You're not anesthetizing yourself for this shoot! No beer!" I then snatched it from her and poured it down the sink. A lot of the men present thought that was a spankable offense in itself, but hey, fair is fair. If I was going to be stone-cold sober for this contest, then she had to be too!

It was decided that we'd shoot it as a cheesy contest ala WWF, with commentators, judges and so forth. Isobel played the emcee and she sat perched on a stool, holding a mike, wearing a black lace negligee and a lot of makeup. The agenda: We'd have 10 two-minute rounds, switching laps after each one, with the spankers both using matching implements (hand, hairbrushes, their belts, etc.) and after that, a solid 15-minute endurance round. Jim and Simon played commentators talking in the background and several of the crew played judges, sitting on the couch and holding up cards after each round with our scores written on them.

It was a crazy, hilarious free-for-all shoot and they encouraged the two of us to be over the top—in other words, scream, kick, insult each other, insult the tops, cuss. We made it through all 10 rounds plus the 15-minute round,

256

and both of us were still willing and able to go on. So how did we end it? Sorry, I'm not telling.

Sierra and I had been so bitchy to each other on camera that as soon as they stopped filming, we fell into each other's arms hugging, as if to say, "I really do love you! I didn't mean it!" It was now nearly midnight and once the adrenaline surge died down, I was so exhausted I could barely hold my head up. I wanted to stay for the Western screening, but then realized that we had to get up in about four hours for our flight. Reluctantly, we said our good-byes all around and were driven back to the townhouse.

A cab picked us up at 5:00 A.M. and drove us to the airport. The flight was tough; I was tired, disoriented, crabby and squirming in my seat with a very sore bottom, plus we had one of the most badly behaved children I've ever seen in my life right in front of us, a little boy about three. Sierra slept through the entire flight and I don't know how she did it, because between the screaming, the whining, the toddler gibberish, the jumping up and down on the seat, the flinging of toys (one of which hit me in the face) and the high-pitched singing for five hours, I couldn't have slept if my life depended on it. But at long last, it was over, I was home, and when I finally staggered in my door I went straight to bed, even though it was only noon.

The trilogy was edited and released, one portion at a time, and the reviews were good. Nothing quite like this had ever been done before in the spanking video industry; it was unique and ambitious, and I was very proud to have been a part of it.

After the trilogy, *Spanking Epics* produced a few more spanklets and one more full-length DVD, and then that was it. I don't know why, but I suspect it was because their production values were so high and therefore their expenditures great, and they probably discovered that the revenue earned by the DVD sales did not offset the production costs. It's a shame, because there's a wealth of untapped subject matter out there into which they could have delved. However, perhaps nowadays, with Spanking Tube and Clips4Sale, people's attention spans are too short to appreciate longer, more detailed videos with intricate plots.

A side note to wrap up an earlier story: While in New Hampshire, I talked with one of the other women (I will not name her), who shared with me that she was an ex of Ben, the cameraman. The story then came out that he had harassed her during the trilogy shoot and that's why he was not present at this one.

I felt sick hearing about this, remembering yet another interaction I'd had with him at the camp. On our last morning there, I saw him on the porch in front of the lodge, sitting bent forward with his head in his lap. I sat next to him and realized he was crying, so I asked what was wrong. His muffled voice answered, "Why do you guys do it?" "Who? Do what?" I asked. "You women," he said. "Why do you torment us so much?" I had no idea what he was talking about, so I said nothing, just sat there quietly and rubbed his back. Then others came outside and he pulled himself together.

But that wasn't to be the last I heard about Ben. Later that month, he was arrested for the strangulation death of a 17-year-old college girl, whose body he had dumped on an abandoned property. He claimed it was an accident and happened during a consensual sex act (erotic asphyxiation) and then he had panicked. The prosecution and the girl's mother thought otherwise. He ended up taking an Alford plea to second-degree murder, bypassing a trial, and was given a 30-year prison sentence.

I couldn't believe it. My mind replayed that conversation we'd had back in June, when I told him he was an accident waiting to happen. I still have no idea why I said that, and I certainly didn't know just how tragically that prediction would play out. I thought at the most he was a danger to himself, not to others.

For a while, I obsessively read everything I could find about the case; every detail, all the interviews, the timelines. I remembered about his bipolar illness and how he had gone off his medication. From all my years in EA, I am familiar with the chaos that can ensue when necessary psychotropic meds are abruptly discontinued.

For what it's worth... I believe it was indeed an accident, not premeditated. The man I encountered during those

258

five days in June was severely unbalanced and may have had a psychotic breakdown, but he did not strike me as a cold-blooded killer. I watched him cuddling a five-week-old infant, holding her close to his chest because he said babies were soothed by the sound of a heartbeat. I know mine is a very unpopular view, but I cannot help it. It's what my gut tells me. However, I'll never know for certain.

I will always be grateful to Bethany and everyone involved in Spanking Epics for the fun experiences and the treasured memories. After the trilogy came out, some people referred to Keith and me as the "Tracy and Hepburn of spanking videos." I couldn't have asked for a better compliment, our being likened to such a classic pair.

THE SPANKING BLOGOSPHERE

"My MSN group is being transferred to World Groups, because MSN is shutting down all adult-themed groups (thank you, Mr. Bush, and your stupid conservative Big-Brother administration). The fucking country is falling apart and you guys are after a few harmless little span-kos. Arrrrrggghhh. Anyway, the transition was supposed to be 'seamless, just a few clicks of the mouse,' and it's been anything but....Out of 15,000+ members, a whopping 21 have been able to transfer over, so far. Seamless, my ass."
—from my *MySpace* blog, March 30, 2006

Southern California Spanked Wives and Girlfriends had a very good run, but a transition was taking place online. The popularity of discussion forums began to wane, over-taken by individual blogs and social networking sites such as MySpace and Facebook. Becca, whom I had always considered as our Fearless Leader, had bowed out, as her life took another direction (motherhood). I had a couple of excellent assistant managers (including Dave Wolfe, the sweet and talented man behind *WolfieToons*), but I felt I didn't have Becca's leadership skills. However, I didn't have much choice. I certainly didn't want to abandon my post as manager.

So SCSW went along for another year or so, not as busy as it once had been, but not completely dead either. And then MSN decided they were going to drop all their adult groups.

This did not happen abruptly; we were given months of notice and told that our groups would be transferred intact to a new site called World Groups. The various boards buzzed with questions and lamentations, everyone wonder-ing about our fate. MSN promised the transition would be smooth; we'd simply be picked up and plunked down onto another forum and we could carry on as before.

Hardly.

Very long story short, when the transition finally hap-pened in March 2006, it didn't go well at all. There were glitches and problems and complaints galore. And no one, myself included, liked World Groups. It was not user-friendly, it was painfully slow, and we were surrounded by hard-core porn groups. It took a few months, but the writing was on the wall. SCSW was dying.

Late in 2005, I had joined MySpace, which was *the* place to be at the time. I noticed that several fellow spankos were on there and I began building my profile and gathering friends. In December, I blogged for the first time.

I was no stranger to journaling, of course; I'd been doing it since I was a teenager. But this was the first time I'd done it publicly. It took a while for me to get my footing; for a long time, my audience was very small and my comments were few to nonexistent. Then Bonnie happened.

Bonnie, affectionately known by many as Queen of the Spanking Blogs, has a popular site called *My Bottom Smarts*, and she has always made a practice of linking to as many other spanking blogs as she can find. Periodically, she'll feature a list of the newer ones in a column she calls "In With the New." Getting listed and linked on Bonnie's blog guarantees an upward surge in your own blog's hits, and mine was no exception when she found it and added me to her list.

Slowly but surely, I got more viewers, comments and friend requests. I took Bonnie's advice about replying to each comment I received; I hadn't been doing that before. And my audience continued to grow. In December 2006, Adele Haze, another popular blogger, asked to interview me. She sent me a list of questions, which I answered and sent back along with several pictures. When that was posted, my blog views skyrocketed. More bloggers linked to me and the ripples continued outward.

It was fun! I felt like I was part of a whole new community. However, MySpace had a lot of limits. I could not link to others, even though they could link to me. In order to comment, people had to be MySpace members (although that wasn't much of a problem back then, as many were). And I had to be extremely cautious about getting too graphic about what I posted. Many of my spanko friends were getting deleted or having their profiles/blogs/photos censored. I had a few of my own photos deleted, with no warning or notice that it had been done. I simply had to discover that they were gone. Nudity was forbidden, but anything that suggested "violence" was also. So, pictures that depicted hard spanking, even if the bottom was covered, were deleted often.

But even with these pitfalls, I persevered and continued to grow in the blogosphere. Unfortunately, as my positive feedback grew, there was also an increase in unsavory messages. Via email, in instant messages, in comments and messages on MySpace and other forums where I posted, stupidity, illiteracy and obscenity made regular appearances. Sometimes I laughed, but most of the time, I reacted with annoyance and even anger. Where did these people get off, writing this garbage to me? What were they thinking? *Were* they thinking? I didn't reply to them, but inwardly I seethed, wishing I could tell them off.

But wait. In a way, I could—and at the same time, entertain my readers as well. And that was how my *Correspondence Hall of Shame* was born.

Every time I got a comment that was offensive in one way or another, I would paste it into a Word document I'd created just for that purpose. On Friday, April 20, 2007, I began my CHoS feature. Once a week, I'd take the comments I'd accumulated, eliminate any identifiers (names, addresses, etc.) and then post them on my blog. After each one, I'd write what I'd *like* to reply to them, being my most sarcastic and pithy self.

Here are a few examples:

Verbatim comment: *wana c me rub my dik for u on cam?*
My "reply": *First of all, if you can't even spell the appendage, you probably have no idea how to use it. And second, shouldn't you ask Cam first? Maybe he/she doesn't want you to rub your dik on him/her.*

Comment: *oh yeah....can ya send me some nudes???*
Me: *Sure... just give me your address and prison cell number.*

Comment: *I would luv to spank your ass with my cock!!!!!*
Me: *(yawn) OK, but would I even feel that?*

Comment: *YOUR ASS DON'T NEED NO COLOR, JUST THIS DICK.*
Me: *Thank you for the diagnosis, Doctor Bumbanger. I'll be sure to file your suggestion in the appropriate place. ***plunk****

This feature took off; my Friday hits soared. People told me they didn't know what was funnier—the comments or my answers to them. That's exactly how I wanted it. The CHoS continues to this day, although it's no longer weekly. I do believe a lot of the perverts caught on to me and don't send those types of comments as often as they used to.

I *never* make fun of someone if what they write to me is sincere and polite. Some people cannot spell, some are dyslexic. And for others, English is their second language. I understand this and I will not exploit it. But if what they write to me is obscene, arrogant, presumptuous or just plain rude, anything is fair game.

Early on, I had to decide in which direction I wanted my blog to go. Many who had done spanking videos had blogs detailing their various scene experiences, with shoots and parties and sessions and so forth. I had some of that myself. But I wanted this to be about more than just Erica Scott; I wanted to include the real Erica. So, interspersed with tales of spankings, I revealed more personal details, warts and all. I discussed my battles with depression and eating disorders. I freely admitted to being moody, irritable, critical and a die-hard loner. I spoke of past relationships, including (especially) the dysfunctional ones, and of my current one with John. I confessed to mistakes and missteps, both in the scene and in general life.

Why? Because I knew how I'd felt when I was new in the scene; I looked at the "models" and thought they were larger than life, somewhat removed from mere mortals and elevated on a special platform. Which, of course, was ridiculous, but a common misconception nonetheless. I wanted readers to know I was a real, flawed human being with

263

foibles, insecurities, bitchy moments and vulnerabilities. It was a risk, baring myself in this manner, but I never regretted it.

Occasionally a malcontent would use my revelations against me. A couple of years ago, a man started leaving very nasty and personal comments on my blog, attacking my character. He wasn't one of the illiterates; he wrote quite well and clearly had been following me and knew details about me. I looked up his profile, but there was no picture. According to his description, he lived in some Podunk town in PA and claimed he was a proud parent, grandparent and Christian. However, the comments he was posting to me were anything but Christian.

People told me to ignore him, but I couldn't; knowing there was someone out there who hated me that much ate at me. I changed my blog settings so he could no longer comment, but soon discovered that he was now going after me on his own page. I'd check now and then and see status updates such as "Erica Scott needs to retire," "Erica Scott needs therapy," and, ugliest one of all, "Erica Scott is a home-wrecker who helps married men cheat on their wives." Talk about libel!

I had the last word, though. I collected these comments and forwarded them to MySpace Help. After I did that three consecutive times, MySpace apparently kicked him off, because his profile was deleted. I never did find out who he was. The downside of the Internet: It enables you to connect with amazing people worldwide, folks you'd never know otherwise. But it also makes you available to some vile characters. So, exercise due caution, always.

Still, I wasn't going to let one hater shut me down. So when I felt like being snarky, I was. Readers came to expect and appreciate my periodic rants, particularly at two times during the year: summertime, because the heat made me cranky, and the holiday season, which I detest. I found these types of posts to be therapeutic, plus they had the side benefit of making people laugh.

Here's a favorite holiday rant, from November 2, 2007:

For those of you who are fairly new to my blog, wel-come to my nightmare, and two months of bitching. I detest the holiday season. It's so commercialized and pressurized and Hallmarked to death. Yes, the world may be falling apart, the war is raging, crime and diseases continue, every damned day they discover a new food that will poison you... but HEY! Let's put that all off and paste on those big fake smiles and put on that holiday cheer! What... it's November 2 and you haven't taken your carefully-posed-to-look-genuinely-happy holiday picture yet? Oh, and don't forget, it's all holiday *now—you can't say* Christmas. *There's a writers' strike about to start up and thousands of people will be out of work. But hey, what do we care? Who watch-es original programming at holiday time anyway? Let's watch* It's a Wonderful Life *for the 500th time! So you hate your relatives, your co-workers make you sick... forget about that! For two months, you get to pretend you love these people! Max out your credit cards, wreck your diets, stress yourselves to the bone, camp out in the mall parking lots, shop 'til you drop, deck those halls, nog those eggs, yule those tides. You can deal with your debts and 10 extra pounds and your hangovers and your kids whining that they didn't get the latest XBox or iPhone or whatever the fuck they wanted, come January 2.*

On the flip side, when I was struggling with something, I laid myself bare, even when it wasn't pretty. Here's a snippet from a May 9, 2007 blog. Poor John had lost his job and I was consumed with worry over him.

I have someone who loves me dearly. But right now, he is needy. And I have to be strong and supportive for him. Love is so much more than sex, spanking and romantic joy. It is compromise, peaks and valleys, heartache, hard work, giving and taking, widening your heart and your world to include another person and all their foibles and weaknesses as well as their strengths. I understand this, and I know I am richer for the experience. But some days... I don't know... I just want a strong force in my life to take care of me, and not need anything in return but my gratitude. Is

265

that selfish and horrible of me, or does everyone feel like that sometimes?

When I indulged in this manner, I'd try to soften it a bit later, so I didn't come off like a complete whiner. At the end of this same entry, I wrote this:

Ever since the incomparable Adele Haze, Jujubees and Bonnie linked my blog to theirs, I have been getting hundreds of hits a day. For those of you just joining me, I promise you, I'm not always this heavy. Sometimes I'm quite amusing. Sometimes I'm mischievous. Sometimes I just observe life and people and all the BS and minutiae that make up the days. So if you're thinking, oh Christ, this woman is a sobfest, please stick around. This will pass.

MySpace was hopping for a long time and I enjoyed my niche there. But its popularity started to wane, then drop drastically. Messages and comments dwindled, and friends left the site. For reasons I will never understand, Facebook became the site of choice. I didn't and still don't care for it, even though I have a profile there; it's extremely vanilla and riddled with silly games and applications. Many of my spanking friends are there, but they use their real names and link to their families, coworkers and so on, so they don't want the association with my kinky profile, even though I tone down the spanking references a great deal.

I knew I should move my blog elsewhere, but I didn't want to bother. Besides, so many people were linked to me and I was still getting a lot of blog hits, although not as many comments. I figured as long as I stayed on MySpace, people would go there to read my blog if they liked it. I hate change and I will stay in a less-than-ideal situation much longer than I should sometimes.

But then in August 2010, MySpace chose to revamp the site and the blogs, and not one of their changes was for the better. I suppose I could have gotten used to most of the inconveniences, but the blogs were now *FUBAR*.

It used to be that I could reply to each individual comment; that was no longer possible. The order of the com-

266

ments now appeared with the oldest at the bottom and newest at the top, which was thoroughly confusing. And worst of all, comment size was now limited. People couldn't insert photos or links anymore, and if they wrote more than a couple of sentences, they would be informed "comment is too long" and would lose what they'd written. That did it. It takes a lot to get me to make a change, but once I hit my limit and am ready to move on, there's no stopping me.

I set up a new blog on Blogspot and got to work on stylizing it. I posted a link to the new place on my old blog so people would know where to go. Unfortunately, I could not move all my blog archives to the new site, so I left the MySpace account intact in order to keep the old blogs.

Being on Blogspot has been wonderful so far; my friends found me, along with several new people. I love how much more user-friendly it is, how easy it is to include photos and links in my entries. I can now list my friends' blog links. Others don't have to be a member of Blogspot in order to leave comments. Unfortunately, I had to disable the option of anonymous comments for a while, because of one very unpleasant and relentless person who went on a spree of negativity, attacking me and my friends, and wouldn't stop even when I pleaded. However, after a few months, I tentatively re-enabled the anonymous option. So far, I have not had any further trouble.

I am in exceptional company with many great writers, and it's so gratifying!

PLAY PARTNER EXTRAORDINAIRE

"I am completely useless today... sleepy, dreamy, bliss-fully happy, sore, spent, all my senses stimulated and tuned. The average person would read that and think I just had incredible sex. Only my fellow kinks are saying, 'Ah, lucky girl, she just had one hell of a spanking session.' "
—from my *MySpace* blog, January 31, 2006

Throughout my years in the spanking scene, I have always been in love with John and he's been with me for it all—the ups and downs, the good and the bad. I wouldn't want to trade him for anyone else. However, that doesn't preclude my desire to be spanked by other men.

As I mentioned earlier, John and I both play with other partners. For one thing, I am not a switch, so I cannot satisfy his bottoming needs. And for another, while he is a very good spanker, I discovered early on that I could not take him seriously as a *top*. We were too close, I knew him too well, and somehow, I could not get into the right head space with him after we'd been together for a while. Therefore, we both had needs that the other could not fulfill. We had to work out a few bugs along the way and had some arguments and hurt feelings, but overall, we supported this outside play, as long as we both knew our priority (each other).

Here's where it gets a little tricky, and where judgment often rears its ugly head. I have had many play partners over the years. While I am *in* love with John, first and foremost, I have loved some of my play partners as well. Not in the same way; John has my heart and occupies a space within that no one else can touch. But there is a special bond that play partners can form, if they connect on a deeper level and have that unique symbiosis that only a top and bottom can understand.

If I trust a top, if I feel chemistry with him and can put myself in his hands with no hesitation, then he can hurt me, much more than I would ever let John hurt me, and I'll take it willingly. I will experience pain, endorphin surge and

268

emotional release—at times, I will even cry. I do not take this kind of trust lightly and when I have it for a spanker, it is precious indeed.

The naysayers point fingers, call it "emotional cheating" and ponder why "one man isn't enough for me." Guess what? I don't believe any one human being can fulfill all our needs. We are raised from the start to believe in "the One" and many of us spend our lives searching for this Holy Grail. I am of the belief that we have many Ones; that different people can serve different purposes in our lives. Love is infinite; feeling it for one doesn't take it away from another.

Parents with more than one child love them all (one would hope). People love more than one friend. Why is it wrong for me to have loving feelings for more than one man? The only person who should object to that is John himself, and he does not. He knows who he is and where he stands, and that I adore him. He is untouchable; no man is a threat to him. And the more freedom he gives me to wander off and play, the more I want to come back to him. At parties, his attitude is: "You get to play with her; I get to take her home."

Some people get this. Many do not. I will be the first to admit that my view of relationships may be a bit unorthodox. But I look at the statistics on divorce, infidelity and unhappy marriages, and I can't help but think that perhaps my way might work better for some.

Enough of that. I cannot change societal dictates. I gave up on being understood a long time ago; these days, my goal is a degree of acceptance, so I can live to the best of my ability among others who don't necessarily share my views.

I have had ads on many sites for several years. In these, I'm very straightforward—I make it clear that I'm in a relationship and am seeking spanking play and friendship. I also stress that I am not a submissive personality and a man needs a sense of humor in order to play well with me. Between these ads, party connections and my presence from videos, I've been fortunate enough to meet some incredible tops while in the scene. A few became one-on-one partners with whom I played in my apartment, or I went to their homes.

I've used the same formula for years when it comes to meeting men online: 1. Exchange a few introductory messages, IM if possible; 2. Arrange to meet in person publicly, ideally at a coffeehouse, so we can see if there is in-person chemistry. If there is, then we arrange to play. Through trial and error, I learned to never skip the initial meeting, and to never promise play to anyone without seeing them in person first. I don't care how good someone sounds in writing; I won't know how I'll feel about going over their laps until I've seen them and spoken with them. Also, I insist on a photo. Refusal to send me one, even privately, is a huge red flag for me.

Why so insistent on pictures and meetings? Because unfortunately, people do misrepresent themselves.

My favorite example: Several years ago, I had an online correspondence with a gentleman who lived back East. We had many exchanges, both email and IM, and I liked how he sounded: attractive, experienced and confident. He traveled often for business and said he'd probably be in California some point soon. However, he would not send me a picture. He gave me some rigmarole about how he had a very high-profile job and he was paranoid about his photos floating around on the Internet. Plus, he claimed to be a Luddite and that he didn't have any digital photos available anyway. "I can tell you that you won't be disappointed," he assured me. "People tell me I look like George Clooney."

Eventually, he did indeed come to Southern California and was staying at a fancy hotel in Beverly Hills. He invited me to join him for dinner there. That was another red flag; I don't like to meet the first time for a meal, just for coffee. I don't want to feel like I "owe" them anything. But I said yes to this as well. My instincts had been murmuring, and now they were elbowing me, but I pushed them away.

He knew what I looked like, so we agreed to meet in the hotel lobby and he'd find me. I sat nervously waiting, and then a man approached me.

George Clooney, my ass. He looked more like George Jetson. The only thing he shared with Clooney was salt-

and-pepper hair. Upon shaking my hand, he winked at me. *Cute,* I thought, *he's flirting with me.* Then he winked at me again. And again. And all through dinner. The poor man had a nervous tic.

The prices on the menu horrified me and I ordered the cheapest thing I could find (a bowl of soup), which was still ridiculously exorbitant. He insisted on ordering a rich dessert, ice cream with bananas flambéed in butter, rum and sugar. The sound of that didn't appeal to me in the least, so I thought fine, he'll eat most of it. But he pushed it over to me after he ate two bites, saying he was lactose intolerant and if he ate any more of it, we'd both be in trouble. Clearly, the concept of "TMI" was foreign to him. Well, I didn't want it either, so most of it went to waste.

By now, after all these arrangements and this expensive meal, I felt obligated to play with him, so we went to his room. I don't know what happened to the confident and assertive man I'd chatted with, but the man in his place was awkward and inept. The scene fell flat from the start and never got better. After we'd been going on for a bit, he stopped, leaned down to me and whispered, "Help me out here. I don't know how to end this." I had to instruct him, as I lay OTK, on how to bring a scene to an end. Yes, it was as excruciating as it sounds. Afterward, he gave me a nice backrub, but that certainly wasn't what I'd come for.

Long story short? Never again. Meet first, no promises, no obligations.

You may have noticed I didn't mention a phone call. For me, that isn't necessary, as I'm not one who enjoys speaking on the phone. Others differ on this point and insist that phone calls are mandatory, and that's fine. I'd rather see if someone can communicate well through writing and then in person, bypassing the middle step. Of course, sometimes they want me to call them because they need to know if *I'm* for real. (As one man put it, "I want to make sure you're an Erica, not an Eric.")

How do I know, when I first meet these men, if I want to play with them? There's finding them physically appealing, of course, but there's more to it than that. I can't explain it; it's an elusive something-or-other, a sense of chemistry, a certain attraction. I only know that it comes upon me rather quickly, and if it doesn't, I cannot will it to be so. It's either there or it isn't. There have been times when I haven't felt it, but the man was nice and I went ahead and played with him anyway, hoping that spark would generate. It didn't.

Sometimes these encounters happen at parties, when I don't plan on them. At several Shadow Lane parties, I've had what I like to call an "Oh my God, who is *that*" moment, when I see a man and somehow, I know I want to play with him before I even know his name.

Fortunately, sometimes the man's first impression of me is somewhat mutual and then things work out swimmingly. However, there have been times when I notice a man at a party, but I don't even enter his radar. On those occasions, I could play with a dozen or more other men, but I'll fixate longingly on the one with whom I didn't. I'm not particularly proud of this, but I've heard others admit to doing it as well. We're only human.

I learned as I went along that the spanking fetish has just about as many variations as it has members. Orientations, preferences, implements, wood vs. leather, anal or no anal, with sex added or not, hot-button phrases and gestures—the list goes on. With this in mind, it's no wonder that these special connections are not that easy to forge. The process is often trial and error, and can be disheartening. So when I did manage to find these connections, I did not take them for granted.

Unfortunately, a spanking relationship/friendship, while powerful, does not replace a full day-to-day relationship with all the facets, vanilla included. Sometimes, a spanker with whom I connected was single when we started. Then, after I got used to having him in my life, grew accustomed to regular play with him and was enjoying it more and more, he'd meet someone and start dating. And even if this new woman was kinked as well, she did *not* like the idea of him getting together with another woman to spank her. So I was history, even though I wasn't a threat in the least and couldn't understand how any woman could consider me as such. *Femmes fatales* are generally younger and have much better boobs than I do.

I never wanted to take another woman's man. I just wanted to borrow some of them on occasion for a spanking and then give them back. Again, some people got that. But many didn't.

This happened a few times, and it hurt like hell every single time. Many people didn't understand why I felt so bad. "You still have John," they said. Of course I did. But I'd still lost a friend, a bond, a source of intense shared experiences. And the *way* I lost them made me feel quite disposable. My head played and replayed the same message: I was fine to play with until someone better came along. I know that's not what any of them meant, but that's how it felt. From childhood on, I've had abandonment/rejection issues, and whenever a top had to disappear, it felt deeply personal, even though I logically knew that it was not.

Late in 2005, I had an abrupt and unpleasant severance from a favorite top, and a friend was involved as well, so I was reeling from the double loss—my top *and* my friend. The situation was ugly and had far-reaching consequences for quite a while, and if anything came close to driving me out of this scene, that was it. My reputation was damaged, and for no good reason. I was depressed, disinterested in perusing the ads anew and felt like I would never again recapture that special connection.

Then an ad on the Shadow Lane site caught my eye. The poster had included a picture, which is a rarity on the SL ads for some reason. I saw a handsome young man in a suit, casually leaning against a wall with his hands in his pockets. His ad read that he was new to the area, he was scheduled to shoot a video with Shadow Lane within a month, and he had a unique proposal; he wanted to meet local women and learn how to be the best possible spanker he could be. He didn't care if we were 18 or 48 (he was 37); he wanted play partners with whom he could grow as a top and learn all the nuances.

Well… I was 48. I'd made it under the age wire. Intrigued, I wrote to him. I didn't hear from him for a while, but then saw him posting on the Shadow Lane board. I posted to him, "Check your messages," and he posted back, "Erica! I wrote to you! Check your spam box and see if it landed there." I did, and sure enough, there he was. Eagerly, I clicked "This is not spam" and read his email; he was articulate, sounded well-mannered and smart, and I liked the pictures he included as well. Things happened quickly after that—we exchanged another couple of messages, had one phone call and then planned to meet the following Monday for coffee.

Enter Danny Chrighton.

* * *

I met him at a Starbucks near my apartment that Monday afternoon. I was excited, but telling myself not to get my expectations too high; nothing was guaranteed. There was still that defining moment ahead, when I'd first lay eyes on him. I'm reminded of "Mystery Date," that silly board game that was popular when I was growing up. I didn't have it, but I remember the commercials and the jingle: *"Mystery date, are you ready for your mystery date…"* Prepubescent girls would play, each selecting a door to open and seeing if her date was a dream ("Ahhhh!") or a dud ("Uggggh"). Was I about to have an "Ahhhh" or an "Uggggh" moment?

Entering the Starbucks, I scanned the line waiting to order drinks and saw him. He turned, recognized me and smiled.

Definitely an "Ahhhh" moment. So far, so good.

We sat down with our coffees and talked. There was no preliminary awkwardness, no lags in the conversation; it was as if we'd known each other for a long time. I knew we'd be playing that very day, and we did. I drove him back to my place, leaving his car in the strip mall parking lot.

Was our very first play session perfect? No. He was a gentleman and erred on the side of caution; he was too light. I can never fault a top for that; not everyone is as heavy a player as I am and the top has to suss things out before he can ramp them up. But the connection and chemistry were there, and afterward, we talked until long after it had gotten dark. John called to see how my meeting had gone and Danny was still there, so the two of them ended on the phone with each other, chatting away and comparing notes like old friends. Had I just met this man today? It didn't seem like it!

About 9:30, I finally drove him back to his car. Before he got out, he leaned across the seat and gave me a kiss on the cheek. The next day I got a lovely checking-in email from him, waxing enthusiastic about our meeting and saying how much he'd love to continue playing.

Things were off to a very good start.

* * *

We became good friends and regular play partners. Eventually, we developed a standing date: every other Monday, he'd come over. He lived 35 miles from me and it was a bitch of a drive on the 405 freeway, but it had to be my place, since he had a roommate. I figured if he was going to deal with the traffic, the high price of gasoline and the horrible parking on my street, the least I could do was buy him dinner. So we'd go to a little deli around the corner, which became our regular spot.

He never showed up to my place without bringing some sort of chocolate, which we'd share later after our play. Oh, and I got him hooked on my *Dark Shadows* DVDs, so we'd watch several episodes each visit. Danny was extremely smart and had a goofy sense of humor similar to mine, so we never seemed to run out of things to talk about.

He was thoughtful, often bringing me little treats and surprises. Once, he saw a pristine hard-cover copy of my favorite childhood book, *The Phantom Tollbooth*, in a used bookstore and picked it up for me. Another time, he surprised me with a Beatles DVD, one I'd never seen before.

Our play got better and better as we got to know one another. Danny was very laid back and sometimes it took a while to get him into Top Mode, but once he was there, he was a force to be reckoned with. I found I could trust him with anything in his hands: belt, cane, paddles. His aim and technique were amazing; he could read me perfectly, knew when to escalate and when to back off a bit. His hand strengthened and became a formidable implement in itself.

As I came to have more trust in him, I let down my walls, my sarcastic exterior, and allowed him to see my vulnerable side. Oftentimes, our scenes got so intense that I'd cry. He'd get me water and tissues, hold me, soothe me and caress my hair, let me come back from subspace in my own time.

John and Danny met for the first time when several of us were invited to the wedding of a couple of scene friends. They'd already had a few phone chats when Danny was at my place and they hit it off in person. There was no jealousy, no competition. Danny started doing Shadow Lane videos and going to parties, and he grew in the scene. I was more than happy to recommend him to any of my girlfriends and I blogged extensively about our scenes and adventures.

All this was great, but I felt a niggling fear in the back of my mind. He was meeting more people and he was bound to start dating sooner or later. Then what would happen to us, to our friendship, our play? I'd been down this road before and it always ended badly.

By the time his second Shadow Lane party came around, he'd met a young woman and she joined him at the party. She was perfectly nice to me, but I still felt nervous. At his first party, Danny and I had played five times. But this time, every time I saw him, he was playing with her. My insecurities kicked in and I found myself avoiding him; if I went to a room party and saw him in there playing, I'd go somewhere else. I didn't answer the messages he left on my cell phone. A couple of times when he tried to talk to me, I brushed him off, saying I had to be somewhere.

Finally, toward the end of the weekend, he cornered me in someone's suite. "Come with me," he said. "Where?" I asked. "We're going to your room," he replied.

Once we were there, he wasted no time. "What's going on?" And, like a ridiculous child, I burst into tears. Feeling incredibly foolish and embarrassed, I confessed my insecurities to him; told him I was afraid that his new friend wouldn't appreciate having me in the picture and I was going to lose him.

I will never forget what he said to me that night. "Erica, I know how fragile you are, and I would never abandon you. Please believe me—any woman I am with now or in the future will know that you are a part of my life and she will have to accept that."

Hearing those words meant the world to me. I was more than an expendable plaything; I was valued. I felt like I mattered. I felt *loved*. More than our scenes, the copious quantities of chocolate, the video we did together (more on that later), any of his thoughtful gestures—that was the best and most memorable gift he gave me. That's what made him stand out from many of the others.

Thank you, my friend. May you always have all the bacon and pecan pie your heart desires.

WHAT HAPPENS TO NAUGHTY GIRLS?

"It's been less than 24 hours since I put my book on sale, and already, the responses have been overwhelming. Emails, posts, bulletins—so many wonderful compliments from supportive friends. How gratifying this is, and it's only just begun."
—from my *MySpace* blog, June 27, 2007

I have always loved a good spanking story; emphasis on the word *good*. If you go online and search, you will find hundreds, perhaps thousands of spanking stories. Unfortunately, many of them are so badly written, they will make you cringe rather than swoon. Many people are capable of taking or giving a good spanking, or of fantasizing about one. Able to write successfully about said spankings? Not as many. I've seen some writers who fill entire paragraphs with sound effects and sobs.

In spanking fiction, as in the scene itself, there is something for everyone. Chances are, if you like something in your play, you'll like it in your stories. And conversely, if you are averse to a particular type of scene, you will not enjoy reading about it, no matter how good the writing is.

With that in mind, whenever I felt the urge to write a story, I knew I was writing first for myself, because it was a reflection of my orientation, my preferences and desires. If other people happened to like what I'd written, that was wonderful. But I was always going to be true to myself.

I'd seen other writers who delved into various orientations and scenarios for variety and a greater audience appeal. Some wrote and published compilations of stories with something for every taste. However, I never bought these. I found that I'd like maybe one or two stories in the entire book, and my reaction to the remainder would vary from indifference to "ugh." Hardly worth the price.

So every now and then, I'd write a piece of spanking fiction, posting it on SCSW and later on my blog. The feedback was a pleasure; people said that as they read my work, it made them feel like they were there, experiencing my scenario themselves. I value compliments on my writing a great deal.

I didn't plan to write fiction; I didn't sit down with the intent to write a story. It would simply hit me; a plot would percolate in my mind and I'd find myself at the computer with the story spinning out of my fingers. As these tales amassed, people told me I should write a book. I'd reply no, I can't force it. The stories come when they come.

In 2007, I was contacted by a MySpace friend. He'd written a book of spanking stories and was planning on self-publishing it on Lulu; would I be willing to read some of his work and contribute a comment? "What is Lulu?" I asked. He told me about the site where one could upload a book manuscript, sell it and split the profits with Lulu. Lulu got the larger share so it wouldn't be a huge moneymaker, but it was fun to see one's work in print.

By now, I had ten fiction stories in my collection, and this idea intrigued me. What if I wrote two more for an even dozen and then put a book together? I could add two nonfiction stories (my first spanking and my first video shoot). The more I thought about it, the more exciting it felt, and I decided to go for it.

Lulu is a fascinating site. They have an introductory tutorial that takes you through the entire process, which turned out to be more complex than I thought. You not only had to write the book, but you had to format it properly too. They would convert it into a PDF for you, but the formatting had to be precisely to their standards or else the conversion wouldn't go through. Coming up with two more stories was the easy part. Now I had to dig back into my dusty archives of Microsoft Word formatting knowledge and figure out how to prepare this thing for publication. Fortunately, Lulu has a lot of FAQs and help sections available, plus a forum where you can present your challenges to other members and get feedback.

Little by little, it came together. I had to merge all my story files into one large file, insert page breaks and pagination, add page gutters and other technical stuff I'd had no awareness of. I had to format the chapter titles as headers so I could generate a table of contents from them. And I had to create a cover—what on earth was I going to use for that?

There was a popular and talented cartoonist who called himself Endart—he specialized in spanking illustrations and had a pay site. He had drawn caricatures of other spanking models, including a particularly adorable one of Pixie Wells, and I knew one of his efforts would be just the thing for my cover. Of course, I didn't know him, but that didn't stop me.

I looked up his site and got an email address. Nothing ventured, nothing gained, right? The worst that could happen was that he'd say no. So I wrote to him, introducing myself and asking if he'd be willing to create a spanking caricature of me that I could use as a book cover. I'd certainly credit him for it and I'd be very grateful. To my delight, he replied, "Send me a couple of pictures and I'll see what I can do."

I thought it might be a while, but after a fairly short time, he sent another email with an attachment. "Is this what you had in mind?" I opened the attachment and felt like jumping up and down and clapping with glee; it was perfect! I'd sent him a picture from *The Spanking Professor*, so he'd drawn me in the blue denim skirt and white tank top I'd worn in that video. I was draped over a handsome man's lap and he was pulling down my panties. The expression on his face was stern; on mine, mischievous and eager. I loved it.

Recently, Endart retired. I'm so thankful to have been graced by his talent.

Although all my stories were M/F and had the same basic protagonists (strong-willed female vs. even more strong-willed male), they were still varied, I thought. Some were more lighthearted while a couple of others had a serious tone. While some of them could actually happen, others were pure fantasy. I even had one where I merged two of my favorite obsessions—spanking and *Dark Shadows*—and put myself in the fictional Collinwood, circa 1897, facing off with none other than the enigmatic and roguish Quentin Collins.

I'd read the stories multiple times and then read the book in its entirety when it was all pulled together, but even the most thorough of proofreaders have blind spots when it comes to checking their own work. One of my online friends offered to read the manuscript for me so that she could catch the little things I'd missed. I gratefully took her up on the offer and promised her a free copy of the finished book in exchange.

The last thing I did was create the back cover. I wanted my own photo on there, but try as I might, I could not configure my jpeg file to fit in the allowed space. I availed myself of the Lulu help forum, presenting my problem. Within the same day, another member replied; he told me to email him the file and he'd configure it for me. The kindness of strangers! Once that was done, it fit precisely and I was able to take a deep breath, convince myself I'd done everything humanly possible to perfect the book, and hit *send* to have it converted to PDF.

The next step was Lulu printing a single copy and sending it to me for final approval. I received my copy a few days later and was thrilled with how it looked, especially the cover art. I flipped through, checked all the formatting, the chapter breaks, the pagination, everything I could think of, and the only error I found was at the end. For whatever reason, there were several blank pages. I went into the file, figured out what was wrong and adjusted it, then resubmitted the PDF. Once I checked online that the correction had been made, I knew it was finished. I then clicked "Make Available to the Public," and that was that. I had a book on sale.

How exciting this was! I posted about it on my blog and sent a mass email to my friends. I ordered a dozen copies (I got a reduced price) for giveaways, and I watched my Lulu page as other orders came in. A few of the bloggers posted about my book as well, and traffic to the book page surged.

There was a review section for the book, and as friends read it, comments and ratings were posted. But I wanted to go one better; I'd found a site called Erotica Revealed, which wrote monthly reviews of various erotic books, and thought perhaps mine would qualify. Sure enough, after I wrote to one of the editors, she requested that I send her a copy.

My review came out in November and was written by a man named Steven Hart. Erotica Revealed gives either a thumbs-up or a thumbs-down symbol on each review, and I got a thumbs-up. Overall, I was pleased with Mr. Hart's assessment.

> The answer to the title of Erica Scott's collection of stories, What Happens to Naughty Girls? is quite obvious, and that is perfectly all right. They get spanked, of course, after consciously or unconsciously, or semi-consciously having worked themselves over the knee of some firm but luscious hunk.

> Ms. Scott's book is amiably clear about what she is doing and the results are charming, sexy, earthy and direct. She includes fourteen stories that are semi-autobiographical fantasies about spankings that she claims to have been given or thought about getting. Given the spanking details, we are pretty sure she has done just that. The stories are the lively, no-nonsense misadventures of more or less the same girl/woman getting her bottom warmed. In fact they are pretty much the same story with different window dressings, but she makes no pretensions to doing otherwise. Thus finding out what happens to naughty girls is a predictable, effortless jaunt if you feel a spanking is what they need most. She certainly thinks so.

> The femme figure is always naughty, cheeky, arrogant in an adolescent sort of way, and/or bratty, often has bad judgment or is possibly drunk, but she is never mean or tiresome. She may well be cranky, horny, or just in the mood to make trouble. Her characters discover that they think spanking is sexy despite their suffering derrieres.

On the other hand she wants the spankings to lead to sex after genuine punishment for being naughty. Okay. Fair enough. In fact, the spankings often seem pretty extreme as they extend from the lengthy application of an enraged male palm to more alarming use of a hairbrush or strap. We worry about her poor bottom. Still, both Erica and her behind soldier on bravely until her body betrays her arousal. Then of course the focus shifts to a sort of gauzy, romantic sex. That's fine too.

In short, Erica, in all her various forms, gets what she wants and her pussy does too, even though she complains that it damply betrays her inner feelings when being spanked. It does just that and we are not unhappy about it. Just how naughty can such a girl be after all? Having worked that hard to get spanked, she really deserves some more tender attention.

Ms. Scott is a very straightforward, likeable writer though her work discloses nothing much about the inner life of her characters or, by extension, herself. Her men are all paternal, clearly very hot numbers to her way of thinking (and why not?), and beyond that largely ciphers. They do what she wants which is to be very dominating for an hour or two, spank her soundly, screw her attentively, and then hit the road.

As such What Happens to Naughty Girls? is an oddly feminist work. Nothing that happens in it is beyond the control of the female characters all of whom provoke and orchestrate the action. The Ken-doll spankers hardly seem to sense they are being manipulated even when they are told as much. So what one likes about this book is that while all these spankings must *be very painful, they are exactly in the form she wants them. She is never in any danger, never truly bullied more than she wants, and she retains throughout the attitude of a darling little wise ass—who really ought to be spanked.*

I've certainly been called worse than a "darling little wise ass," so I consider that a compliment. And I'm glad to be acknowledged as a likeable writer. I think this guy got me, for the most part. He completely understood that my protagonists seek to provoke a spanking, but never intend to be mean or destructive. But there were a couple of points with which I mildly disagreed. Nothing horrible, just minor misunderstandings on his part, I believe.

First, I didn't *always* have the spankings lead to sex. Sometimes I did, because I know that's what many people want to read. Sex makes the story hotter and broadens its audience appeal. But the sex was often suggested more than executed, usually at the end as a fade-out. The spanking was definitely the focus, rather than a means to an end.

Second, are all the men in my stories really Ken dolls and ciphers (numbers; non-entities)? I can't deny that my fantasy spankers all seem to fit a particular mold—they are handsome, confident, strong, dominant but compassionate, and they know just what to do with me. But isn't that the purpose of fantasies?

I'm certainly not alone in writing about an ideal male. Look at the thousands of romance novels out there—the men in those are quite formulaic and interchangeable, with fake-sounding macho names. So my style was not exactly an anomaly. Find me a romance novel where the heroine is plain, the villain looks like Clive Owen and the hero looks like Chris Farley, and I'll admit I'm wrong.

However, if the reviewer really thought I consider my spankers to be simple, interchangeable ciphers, he was mistaken. My readers know otherwise.

And finally—my men are all paternal? No, no, *no*.

Despite these trivial contentions, I did like this review and I wrote to Mr. Hart to thank him.

When I first embraced the spanking kink, I decided I wanted to experience everything I possibly could within it. It had now been eleven years, and I had:

- gone to spanking parties and played publicly;
- been in videos;
- written video scripts;
- worked in a dungeon;
- my pictures published in a magazine;
- been a spanking forum manager;
- kept a spanking-oriented blog; and
- been through the process of writing a book, start to finish.

Granted, the book was self-published. I know that going through a self-publisher or a "vanity press" is not the same as having one's book accepted and produced by a bona fide, mainstream publishing company. Still, I was proud of it. I was told that if it sold even one copy, I could call myself a "published author." As of this writing, *What Happens to Naughty Girls?* has sold 197 copies.

Certainly not bad for a little book of spanking stories. I confess, though, that I hope *this* book does a little better.

WHEN DANNY MET ERICA

"We both thought the script was hot, and covered terri-
tory no company has ever ventured into before. I still won-
der... is this untapped territory going to be welcomed with
enthusiasm, or will it fall flat? Was the fantasy just in my
own head, and in no one else's? (sigh) I can't go there
now. Just have to wait and see what kind of finished prod-
uct we end up with. To my comfort, Chelsea's reaction
when I sent her the script was, 'This is HOT!' "
—from my *MySpace* blog, May 22, 2008

As our friendship and play-partnership blossomed,
Danny and I had a lot of fun with board posts and stories
we wrote together, plus some goofy pictorials. For example, on his birthday we played out a scene (and took pictures) of sharing some chocolate cake, and I mischievously
smeared a forkful of it across his face. He commanded me
to lick it off, then he spanked me as I bent over the kitchen
sink.

Just for giggles (and to drive the gossipers and specula-
tors crazy), we decided to co-write a fictionalized account
of our first meeting. We called it *When Danny Met Erica*,
and the basic premise was true (he placed an ad, I answered
it, we met for coffee). But after that, we spun it into a tale
in which our roles were clearly defined: I was the older,
more experienced spankee, haughty and condescending,
and he was the younger top, new in town and unsure of
himself. In the course of the story, he gained confidence
and transformed, putting me in my place.

We took our first foray into play and built on it, adding
a strapping and severe hairbrushing, plus some sexual activity at the end. Of course, we both knew this was fictional, since the most forward thing he'd done that initial
meeting was kiss me on the cheek. But no one *else* knew
that.

Yes, perhaps it was a bit childish of us. However, we
figured we were doing a service as well. After all, those
who live to focus on other people's lives aren't happy un-

less they have some potential dirt to roll around in, so who were we to deny them?

Sure enough, a girlfriend and I were instant messaging and she told me that the Shadow Lane chat room had been abuzz with speculation about Danny and me. To quote her, some people were positive that the two of us were "fucking like bunnies."

Myths and rumors circulated; my personal favorite was from Danny's first SL party. He had gone a day early, as many do, and he was sharing a room with a female friend. The next morning, she got up to shower and dress and he called me to say hi and find out when John and I were hitting the road for Vegas. This innocent act somehow morphed into "Danny had the nerve to call Erica while he was in bed with so-and-so." Never happened, folks. But we got a perverse kick out of the attention. I never considered myself as interesting gossip fodder, so this was flattering in a twisted way.

* * *

Time passed and Danny shot one Shadow Lane video after another, eventually totaling five. I was very proud of him and loved to watch him on video, but that made me yearn to be on camera with him. I really wanted to shoot again and I couldn't think of anyone else with whom I'd rather co-star. People who watched us play at parties said we looked great and our chemistry was extraordinary, so I figured if we could capture it on film, we'd have a wonderful product, crackling with clever dialogue and thorough spanking. And our storyline was already written; we could use *When Danny Met Erica* and convert it into a video script.

So toward the end of 2006, I took our story and did just that. I sent it to Danny, who then added his feedback and dialogue tweaks. After going back and forth a few times, we now had a script we both liked and were quite excited about it. We felt certain we had a potentially hot video on our hands and there would be interest in shooting it.

We were mistaken.

For one thing, no one wanted to veer from the tried-and-true video standards and tackle this unusual twist—older female bottom with younger male top. Of course, you could have a barely legal woman being spanked by a man old enough to be her grandfather, and you could have older female tops spanking younger male bottoms. But a haughty older woman being taken down a few pegs by a strong, confident man a few years her junior? Unheard of, and apparently untouchable.

And second, although no one said this to me in so many words, the message received repeatedly was clear: I was too old. In this industry, the average cut-off age for a female spankee is 35. I'd already bucked the system and shot videos in my 40s, but now I was pushing 50. It didn't matter how much I worked out, how hard a spanking I could take, how well I could handle lines and perform for the cameras. If I wanted to top, I could continue. As a bottom, apparently I was done. The only company who had thought otherwise was Spanking Epics and they were no longer producing.

I went into a terrible funk, which progressed into a spectacular mid-life crisis overall. I felt like a has-been—old, unattractive, no longer useful in an industry I adored. In my mind, the depressing melodrama played over and over—all my life, I'd felt insignificant, like a non-entity, a nobody. For a few years, I was "somebody"—granted, in a rather unusual way, but still, it meant a lot to me. More than it should have, perhaps. Now I felt like a nobody once again, and I was crushed.

Poor John, and poor Danny. They put up with my crying jags, my rants, my obsessing over my aging face and inevitable bodily changes. My blog readers endured a lot of pity parties as well. I tried to keep my humor intact along with the honest revelations of my feelings, but I look back at some older writing and some of it was over the top. But I couldn't help myself. At the time, it was an all-consuming hurt. The spanking video industry had helped boost my self-esteem in ways I'd never experienced before. Now I felt like it was rejecting me.

When I was finally starting to accept that this video would not happen, a friend offered to shoot us. Needless to say, I was over the moon; I sent her our script, printed one out and started memorizing my lines. My mind buzzed with ad-libs, I planned outfits, and we set a date, or so we thought.

The shoot fell through at the last minute. Having come so close, I was even more depressed when it was yanked away.

* * *

Cut to early 2008; although I'd stopped kicking and screaming over it, the idea of shooting our script never completely left my mind. I made one more attempt to sell the idea, presenting my most compelling argument in favor of producing the video and confidently claiming that it would sell well, as it was a fresh and new type of pairing, unchartered territory in the industry, and Danny and I would blow the cameras out with our chemistry.

The response pulled no punches. I suppose I brought it on myself by pushing so hard, but still. Following the hurtful words was the gentler suggestion that if I wanted this filmed so badly, I should arrange to shoot it myself. I knew enough about the industry and how things worked, and I could do it the way I envisioned it.

I could not blog about this; it was too personal. Fortunately, Danny was coming over later that day. When he arrived, I told him what had happened and wept copiously.

"Let's do it," he said, holding me. "Let's shoot this thing ourselves."

"Huh? How could we do that?"

"We know people. We have friends who know how to shoot video. Let's get someone to shoot us, I'll edit it and finalize it, and we'll figure out how to distribute it."

At first I thought this was too far-fetched and we'd never be able to pull it off, but as we discussed it further, it began to sound feasible. We'd save a ton of money, since Danny knew all about film editing. If we could just get this thing shot by someone we liked and trusted, that would be the biggest hurdle. What to do with it would be decided later; one thing at a time.

We went to dinner and knocked about some ideas, but our first choice stood alone, far above the others: Chelsea Pfeiffer. She and her husband Larry produced their own videos and had been doing so for years, they were skilled and experienced, and we liked them both a great deal. And they were local.

I wasted no time. I wrote to Chelsea, telling her of our product, proposing that they shoot us and asking what they would charge us. It would be just one afternoon, film only, since Danny would take over with the editing. I attached the script so she could read it and get some idea of how much work it would entail.

I received her answer almost immediately—she said it sounded like fun, the script was hot and they'd be very happy to shoot it for us. She asked for $300, which was more than reasonable; they could have gotten up to five times that amount, I believe.

We scheduled our shoot for May 1. Could this actually be happening, after wanting it for so long? It nearly didn't. That morning I got up early, washed and blew out my hair, and started pulling together outfits and makeup. Then Danny called. Very sheepishly, he told me that the night before he'd been playing softball after work with some friends. He'd worn his street shoes and of course, he slipped and fell. Sprained his right wrist. The shoot would have to be postponed.

We rescheduled for May 22. By now, I was convinced that this was not meant to be and something else would come up to sideline it. I studied the script anew and prepared myself, all the while thinking that any minute now, I'd get some sort of bad news, either from Danny or from Chelsea and Larry. *Don't get your hopes up, Erica. Don't get too excited. You've wanted this for what, over two years now? You've gotten to make so many of your fantasies into reality. Perhaps this is the one you simply cannot have.*

But the bad news never came and the date arrived.

We were due at Chelsea and Larry's at 2:30, and Danny came over to my place early so we could run our lines and make any last-minute changes. I had made a change myself, to the final scene, the one in which I finally surrender and apologize. I decided I was going to do this scene completely naked.

I'd never been fully nude on video before; my breasts had always been covered, I had shoes and/or stockings on, etc. For the most part, I thought spankee nudity on film was gratuitous, unless the scenario was between intimate partners. After all, what did bare breasts have to do with spanking? But in this case, it was about humbling me and I thought being naked would play that up.

Plus, I had a more personal reason. My appearing on camera naked was my way of flipping the bird to the industry that no longer acknowledged me as a viable and attractive bottom. "*This* is what 50 looks like, you fucking ageists!" Yes, I know; once again, rather childish. But it sure felt good.

After we arrived at Chelsea's, the four of us discussed the particulars. I was used to Shadow Lane and Spanking Epics, who both shot the same way—with three cameras at once, each filming their own angle, and then all three would be cut together and edited for the final. Larry used one camera, but he was so thorough with it, the finished products ended up looking like several cameras were used.

They explained the procedure: Instead of shooting each scene straight through, we would do it bits at a time, a couple of lines, pause, then he'd shoot another angle, getting facial reactions, close-ups on the bottom, wide shots, etc. Chelsea acknowledged that it *sounded* like a choppy way to do it, but we'd be surprised at how quickly we'd adapt to the process and how well it would turn out.

As we got ready, I was my usual pre-shoot nervous wreck. Actually, even more so. This one was different—this was *mine*. It was more personal.

Danny got into his shoot clothes and sprawled on a couch in the back room, completely relaxed. I, on the other hand, flitted around like a caged bird. A clumsy caged bird at that; I walked right into a low glass coffee table, smacking both shins so hard, they both turned purple immediately and one bled. I had made a conscious effort the past week

291

or so to be extra careful, to not bump into anything so I wouldn't have any bruises... and now this. Oh well—as Chelsea put it, no one would be looking at my shins. I put some concealer and powder on the discolorations and then changed into my outfit.

We began the shoot, and as Chelsea had promised, it was quite easy to get into the flow of Larry's method. Anytime he wanted a repeat of something, he'd "freeze" us. "Give me that face again." "Let's shoot from such-and-such line again; I want to get that foot stamp."

As Larry went back and forth with the camera, Chelsea directed and fed us lines. She was very helpful, suggesting little tweaks. If she thought a line wasn't read with the right inflection or simply could have been done better, she'd say do it again. During the strapping scene, she called "cut" so that she could straighten my stocking tops. If a particular angle didn't look quite right, she'd suggest another.

The afternoon flew by and we were done in three-and-a-half hours, just in time for dinner. The four of us went to a nearby Italian restaurant and as an added thank-you, Danny and I treated Larry and Chelsea.

The sole glitch of the day was minor. Danny had brought along his external hard drive so Larry could transfer the video directly to it, and then Danny could go home and load it onto his own system. However, Larry's computer would not recognize Danny's device; some sort of incompatibility, and I have no idea how these things work, so I can't explain it. Larry gave Danny the video on some small portable type of file, and kept it on his own system as backup, so there was no way we'd lose it. As it happened, the portable device didn't work either, so Danny went to Larry and Chelsea's at a later date, bringing his laptop. This time, the transfer was successful.

I didn't even see Danny for the next two months—he got extremely busy with work and he was doing freelance work on the side as well. Plus, it was summertime and very hot, and my apartment's A/C isn't strong enough to handle the 90s+ days, so we decided to pass on playing for a while anyway.

Finally, on July 21, Danny came over with his laptop and showed me a rough cut of the first 20 minutes, edited. What a trip to finally see the two of us on camera! I was beyond thrilled and loved how well it was coming together so far. Clare Fonda and Tony Elka had been helpful, informing Danny about the necessary legalese he'd need to insert, and he and I went through the music he had downloaded to choose something for the opening credits. I'd opened the floor on my blog as for ideas in naming our "production company." (I wanted to call it "Mrs. Robinson Productions" but Danny wouldn't have any of that.) We received many good names, but our friend Dave Wolfe won with his suggestion of "StarStruck Productions."

By August, he'd finished editing the DVD and had added credits, the FBI warning and so forth. He brought it to my place and we watched; wow! There we were! There was our chemistry and camaraderie, my sass, his spanking prowess, my transition into contrition, all perfectly captured for posterity. I was so pleased that I didn't even flinch while watching myself naked.

There were only two minor glitches and they were easy fixes. One of them? He'd misspelled his own name in the credits! And yes, if you think I got a lot of fun-poking mileage out of that one, you are correct. Once he'd fixed the master, he burned a couple of copies and then sent one to Larry and Chelsea, one to Tony and Eve.

And right after he did that, he moved away.

It happened very suddenly, starting with a job loss and ending with an offer from friends in Denver, where he'd been living before—they had a house he could move into. He was familiar with the area, knew a lot of people there, and the cost of living was much lower than Southern California. Long story short, he packed up some of his things, sold some others on Craigslist, and then he took off. I barely had a chance to say goodbye.

A week later, he did fly back to collect some more of his things, and I picked him up at the airport. So we did get to say a proper goodbye after all, but of course, I was heartbroken. He wasn't just a play partner; he was my best friend, next to John.

Tony and Eve liked the DVD and made an offer to distribute it for us. We figured it couldn't be in a better place, since we were both closely associated with SL (he'd done five videos for them; I'd done four), we'd met through their ad site, etc. They would do all the packaging, duplicating and mailing, so we didn't have to do another thing. At first, there was a holdup because Tony wanted the video in another format, but there was no way Danny could do that now, since he had way too much on his plate with the move. So Tony said he'd make things work with the copy he had.

On October 2, 2008, *When Danny Met Erica* officially went on sale. Eve had written to me, requesting pictures and a written synopsis. However, writing promotional material is not my forte, and she ended up punching it up a great deal and making it sound great, for which I was grateful. Butch took the photos I'd sent and Eve's text and created a beautiful five-page spread for the catalog.

Practically from the first day I met Danny Chrighton, I wanted to shoot with him. This DVD was a labor of love between two great friends and play partners, and I was over the moon seeing it finally come to fruition. The only thing that could have made me even happier would be having him there with me so we could celebrate together, but that wasn't to be. I cried a lot when he left and missed him terribly. But he ended up making a good life for himself in Denver; it was the right move for him and I'm happy it worked out.

Still, we remain great friends and keep in touch, and I see him and his lovely play partner Sophie at Shadow Lane parties. And *When Danny Met Erica* will forever be my personal favorite among the films I've done. Once I'd accomplished that, I figured it was the end of my video adventures. If I never shot again, I wouldn't mind; I'd made my dream video, exactly the way I wanted it, and I could add "producer" to my list of spanking accomplishments. I didn't need to do any more.

However, a spanking video production company from across the pond would bring me out of retirement in 2009.

NORTHERN SPANKING INSTITUTE

"They told me Stephen and I were doing a hus-band/wife scenario. I'm American and he's English, and I hate living in the UK. We've been to a party with his col-leagues and my attitude has embarrassed him, so we're having a huge fight over it. I had carte blanche to insult him and his culture all I wanted, and vice versa. No script, just go with it, ad lib and have fun. Fine by me!"
—from my MySpace blog, March 10, 2009

Shadow Lane hadn't had two parties a year in a long time, but in 2009, they decided to do so. Because it was in March, it became a St. Paddles (Patrick's) party and green was the color of the weekend. I managed to find a green-and-black print dress on sale at Macy's, a place where I never shop but I couldn't find anything green elsewhere. I don't usually follow the party dress themes, but wanted to this time.

I'd heard that we were going to have special visitors this time: A group of people from the Northern Spanking Institute video company in the UK. I was familiar with the name, but didn't know any of them and had never seen their work.

A few years prior, another group (whose company shall remain nameless) came to a Shadow Lane party and were completely aloof and exclusionary, keeping to themselves and staying in a separate hotel from our party (and hijack-ing the SL guests to come to *their* party). I certainly hoped this group wasn't going to behave in that manner.

My concern turned out to be completely unfounded; they were delightful people. Warm, lively, friendly and ex-uberant, genuinely happy to be here, mingling with every-one and inviting us to their suite the next day for a party.

However, the rest of the party didn't seem like it was starting out well. They'd tried a different hotel this time because it was much cheaper, and it was the pits. The rooms were small, the bathrooms tiny, and the A/C was a loud wall unit, not central. The suites, which were supposed to be large for our group parties, were barely bigger than the regular rooms.

Also, a lot of people we'd hoped to see didn't show up. Friday night, which is usually hopping at these gatherings, was quite low-key and there was only one room party we could find, which was completely packed (people sitting on the carpet) and uncomfortably warm. I went to bed that night feeling let down and disappointed, fearing that the rest of the weekend was going to be as much of a bust as this evening had been.

John and I have a well-established routine at these weekend parties. In the mornings, I sleep in while he gets up to find the hotel gym and work out. He usually finds some other party-goers in there and chats them up, gathering tidbits about who's doing what, where the suite parties are, who wants to go to lunch, and so forth; then he comes back to our room, wakes me up and fills me in before we go shower and dress.

That Saturday morning was no different; I snoozed away while he went to exercise, and when he woke me up, I felt the heaviness of the letdown settle onto me once again. Sighing and stretching, I asked him how his morning went.

"Oh, I've been busy," he said. "I worked out, saw so-and-so, made a lunch date for us with so-and-so, found out where there's a room party from noon to 2:00, got you a video shoot, talked with…"

"You *what*?" I screeched, now wide awake.

He smiled innocently at me. "I said, I found out where there's a room party at—"

"Not *that*," I interrupted. "Before that!"

"You mean, our lunch date with—"

"JOHN!"

"OK, OK," he said, grinning. He then told me how, while he was at the gym, he struck up a conversation with a lovely blond woman. He wondered if she was with our party and discreetly managed to find out that indeed she was, and then asked her if she was part of the "British Invasion group," since she had an accent. She laughed and answered yes.

They introduced themselves to each other—her name was Lucy. John added, "I don't know whether or not you know of her, but I'm here with Erica Scott—"

"*Erica Scott?*" Lucy shrieked. "Oh my God, I love her! She's incredible! She's here? You're with her? Oh, do you think she might shoot with us?"

Wow. Turns out she was *the* Lucy, of Lucy and Paul, the couple who are behind Northern Spanking. John said he could certainly run that by me, but she had to keep in mind that I only play with men. No problem, she said.

Unbelievable. I'd figured my shooting days were over; now here was this company who wanted me. Who still thought I was sexy and fun and quite shoot-able. I was stunned at first, then that gave way to massive excitement. Suddenly, the weekend was looking up.

After I showered and dressed and we grabbed a bite to eat, we headed for the Northern Spanking suite at 12:30. The place was filled with people watching an impromptu skit the NS folks were putting on for us. John and I found a spot on the carpet near the "stage" and sat down to enjoy. They were hilarious; I had to put my hand over my mouth frequently to stifle my loud and distinctive guffaws.

When they wrapped it up, we waited patiently for our turn to speak to Lucy. It took a while, but when we finally reached her, she beamed at me, gave me a huge hug and cried, "I love you; you're awesome! I want to shoot with you!" Greetings don't get much better than that. We agreed that we'd touch base later and see if we could set something up. They were doing several small shoots the next day, but weren't sure of the time frame yet.

However, by 4:00 the next day, I still had not heard from them, and I was starting to think the shoot might fall through. We were invited to a suite party at 6:00, so I called Lucy and Paul's room to leave a message and then we left.

As soon as we walked into the crowded room, one of the NS ladies saw me and dashed over. "Did Lucy and Paul connect with you? They want to shoot with you tonight!"

"They do? Really? When, where? I've been trying to find them!" I cried.

She said she thought they were up in the 10th floor suite shooting, and she'd go slip a note under the door and tell them yes, I was up for shooting later. What a doll! She left, and then returned a few minutes later, telling me that she'd seen them and yes, they were in 1058 and I should just pop up there and knock on the door. I thanked her profusely and fairly ran up to 1058.

Paul and Stephen were up there shooting with Bailey Sullivan. Paul asked if I could come back in an hour. I looked at my watch—it was now 6:45. We were supposed to go to dinner with a group at 7:00. I asked him if there was any way we could do it a little later; he said he was sorry, but they had somewhere to go later this evening. So I said yes, absolutely, I will be there.

I dashed back downstairs to tell John and our friends that I was sorry, but I couldn't have dinner with them, and they should go without me and I'd grab something for myself later. They insisted they'd do nothing of the sort; they'd wait for me to finish the shoot and then we'd have a late dinner, so I could tell them all about it.

I went back into our room to change; I already had some makeup on so I just had to touch it up and fix my hair. I decided to wear the dress I'd had on the night before; a skin-tight, long-sleeved black mini-dress. My hands were shaking so badly, I tore my stocking as I pulled it on, but fortunately I had a spare pair. Amazing how the pre-shoot nerves were as powerful as ever.

I got back to 1058 at 6:45 on the button, but they were running a bit late with Bailey's shoot, so I sat quietly and watched the end of it. Then it was my turn. They gave me the setup: husband/wife, UK vs. America. I had married him and come to live in the UK, and I didn't like it there. We were just arriving home from a business dinner, during which I'd embarrassed him.

It was a short scene since their time was limited, but it was so much fun. After some preliminary arguing, we started with OTK on the couch, then he "slippered" me while I knelt on the couch. The insults were flying. Stephen claimed he couldn't keep up with me because I was too quick, but I think he made some marvelous comebacks.

When I was snarking about how Brits have such lousy oral hygiene, he snapped, "I'll have you know that I floss once a year!" To which I replied, "Yeah, all three of your real teeth!"

Paul told me afterward that they'd made so many wonderful connections with American models on this trip, they wanted to come back soon, hopefully next year. I said if they did, it would be my honor to work with them again. Our video was named *Cultural Exchange* and was posted on their site in three parts, along with several pictures.

Toward the end of 2009, I received a surprise package from Lucy: My DVD and a Christmas present. She also wrote to me and said they planned to return in 2010 for the Shadow Lane Labor Day party; might I have some time to shoot with them again if I was going? I didn't have to give that question any thought; of course, the answer was yes.

* * *

In August 2010, prior to the Shadow Lane party, flurries of emails went back and forth; Lucy and I confirming our shoot and setting a time, and Stephen and I trading ideas about scenarios. He suggested that I be a temperamental and egotistical diva actress and he would be my long-suffering agent, fed up with my screwing up every job he gets for me. We'd play it over the top for humor. I loved it; any opportunity to chew up the scenery and play a bitch from hell to the hilt had great potential for me.

My mind worked feverishly, conjuring scathing lines to throw at Stephen, and I came up with what I thought would be the perfect *coup de grâce* to push him into starting the spanking. I'd have a hissy fit because I'd requested peanut M&Ms in my hotel room and I'd received plain instead. When he failed to see how critical this was, I would dump the bowl of the offending sweets over his head. I figured M&Ms would be perfect, since they wouldn't mess up his clothes or our surroundings; when we were done, we'd simply pick them back up. I ran the idea past Stephen and he approved it.

Party time arrived; the usual whirlwind of greetings and hugs, nerves and thrills. My shoot with Northern was scheduled for 1:00 on Saturday afternoon, which was ideal. After a light lunch with John and some of our friends, I wandered up to the NS suite right on time. They were shooting in one of the bedrooms with Jenni Mack and running a little overtime, so Lucy and I sat in the front room, chatting quietly until they were ready for me.

We decided to use the bedroom for our scene as well, since the lighting in there was perfect and the bedspread was white, marvelous for shooting against. The video would start with me sprawled on the bed passed out, an empty champagne bottle at my hand—I'd have missed yet another call my agent had set up for me by getting drunk in my hotel room, and Stephen was there to angrily rouse me and read me the riot act. Some camera blocking and lighting checks, and we got right into it.

Lucy had said they felt Stephen was the best of their men to pair with me, since he was so good with ad-libbing and he could keep up with my banter. Could he ever—I even had a couple of times when I had no comebacks! We had a lively scene with a lot of kicking and squalling and wonderful insults, until my poor beleaguered agent managed to convince me that I should accept the jobs he gets for me and knock it off with the highfalutin attitude. And in the interest of the top winning, the finale and fade-out was my getting onto my hands and knees and picking up all the M&Ms while he watched.

And there it was; I'd just shot another spanking video. At three weeks short of age 53. I felt triumphant, and at the same time thankful, as if I'd been given an unexpected and lovely present. I really did think that after *When Danny Met Erica*, I was done.

That wasn't my only shoot that weekend. The prolific blogger Richard Windsor, whose writings I've enjoyed for quite some time, was doing interviews at the party and had requested to do one with me. We did so in his room on Friday evening; the intent was to have it go out live on streaming webcam and tape it as well for Spanking Tube, but the streaming didn't work, unfortunately. But we had a fun chat, and what was originally meant to be about 15–20 minutes stretched into 40! So Richard broke it up into two parts and posted it on Spanking Tube the following week. The lighting was a bit dark, but the sound was perfect and the two of us were animated and easy with each other. I was very pleased with how it came out and honored that I'd been asked.

On camera twice in one weekend! And I'd even received yet a third request, to do a shoot with the Strictly Spanking New York folks, but I had to turn that down. It would have been a hard discipline scene and I didn't really want to get into that headspace on a party weekend. But still, it was gratifying to be wanted. Perhaps I could put my has-been insecurities to bed after all. They were growing rather tiresome, anyway.

In March 2011, my second Northern Spanking video was released on their site; Lucy demonstrated her cheeky humor with its title. One of the best exchanges in the film occurs when I am complaining about the M&Ms. Stephen asks what's wrong with them, and I say, "They're plain. They're boring. They're nutless. Much like you!"

The video's title? *Nutless*.

THE KINDNESS OF TOPS

"Fantasies do become realities, if you hang with the right people. My heart is full."
—from my *MySpace* blog, June 3, 2009

Over the years, I've had countless wonderful scenes, some of which I've described in previous chapters. However, I also have many fond memories of tops' sweet gestures and surprises that went beyond spanking, illustrating that there is much more to these special relationships than meets the eye. I certainly can't write about all of them, but I want to give two of them a special mention.

One of the first spanking stories I ever wrote was called *A Discipline Fantasy*. The plot was simple: I felt I needed a strong discipline session and I asked a trusted friend to give me one, even though I'd never had one before and didn't know what to expect. I wrote it as I envisioned something like that would play out, with a lot of implements, my friend being very strict and the punishment painful, and with my ending up in tears. When it was over, he soothed me and left me to sleep peacefully, and the next day I received a floral delivery, with a note saying thanks for trusting him and that he was proud of me. I included this story in my book years later.

Cut to 2009, when I was playing regularly with a gentleman known as Craig Aych on the various kink sites. He and I had met at a Shadow Lane party, his first, and John and I would get together with him and his wife periodically to play at a local dungeon. We had developed a bond with a great deal of trust and I felt safe in going to new and different emotional and physical places with him.

So when he and I had a misunderstanding, he asked me (after we'd patched things up) how I felt about dealing with it through one of our play times at the Lair; in other words, making it a real discipline session. The idea was scary but intriguing, and I certainly trusted him enough to engage on that level. I said yes, let's do it.

The scene was intense in all ways, he was extremely strict (but checked in regularly), used multiple implements and I wept a great deal afterward. Craig was very good with aftercare and allowed me to process the sensory overload as I needed to, taking as much time as necessary. He wrapped me in a fur blanket, brought me tissues and stroked my hair, murmured sweet words about how proud he was of me. That would have been more than enough.

But then, three days after our scene, I received a surprise—a delivery of beautiful multi-colored roses. When I opened the card, the message started with: "See… I do pay attention." It was Craig. He wanted to make my fantasy story come true, right down to the flowers.

To say I was deeply touched by his thoughtfulness would be a gross understatement. I will never forget it. And of course, I blogged about it. In the scene grapevine, Craig became "the guy who sent Erica flowers."

He also once had chicken soup, crackers and orange juice delivered to me when I was sick. I was starting to feel a little better, but not well enough to venture out and buy food, and I can't tell you how perfect that soup tasted.

* * *

Most people who know me (or have read my blogs, my stories, etc.) know that I am still as much in love with *Dark Shadows* as I was when I was 12 years old and swooning over it with my best friend. On the Shadow Lane bulletin board, a man who went by the name Irish Mike would comment to me at times, mentioning that he was a big fan of the show as well and he had some fun artifacts that I would probably enjoy. He seemed like a lovely man, always with compliments and friendly words at the ready. So when I found out he was coming to a Shadow Lane party, I was eager to meet him.

On *Dark Shadows*, the popular character of vampire Barnabas Collins had two props familiar to all fans: one was the onyx ring he wore on his left index finger and the other was his silver-topped wolf's-head cane. Mike told me that he had one of these canes and promised to bring it to the party to show me.

What a sweetheart he turned out to be! He seemed like a throwback to another time; one doesn't use the word "courtly" much these days, but it described him perfectly. Diminutive and in his 50s, he had an old-world charm, a gentle demeanor and a soft voice with a lilting brogue.

On Saturday night during the party weekend, he approached me in the ballroom, carrying the Barnabas cane. I'd seen this cane hundreds of times on television, but it was quite another thing to see one for real. It was a beautiful piece and I was genuinely enthused about looking at it up close and getting to hold it. After I was through *ooh*-ing and *ahh*-ing, I reluctantly handed it back to him—and he gave it right back. "It's yours," he said.

Huh??

I thought I'd misunderstood him; there was no way he was giving the cane to me. But indeed he was. No matter how much I protested, he insisted. I thanked him profusely with tears in my eyes.

When I got home, I searched the cane online. It is a collector's item and not cheap; Mike had given me quite the generous gift. But, as I learned, such was his nature.

I got to see him again in June 2010, when we both attended the Florida Moonshine party in Tampa. When he left on Sunday afternoon, I gave him a warm hug and a kiss and told him how much he made me smile with his sunny presence.

I'm so glad I had the opportunity to do that. After we all got home and the post-party buzz was flying around on the FetLife forum, Irish Mike was conspicuously absent. After doing some poking around, one of our friends found out he'd had a massive heart attack and passed away at age 54.

His profile is still up at FetLife and his wall is covered with loving messages. Every time I look at my Barnabas cane, I think of him.

Ar dheis Dé go raibh a anam (may he rest in peace).

MY 50S AND BEYOND

"To my loyal friends who have proven themselves to me over and over, who support and uplift me, who have taken me into their worlds and shared themselves with me, who accept me as I am, who know the real Erica and not just 'the spanking model,' who touch my heart—you know who you are, and I LOVE YOU!"
—from my *MySpace* blog, November 9, 2006

I've come to the last chapter of my book—now what? I debated about how to end this, how to wrap it up neatly, then realized I can't. For one thing, this isn't a novel or a sitcom; life doesn't wrap up neatly. And for another, I'm still very much present, so my story isn't over yet.

Why did I write this? Several reasons, I suppose. I wanted a record of my adventures, of my ups and downs and how my life has played out. I wanted to entertain, titillate and touch people. I wanted others to relate to me in one way or another, to see the real person with all the flaws and insecurities. And I felt I had something to share.

What is a successful life? Many define it by societal standards; for example, success is quantified by such things as getting married, raising children, having an important career, or owning a home. I have done not one of those. I've never invented anything, saved a life, composed music, or discovered a cure for cancer. However, I have:

- endured pain, loss, and very dark days, and survived to see better ones;
- loved and been loved;
- made people laugh. As one who believes that humor is one of life's saving graces, I consider this of great worth;
- lived long enough to realize that, through trial and error, being a square peg in a round world isn't the worst thing to happen to a person, if you learn how to work with your differences instead of fighting them;

- made many of my fantasies and dreams into reality. How many people get to do that?

My value is not measured by my accomplishments or what I have amassed, but by who I am.

This is not intended to be a "message" book. I am not suggesting that anyone with self-esteem issues or eating disorders has but to find the right drug and their problems will be behind them. Nor am I telling anyone, "Embrace your kinky side and your life will change miraculously!" That would be too easy and an insult to anyone reading.

This book is about my own journey and experiences, not magic bullets or happy endings. However, if any part of it strikes a chord, gives someone food for thought, provides a degree of comfort, or makes even one person feel less alone in dealing with struggles and challenges, then my efforts are further validated.

I've milked a great deal of humor from the outrageous correspondence I've received over the years, but at this point, I'd like to acknowledge all the wonderful emails, comments and posts that people have sent to me or written about me. They've made me laugh and beam with delight, touched me, even moved me to tears. For a woman who spent much of life feeling invisible and inconsequential, these compliments and accolades are priceless.

Sadly, it's all too easy to criticize and condemn, particularly on the Internet where one can hurl anonymous potshots. So when someone takes the time and makes the effort to say something nice, that tells me a lot about their character. For example, I'm quite sure I would like the gentleman who sent me this "fan letter":

> *Hi, Erica. My name is [name deleted] and I'm a longtime fan of yours, although from afar. I love your spanking videos and think you may very well have one of the most spankable bottoms ever captured on tape! Combine that with your quick wit and irrepressible "inner brat" and you are truly an icon in the spanko community! As a member of "Southern California Spanked Wives Club" and "The Brats' Place for Spanking" groups I've always enjoyed your posts and re-*

ports on the Shadow Lane parties and your latest video filming experiences.

I just wanted to take this opportunity to salute you and to express my appreciation for ALL of your contributions to this wonderful, whimsical, wild, world of spanking that we all enjoy so much! Your bottom has paid the price so we could all enjoy our kink vicariously through you! It's nice to know that beautiful, sweet, sexy, NICE people like you are a part of our community! Thanks again for being you!

On a more personal note: A couple of years ago after blogging my frustration over ageism and societal double standards, I received the following from a man whom I've never met, but with whom I've had many lovely exchanges. I think you'll agree it was a keeper:

As a man, I cannot understand what women go through at many levels. As we have discussed before, women do not have the advantages men do as the aging process takes place, but I can assure you without a hint of pity or patronization that you are indeed a vital, beautiful desirable woman. You have worked hard at it to maintain your physical beauty, but that is what one must do and your "friends" who are so negative seem to have missed the fact that they simply have not paid the dues to find themselves as delicious as you are. ...So many of us are attracted to you because of how beautiful you are, because you are the model of the perfect feminine form, because your bottom is the most spankable bottom to ever grace a woman. Your eyes are kind, mischievous, and even carry a hint of sadness and vulnerability that make you one of the most beautiful women I have ever seen. But your beauty transcends the physical form. Your mind and heart are and always will be what makes Erica so loved by so many.

You know, I read something like this and that damned old familiar voice still crops up and whispers, "Who is he talking about? It can't be you!" Screw you, old voice. I'm going to accept the compliment graciously and embrace it like a warm hug to my soul, and not question it.

Recently, I found this description of my blog on another forum, written by a friend who was nominating me for Best Spanking Blogger of 2010:

> Erica Scott; Wickedly funny, brutally honest, and infinitely spankable. She blends intelligence and a delightful brattiness, all the time keeping her identity as a real and vulnerable person who happens to love this thing we do.

It didn't matter whether or not I won that award, or even got votes. That compliment is a treasure.

And finally, if ever I have a down day where I feel like I've neither accomplished nor contributed anything in life, all I have to do is read the following:

> Erica,
>
> We have never met, I doubt we ever shall, but you will always have a warm spot in my heart. For you are among the cherished few who helped me see that I was not alone in the universe.
>
> Growing up in a very politically correct and comfortable home I could never understand why I felt the way I did. Later at boarding school, in college, and later law school I was surrounded by other young women just embracing feminism and longing to be all that they could be. Their hopes, aspirations, expectations so different from mine. My parents would never think of spanking a child. The men I knew flattered me, spoiled me, fell over themselves doing for me, but take me in hand? Not a

chance. And then searching the internet looking for something else I found the trail that led to you.

I hope you will not misunderstand when I say you seemed to me just the perfect younger aunt or older sister who given the chance could have saved me so much grief, loneliness and misunderstanding. So if you are ever in doubt about your contribution to humankind, be assured that somewhere there is a young woman who looks up to you and thanks you from the bottom of her heart for your contribution to her life. I am sure that there are many others just like me. That is the gift you gave me.

With true affection,
[name deleted]

That letter touches me every time I read it. To this special young woman, if you happen to be reading this: You gave me one hell of a gift yourself. Thank you.

* * *

What is next for me? At the time of this writing, I am 53 years old. In taking stock of my life, here are a few points I'd like to touch upon.

John and I are still together, still happily *not* cohabitating. Relationships are hard work and there are times when I still wonder if I'm cut out for one. But then I remember that I've been in this one for nearly 15 years, so I guess that means I am. I also remember the many years when I believed there was no man in existence who would love and accept me as I am.

John likes to say he knows me better than I know myself, and sometimes I think he's right. He still makes me laugh like no other, and my heart still leaps in my chest when I see him across a crowded room and know that beautiful man is with me. He is the love of my life.

I worry about him, because he has a heart condition. He was recently hospitalized with a strep infection that further damaged his weak mitral valve. Eventually, he is going to need surgery to replace it. Therefore, I don't know what the future holds and I don't like to dwell on it much. I am endeavoring to stay in the moment, a day at a time, and treasure what I have now.

My mother and stepfather are still alive; Mom is 89 and M is 93. About five years ago, my mother had a series of small strokes that affected her brain and began a slow progression of dementia. She became delusional and bitterly hostile, saying horrible things to us, calling the police and claiming M was her captor, wandering out in the middle of the night and falling in the street. M took care of her for as long as he could, but when she got too far out of control and was a danger to both of them, he had no choice but to put her in an assisted-care facility.

Aside from her ever-increasing dementia, she is in good health and could linger on like this for years. She is on various medications that keep her docile, so the rage is no longer an issue, but she is completely incontinent. The part of her brain that controls those bodily functions was damaged by the strokes. She remembers nothing of the dreadful episodes that necessitated her move into assisted care.

I look at her and admit to feeling scared to death; I have her genes, after all. My belief in quality over quantity extends to life itself and I do not want to end mine in such indignity. But I can't allow myself to dwell too much on that either. My life is now, and for now, I am healthy, whole and independent.

I cannot bring myself to visit her. I'm not proud of this, but I can't help it. Seeing her like this disturbs me deeply and I'm in a funk for days afterward. I would rather remember her as she was: vital, energetic, a force to be reckoned with, even though she could drive me crazy. That woman is already gone.

Some people consider the cycle of life to be that you grow up and take care of your parents, because they took care of you. Once again, I don't fit into this mold; I didn't ask to be born. My parents chose to have me, and with that choice comes a certain responsibility. I love my mother, and I've made a degree of peace with our past and how critical she was of me. I know she did the best she could. But I don't feel like I owe her anything.

A couple of years ago on a whim, I Googled my former stepmother S and found a website created for her by a fan. I eagerly read all the pages, viewed her beautiful photos and her various clips, and reminisced about how I had adored her. And then there it was—a contact page. I wrote to her, not knowing quite what to expect, and was highly gratified when she wrote back, bubbling with excitement and joy at having heard from me and wanting to get together.

I know she made mistakes and did some hurtful things. But I was able to forgive her, as I did my father.

She is now 80 and lives about 25 miles from me. We have had several lunches and long talks and I'm so grateful she's in my life once more. Last year, we were both invited to a holiday gathering at the home of an old friend and colleague of my father's. In conversation at this party, she referred to me as "her kid." I guess there's a part of me that will always wish I were indeed her kid.

* * *

In September 2010, a man answered one of my spanking ads and we met. Our first scene was right after my birthday and he brought me a rose and a balloon. He has been my play partner ever since; we meet every Monday and have had incredible adventures, all of which I chronicle on my blog with pictures. We've even videotaped a few of our scenes and I've posted clips of them.

When I first started writing about him, he didn't wish to have his name revealed, so I called him New Guy, and the name stuck, even though he is no longer new. He is an amazing top and a wonderful guy, and we've forged a close and trusting friendship. I feel very lucky to have met him and I hope to play with him for a long time.

In January 2011, I was flown to Connecticut for four days to work with Sarah Gregory and a delightful gentleman named Paul (also known in the scene as "Tubaman"), who is creating a spanking website and is in the process of shooting content for it. So I shot three scenarios for Sarah's video site and several more for Paul's future site. We all stayed at their friend K's home, complete with two dogs.

They were so kind to me, made me feel like a superstar and I had a fabulous time. When we weren't shooting, we were just hanging out, telling stories and sharing laughs, and having wonderful meals (they even treated me to a lobster dinner on my last night). Once again, I'd thought I was done, but I was mistaken. And they want me to come back and shoot more at another time.

At the time of this writing, I recently shot a cover photo for Devlin O'Neill's new book, *Spanked in Her Dreams*, per his request; I was beyond flattered and honored to do so. And I am going to work for a relatively new site, Spanking Court, very soon. It looks like I'm going to continue thumbing my nose at the ageists for a little while longer. I still want to pinch myself at times, because I feel I'm living a dream, scene-wise.

Despite all the progress I've made, I know there are certain things that will not change; certain traits that are indelibly stamped upon my psyche. I'll always be a storm cloud instead of a ray of sunshine. I will probably always feel fear about way too many things; the difference is I've learned the meaning of "feel the fear and do it anyway."

Self-centeredness will most likely remain a solid facet of my personality. And I suspect my view of the glass will remain half-empty rather than half-full. However, considering that for most of my life, my glass was completely empty, I'm not going to beat myself up over that one. There will still be mornings when I wake up and groan, unwilling to face the day. But "Ugh, I'm still alive" is no longer my first thought.

I still take medication and I anticipate that I always will. I have no problem with that.

I will always have quirks and little issues around food; you never fully recover from an eating disorder, just as you don't recover from alcoholism. But you learn to live with it and keep the demons at bay. I still count calories in my head every time I eat something. I still play with my food,

312

using the old anorexic tricks of making whatever I'm eating last longer. For example, if I eat a bowl of vegetable soup, I eat one vegetable at a time—pick out and eat all the peas, then the carrots, and so on. But the only person who is allowed to tease me about any of that is John. My food shtick is off limits for others.

My worst days now are still better than my best days were back then. As long as I remain cognizant of that, I will maintain perspective.

There are times when I wish things could have been different. During the depressive periods when my mind goes to dark places, my youth seems wasted, and my frantic efforts in later years to make up for lost time feel somewhat forced and pathetic. I gaze at my face and body and wish I could erase time so that I looked as young as I feel in my psyche.

Then I realize those are old negative tapes replaying and I do my best to shut them off. The pain and emptiness of my youth made the later accomplishments sweeter. The struggles made me appreciate the victories all the more. From grief blooms strength and empathy. And when I pick myself apart physically, I am channeling my mother, which is an unhealthy thing to do.

For any spanko who may be reading this, do yourself a favor: Don't question the whys and wherefores or over-analyze to death this thing we do. Just enjoy the hell out of it. Spanking is *fun*, and for people like us, it provides a physical and emotional fulfillment that defies explanation. Experience as much or as little of it as you want, and learn which variations appeal to you—and which ones do not. Remember, beyond observing the basics of SSC (Safe, Sane and Consensual), there isn't a right or wrong way to engage in spanking, only the way that works for you, from naughty playfulness to intense discipline. *There is nothing wrong with you.* Embrace your kink and rejoice in it, without any shame or second-guessing. Life is too short for that.

And to my fellow late bloomers: Celebrate your blossoming, whenever it is, however it may happen. I promise I will continue to do so as well.

www.ingramcontent.com/pod-product-compliance
Lightning Source LLC
Chambersburg PA
CBHW071407050326
40689CB00010B/1785